PERSONAL CAPITALISM AND CORPORATE GOVERNANCE

Modern Economic and Social History Series

General Editor: Derek H. Aldcroft

Titles in this series include:

Alfred Herbert Ltd and the British Machine Tool Industry, 1887–1983
Roger Lloyd-Jones and M.J. Lewis

Rethinking Nineteenth-Century Liberalism
Richard Cobden Bicentenary Essays
Edited by Anthony Howe and Simon Morgan

Governance, Growth and Global Leadership
The Role of the State in Technological Progress, 1750–2000
Espen Moe

Triumph of the South
A Regional Economic History of Early Twentieth Century Britain
Peter Scott

Aspects of Independent Romania's Economic History with Particular Reference
to Transition for EU Accession
David Turnock

Estates, Enterprise and Investment at the Dawn of the Industrial Revolution
Estate Management and Accounting in the North-East of England, c.1700–1780
David Oldroyd

Across the Borders
Financing the World's Railways in the Nineteenth and Twentieth Centuries
Edited by Ralf Roth and Günter Dinhobl

Economics in Russia
Studies in Intellectual History
Edited by Vincent Barnett and Joachim Zweynert

Mining Tycoons in the Age of Empire, 1870–1945
Entrepreneurship, High Finance, Politics and Territorial Expansion
Edited by Raymond E. Dumett

British Conservatism and Trade Unionism, 1945–1964
Peter Dorey

Personal Capitalism and Corporate Governance

British Manufacturing in the First Half of the Twentieth Century

MYRDDIN JOHN LEWIS
Sheffield Hallam University, UK

ROGER LLOYD-JONES
Sheffield Hallam University, UK

JOSEPHINE MALTBY
University of York, UK

and

MARK DAVID MATTHEWS
Sheffield Hallam University, UK

ASHGATE

Published by
Ashgate Publishing Limited
Wey Court East
Union Road
Farnham
Surrey, GU9 7PT
England

Ashgate Publishing Company
Suite 420
101 Cherry Street
Burlington
VT 05401-4405
USA

www.ashgate.com

British Library Cataloguing in Publication Data
Personal capitalism and corporate governance : British manufacturing in the first half of the twentieth century. – (Modern economic and social history)
   1. Corporate governance–Great Britain–History–20th century–Case studies. 2. Manufacturing industries–Great Britain–Finance–History–20th century–Case studies. 3. Private companies–Great Britain–History–20th century–Case studies.
   I. Series II. Lloyd-Jones, Roger, 1944–
   338.6'041'0941-dc22

Library of Congress Cataloging-in-Publication Data
Personal capitalism and corporate governance : British manufacturing in the first half of the twentieth century / Roger Lloyd-Jones ... [et al.].
      p. cm. — (Modern economic and social history)
   Includes bibliographical references and index.
   ISBN 978-0-7546-5587-9 (hbk. : alk. paper) — ISBN 978-1-4094-1758-3 (ebook) 1. Manufacturing industries—Great Britain—Management—History—20th century. 2. Corporate governance—Great Britain—History—20th century. 3. Corporate governance—Great Britain—Case studies. I. Lloyd-Jones, Roger, 1944—
   HD9731.5.P47 2010
   338.094109'04—dc22
                                                                                    2010031152
ISBN 9780754655879 (hbk)
ISBN 9781409417583 (ebk)

Printed and bound in Great Britain by the
MPG Books Group, UK

Contents

List of Tables

Acknowledgements

This research was funded by the Leverhulme Trust, and we would like to thank them for their support that made this research possible. The final stages of the research were also aided by the sabbatical awarded to Dr Merv Lewis at Sheffield Hallam University. Numerous archives were visited and we would especially like to thank the staff of the Sheffield Archive for their co-operation in making available as yet un-catalogued material; also the staff at Nottinghamshire Archive, Coventry Archive, Birmingham Archive, Solihull Library, and West Yorkshire Archive Leeds.

Modern Economic and Social History Series
General Editor's Preface

Economic and social history has been a flourishing subject of scholarly study during recent decades. Not only has the volume of literature increased enormously but the range of interest in time, space and subject matter has broadened considerably so that today there are many sub-branches of the subject which have developed considerable status in their own right.

One of the aims of this series is to encourage the publication of scholarly monographs on any aspect of modern economic and social history. The geographical coverage is world-wide and contributions on the non-British themes will be especially welcome. While emphasis will be placed on works embodying original research, it is also intended that the series should provide the opportunity to publish studies of a more general thematic nature which offer a reappraisal or critical analysis of major issues of debate.

Derek H. Aldcroft
University of Leicester

Chapter 1

Introduction: Corporate Governance, Personal Capitalism, and British Manufacturing in the First Half of the Twentieth Century

Introduction

An examination of corporate governance involves a study of the 'the institutions that influence how business corporations allocate resources and returns. [A] system of corporate governance shapes who makes investment decisions in a corporation, what type of decisions they make, and how returns from investment are distributed'.[1] In Britain, limited companies have been an increasingly important part of economic activity since the 1855 Limited Liability Act, but it is only more recently that there has been an increasing interest by academics in the historical evolution of corporate governance.

Writing in 1984, Tricker argued that interest in the issue of corporate governance appeared to be of recent origin, perhaps because 'In the past there seemed little challenge to management's prerogative to run the company unimpeded, no demand for independent supervision or disclosure, no intervention in matters of accountability, no questioning of corporate power and legitimacy, little interest in involvement or participation in management decisions.'[2] More recently, Sheikh and Chatterjee have claimed that while corporate governance is a well recognised concept in Australia, New Zealand, the USA and some European countries, 'it has received hardly any attention in Britain, primarily because of the traditional view maintained by the [corporate governance] system that directors are responsible to maximise profits for their shareholders, as the interests of the latter are paramount to directors'.[3] Corporate governance, according to Keasey, Thompson and Wright,

---

[1]   M. O'Sullivan, *Contests for Corporate Control: Corporate Governance and Economic Performance in the USA and Germany* (Oxford, Oxford University Press, 2001), p. 1.

[2]   R. I. Tricker, *Corporate Governance* (Aldershot, Gower, 1984), p. 5.

[3]   S. Sheikh and S. K. Chatterjee, 'Perspectives on Corporate Governance', in S. Sheikh and W. Rees (eds), *Corporate Governance and Corporate Control* (London, Cavendish, 1995), p. 1.

was 'a term that scarcely existed before the 1990s', a decade which forms the starting point of their discussion.[4]

The analysis of governance structures 'is not simply a gimmick or ... an intellectual fashion or an ideological tool', but is a topic 'high on the agenda of [the] business historian'.[5] It deserves this place because of its crucial importance in understanding important issues associated with systems for internal promotion of executives, the distribution of profits to executives and shareholders, and the accountability of the directors to stakeholders within the organisation.[6] These are features of a company's culture which help determine the performance of top management in setting the strategic direction of the firm, building the core capabilities of organisations, and responding to changes and to business adversity.[7]

The decades since 1990 have seen a growing concern in the UK with the significance of corporate governance for business performance, resulting in extensive debates about its regulation. The financial scandals of the 1980s and 1990s 'coincided with the privatisation of nationalised industries and the actions of governments in rolling back regulatory market mechanisms'.[8] Examples in Britain during the 1990s included the 1990 downfall of Polly Peck, a diversified conglomerate whose chief executive promptly fled to Northern Cyprus to avoid extradition; the closure in 1991 of the Bank of Credit and Commerce International, described in 1999 as then the 'biggest fraud in world history';[9] the discovery of huge losses in the pension fund of Mirror Group Newspapers in 1992, soon after the death of its chief executive, Robert Maxwell; and the 1995 collapse of Barings, one of the oldest British banks, with losses of over £800 million. Distrust of the Anglo-American system of corporate governance intensified with the Enron and WorldCom collapses of 2001–02. The UK reaction was a series of initiatives to regulate governance via regulatory codes produced by a variety of City institutions, addressing the issues of financial reporting and accountability, directors' remuneration and the role of the board of directors, and drawn together in the Combined Code of 1998.[10] The 'comply or explain' principle of corporate

---

[4]   K. Keasey, S. Thompson and M. Wright, 'Introduction', in K. Keasey, S. Thompson and M. Wright (eds), *Corporate Governance* (Oxford, Oxford University Press, 1997), pp. 1–19.

[5]   P. Fridenson, 'Business Failure and the Agenda of Business History', *Enterprise and Society*, Vol. 15, No. 4 (2004), p. 564.

[6]   See D. J. Jeremy, *A Business History of Britain 1900–1990s* (Oxford, Oxford University Press, 1997), pp. 503–505.

[7]   See R. R. Nelson, *The Sources of Economic Growth* (Cambridge, MA, Harvard University Press, 2000), p. 110.

[8]   Jeremy, *A Business History of Britain*, p. 548.

[9]   *Guardian*, 8 January 1999.

[10]   See K. Keasey, H. Short and M. Wright, 'The Development of Corporate Governance Codes', in Keasey, Thompson and Wright (eds), *Corporate Governance*, pp. 21–44.

governance set out by these codes stressed the voluntary nature of good corporate governance practice in the UK. Regulatory codes were backed by increasingly detailed standards for accounting disclosure,[11] and by the Companies Act of 2006, 'the longest Act ever passed,' intended, according to a Government minister, to 'support stronger shareholder involvement and promote a long-term investment culture'.[12]

The global financial crisis of 2008 – 'arguably the greatest crisis in the history of finance capitalism'[13] – again drew attention to the role of corporate governance, in particular in the financial services sector. The Turner Review of 2009 called for reconsideration of the quality of financial services regulation, and a move from a system of supervision that trusted in the ability of the market to correct itself and of senior management to 'make appropriate decisions'.[14] Turner recommended a 'more intrusive and more systemic' supervisory approach with much closer regulatory involvement in 'published accounts and accounting judgements, with far more intense contact with bank management and auditors on these issues'.[15] It remains to be seen whether reaction to the quality of financial services governance will trigger a generally 'more intrusive and more systemic' regulation of corporate governance in general.

As suggested in the preceding brief overview of recent changes, corporate governance is an evolving practice, and one whose changes reflect wider issues in business history: corporate governance is seen as implicated in economic success or failure, so that part of public reaction to an economic crisis is a call for reform of governance practice. This book is specifically aimed at addressing a gap in the study of the evolution of corporate governance in Britain. In particular its key theme, the relationship between corporate governance and personal capitalism in British manufacturing in the first half of the twentieth century, provides the means for a systematic and critical examination of the dominant paradigm of Alfred D. Chandler that the long-run persistence of personal capitalism shaped

---

[11] I. MacNeil and Xiao Lu, 'Comply or Explain: Market Discipline and Non-Compliance with the Combined Code' (2005), *http://papers.ssrn.com/sol3/Delivery.cfm/SSRN_ID726664_ code282794.pdf?abstractid=726664&mirid=1, accessed 10 November 2008.*

[12] Margaret Hodge, 'Fit for Purpose', *Accountancy*, Vol. 139, Issue 1,365 (May 2007), p. 105. In the USA, the Sarbanes–Oxley Act of 2002 was reported to be 'an extraordinary expansion of the United States securities law regulation of *corporate governance*, disclosure, reporting and accounting requirements and penalties'. See M. L. Hermsen, P. J. Niehoff and M. R. Uhrynuk, 'An Extraordinary Expansion', *Accountancy*, Vol. 130, Issue 1,310 (October 2002), pp. 110–12.

[13] The Turner Review: A Regulatory Response to the Global Banking crisis (March 2009), www.fsa.gov.uk/pubs/other/turner_review.pdf, accessed 30 March 2009.

[14] Ibid., p. 87.

[15] Ibid., p. 89.

the governance of British manufacturing firms well into the twentieth century and acted to erode their competitive performance.[16]

Our examination of corporate governance in Britain covers the period c. 1900 to 1950, chosen because it focuses particularly on the responses of business to the impact of two world wars and the turbulent business environment of the inter-war years. A range of organisational types are considered, from the family-controlled firm to the operation of personal capitalism within large holding-company structures.

Financial reporting and corporate governance

The Limited Liability Act, 1855, and the Joint Stock Act, 1856 represented major changes in the legal status of companies, but despite regulation the UK continued to have 'the most permissive commercial law in the whole of Europe.'[17] For companies in general, other than utilities, insurers, and building societies, there was no requirement to make an audited balance sheet available to shareholders until the 1900 Companies Act. It was not until the Companies Act of 1929 that companies were required to publish a profit and loss account, and only the Act of 1947 required audit. There were continuing difficulties until 1947 because of this low level of information, as well as the lack of disclosure about the performance of subsidiaries within a group and the opportunity that was afforded directors to camouflage reserves. Brooks identifies, for instance, fifteen major financial scandals in Europe and the USA in the 1920s and early 1930s, which included in Britain the notorious Royal Mail Steam Packet case, revealing how secret reserves could be used to conceal profit or make transfers between profitable and less successful years.[18] Other than observing dividend performance over a number of years, investors had little chance of gauging profitability or of making fair comparisons between different companies. The major force for disclosure before the statutory requirements of the 1947 Act was the Stock Exchange, which in 1939 required that companies must produce a consolidated balance sheet and profit and loss account in order to be allowed to issue new securities.[19]

---

[16]   See A. D. Chandler Jnr, *Scale and Scope: The Dynamics of Industrial Capitalism* (Cambridge, MA, Harvard University Press, 1990), pp. 12, 392.

[17]   P. L. Cottrell, *Industrial Finance 1830–1914: The Finance and Organisation of British Manufacturing Industry* (London, Methuen, 1980), p. 41.

[18]   Brookes cited in J. Maltby, 'Was the 1947 Companies Act a Response to a National Crisis?', *Accounting History*, Vol. 5, No. 2 (2000), pp. 31–60, esp. pp. 37–8. See also A. J. Arnold and D. R. Matthews, 'Corporate Financial Disclosures in the UK, 1920–1950: The Effects of Legislative Change and Managerial Disclosure', *Accounting and Business Research*, Vol. 32 (2002), pp. 3–16; J. R. Edwards, 'The Accounting Profession and Disclosure in Published Reports, 1925–1932', *Accounting and Business Research*, Vol. 6 (1976), pp. 289–303; J. R. Edwards, *A History of Financial Accounting* (London, Routledge, 1989).

[19]   Maltby, 'Was the 1947 Companies Act…?', p. 44.

Given this absence of statutory regulation, the amount disclosed by the manufacturing companies studied in this book and any changes made in their voluntary disclosure are therefore revealing as an indication of the directors' willingness to highlight or downplay aspects of corporate performance. Hence the level and type of disclosure are symptomatic of the relationship of directors with shareholders and other interested parties. Some directors of large British holding companies during the inter-war years, for example, admitted their reluctance to disclose information to stakeholders. Arthur Chamberlain, for instance, the chairman of Tube Investments, a diverse holding company, announced at the company annual general meeting (AGM) in 1935 that he did not disclose the company's entire profits: the decisive accounting policy was to reveal 'so much as we consider will make a pretty balance sheet'.[20] At Unilever, Britain's largest holding company in the inter-war years, the chairman Francis D'Arcy Cooper, giving evidence before the Greene Committee on company law in 1925, asserted that consolidated balance sheets would convey no meaningful information to shareholders:

> The incorporation of a statement purporting to be the balance sheet of a holding company of the assets and liabilities of other legal entities, would not, in my opinion, be a true statement of the position of the holding company ... It would be a conglomeration of figures, futile as an aid to any person desirous of understanding the true position, and, as far as it was taken seriously misleading'.[21]

There was some pressure within the accounting profession for companies to improve disclosure, because investor confidence was undermined by uninformative accounts,[22] but representatives of major firms were prepared to support the status quo because uninformative accounts defended 'the best interests of shareholders themselves'.[23]

A low level of financial disclosure raises the question why a historical study of corporate governance should engage with financial reporting. If reporting were fundamentally misleading, it could be argued that it should not be included in a historical study – this should be confined to information from other sources, about the management and shareholders, about the performance of the company's products, the evidence of its investment in new plant and technology, its place in business networks and so on. The 'insider' shareholders who wanted information need not necessarily rely on the published accounts – they could use personal contacts with

---

[20]   *The Accountant*, 14 December 1935, p. 812.

[21]   Cited in K. Camfferman and S. A. Zeff, 'The Apotheosis of Holding Company Accounting: Unilever's Financial Reporting Innovations from the 1920s to the 1940s', *Accounting, Business and Financial History*, Vol. 13, No. 2 (2003), p. 175.

[22]   *The Accountant*, 12 December 1931, p. 731.

[23]   J. Kitchen and R. H. Parker, *Accounting Thought and Education: Six English Pioneers* (London, Institute of Chartered Accountants in England and Wales, 1977), p. 80.

the board to find out what they wished to know in much more detail, and the modern historian should attempt to follow the same trails. These are reasonable points with which to challenge the study of financial reporting, but they tend to ignore the point that while financial reports' weaknesses were recognised and criticised in the late nineteenth and early twentieth centuries, they were still taken seriously. The AGM at which financial statements were discussed was given extensive press coverage in local and national newspapers, and financial journals; companies would even pay to have their AGM reported over one or more columns of *The Economist*. For example, the Sheffield steel manufacturers Hadfields Ltd, whose style of corporate governance is examined in Chapter 3, reported its AGMs extensively in the local newspapers, a recognition of the high proportion of local shareholders in the firm. This suggests that boards of directors recognised public interest in their published reports and were at pains to ensure that their own comments on the statements received wide publicity, either to extol good performance to enhance the reputation of the firm, or to pre-empt potential criticism. The amount of disclosure also varied, from company to company and over time, in a manner which attracted comment. It was, for instance, noted that companies which were, or seemed likely to be, making high profits during the First World War chose to reduce the length and informativeness of their financial statements.[24]

Finally and most crucially, shareholders made demands for informative and reliable reports. For example, the *Newton v Chambers* case of 1906 demonstrated the general point: shareholders wanted financial reports to provide them with as much information as possible in a mode that helped them to judge the company's performance. It was recognised that directors were entitled to use their discretion in determining how much disclosure was in the company's interests – it would be in no one's interest to give away trade secrets or help a rival to undercut them. But this did not detract from the view that the production of financial reports was an important means of communication between directors and shareholders. In producing reports, directors were demonstrating that they were prepared to be accountable not only to 'insiders' but also to small investors who did not have the means or opportunity to monitor the company on a daily basis. Relations with shareholders were complex, and a study of governance requires a consideration of the behaviour of shareholders and managers. To this effect, the case studies in the book incorporate the concepts of exit, voice and loyalty, which provide a means of understanding the response of stakeholders to changing business circumstances. Stakeholders in an organisation may choose to leave (exit) the organisation, stay and exercise their voice in reforming managerial and accounting practices, or remain loyal to the goals of executive management.[25]

---

[24]   J. Maltby, 'Hadfields Ltd: Its Annual General Meetings, 1900–1939 and their Relevance to Corporate Social Reporting', *British Accounting Review* (2004), pp. 415–39.

[25]   See J. Foreman-Peck, 'Exit, Voice and Loyalty as Responses to Decline: The Rover Company in the Inter-War Years', *Business History*, Vol. 23, No. 2 (1981), pp. 191–210; A. O. Hirschman, *Exit, Voice and Loyalty. Responses to Decline in Firms, Organisations*

Because of the importance of reporting for the relationship between shareholders and directors, it recurs as a theme throughout the period covered by this book, from the *Newton v Chambers* case which turned on the use of secret reserves, and is discussed in Chapter 4, to the dissatisfaction of shareholders at the bicycle firm of Raleigh in the late 1940s with the level of company disclosure, examined in Chapter 2. The use of financial reporting is explored in detail in this book because, we argue, of its significant role in corporate governance, and because it aids us in understanding the interaction between stakeholders within the organisation.

Key issues

Throughout the variety of companies and industries that this book considers two key issues recur, which form the basis of major debates in business, economic and accounting history. These are briefly outlined below, as a preface to their consideration in the individual case studies; they relate to Chandler's account of the effect of personal capitalism on the trajectory of British industry, and to the nature of share ownership in the first half of the twentieth century.

A. D. Chandler and company culture, ownership and management

The term 'personal capitalism' has become a received notion in the literature of British business history, owing much to Chandler's pioneering work. His argument is based on the observation of the slower separation of ownership and control and emergence of managerial hierarchies in Britain compared to the USA, a factor that he causally relates to the relative decline of Britain's manufacturing sector in the twentieth century. In essence, personal capitalism is equated in Britain with a failure by business to invest sufficiently in manufacturing (mass production), marketing (mass marketing), and crucially in management, and thus British businesses allegedly failed to build the organisational capabilities that would have enabled them to compete more effectively with their American and German counterparts.[26] While this causation is a controversial issue, and it has been argued that Chandler in his comparative analysis underestimates the different market-cum-technological environment facing British firms compared to their counterparts in the USA and Germany,[27] he nevertheless provides a valuable

---

and States (Cambridge, MA, Harvard University Press, 1970); P. C. Konstant, 'Exit, Voice, Loyalty in the Course of Corporate Governance and Counsel's Changing Role', *Journal of Socio-Economics*, Vol. 28 (1999), pp. 203–246; R. Lloyd-Jones et al., 'Corporate Governance in a Major British Holding Company: BSA in the Interwar Years', *Accounting, Business and Financial History*, Vol. 16, No. 1 (2006), pp. 71–2, 77–8.

[26]   Chandler, *Scale and Scope*, pp. 12, 392.

[27]   See R. Church, 'The Limitations of the Personal Capitalism Paradigm', *Business History Review*, Vol. 64, No. 4 (1990), pp. 703–710; L. Hannah, 'Scale and Scope: Towards

insight into the form and evolution of organisational control pertaining in Britain prior to the Second World War. Chandler defines personal capitalism in terms of the 'governance' of organisation and what he calls the 'management style'. The latter is identified with 'management culture', while the former is equated with the managerial structures of organisations, and how they evolve over time in relation to the separation of ownership and control in companies. Thus, Chandler identifies three distinct but overlapping stages of governance, based upon changes in the structure of managerial organisation. In the first phase, in what he terms the 'personal enterprise' type of company, founders, often family founders, are instrumental in the management of the firm, and administer operations 'without benefit of an extensive managerial hierarchy'. In the second phase, 'the entrepreneurial or family-controlled enterprise' emerges, in which 'the founders and their heirs recruited managerial hierarchies but continued to be influential stockholders and senior executives in their companies'. Finally, in the third phase the 'managerial' form of industrial enterprise evolves, 'in which the executives in the administrative hierarchy have no connection with the founders or their families and have little or no equity in the company'.[28]

For Chandler the managerial form of organisation represented an ideal type, which he claims to have been slow to emerge in Britain compared to the USA and Germany. Consequently, British enterprises differ from their American and German counterparts because British family dynasties 'assembled smaller managerial teams, and until well after World War II they and their heirs continued to play a larger role in the making of middle- and top-management decisions'.[29] As John Quail has argued, in Britain the 'separate roles and prerogatives of the directors … led to a fixity of structure' which acted to limit the evolution of 'managerial hierarchies beyond the departmental or functional level' and also restricted the growth of firms 'beyond a certain size or complexity of operation'.[30]

Business history case studies demonstrate that prior to the Second World War family influence remained important, despite the creation of managerial hierarchies of professional managers in British business. Family control, as Roy

a European Visible Hand', *Business History*, Vol. 32 (1991), pp. 297–310; B. Supple, 'Scale and Scope: Alfred Chandler and the Dynamics of Industrial Capitalism', *Economic History Review*, Vol. 44, No. 3 (1990), pp. 500–514; J. F. Wilson, *British Business History, 1720–1994* (Manchester, Manchester University Press, 1995), pp. 9, 87–8; J. F. Wilson and A. W. J. Thompson, *The Making of Modern Management in Historical Perspective* (Oxford, Oxford University Press, 2006), pp. 60–64.

[28]   Chandler, *Scale and Scope*, p. 240. For an examination and assessment of Chandler's stage model see Wilson, *British Business History*, pp. 10–15; C. Schmitz, *The Growth of Big Business in the United States and Western Europe, 1850–1939* (London, Macmillan, 1993), pp. 37–46.

[29]   Chandler, *Scale and Scope*, p. 240.

[30]   J. Quail, 'The Proprietorial Theory of the Firm and its Consequences', *Journal of Industrial History*, Vol. 3, No. 1 (2000), p. 21.

Church reminds us, was not a unique feature of the British business scene from the late nineteenth century to the 1940s, and persisted in many other economies, including the USA.[31] Indeed, it is probable that 40 to 50 per cent of America's largest mining and manufacturing firms were under family control in 1936,[32] and in 1956 a study by Bendix 'revealed how, in a sample of approximately 1,000 businessmen, original entrepreneurs and their heirs remained in the majority of chief executives well into the twentieth century'.[33] While family control was not unique to the British business scene, Church does acknowledge the persistence of family control in British business organisation, the continued role of founders and their heirs in the promotion of professional managers in the company, and the fact that they retained leading directorships and continued to have a significant 'influence on company policy'.[34] In 1950, as Channon showed, family concerns in Britain, defined 'as one where a family member was the chief executive officer, where there had been two generations of family control, and where a family or its trusts still held 5 per cent of voting shares', still accounted for 50 out of the largest 92 companies in the UK.[35] As Wilson and Thompson comment, 'a reluctance to delegate was a pattern that continued well into the twentieth century, providing the central organisational pattern of both personal and proprietorial capitalism'.[36]

Enduring family control is an important characteristic of the firms examined in this book. Raleigh was founded by Frank Bowden in 1887, and the family succession to his son Harold was secured by the creation of a private limited company in 1908, creating a tightly knit family partnership. At Hadfields, during the inter-war years, Sir Robert A. Hadfield, who had succeeded his father, pursued an autocratic style of management, governing the company with a trusted board of directors. The comparison in Chapter 6 between governance at Hadfields and Greenwood & Batley, a diverse engineering firm in Leeds, also shows how members of the Greenwood and Batley families remained prominent directors of that company during the inter-war years. The persistence of personal control linked to a family founder is personified in the case study of Sir Alfred Herbert in Chapter 5. Sir Alfred's individualistic style of leadership dominated the history of Britain's largest machine tool manufacturer, and he remained the 'governing director' of the company, supported by a hand-picked group of 'departmental directors', until his death in 1957, aged 90, having originally founded the company in 1887. Businessmen such as Alfred Herbert and Robert A. Hadfield personified a

---

[31]   R. Church, 'The Family Firm in Industrial Capitalism: International Perspectives on Hypothesis and History', *Business History*, Vol. 35, No. 4 (1993), p. 18.

[32]   Church, 'The Limitations of the Personal Capitalism Paradigm', p. 706; Jeremy, *A Business History of Britain*, p. 186.

[33]   R. Bendix, *Work and Authority in Industry* (New York, Wiley, 1956), pp. 211–12.

[34]   Church, 'The Family Firm in Industrial Capitalism', p. 18.

[35]   D. F. Channon, *The Strategy and Structure of British Enterprise* (London, Macmillan, 1973), cited in Jeremy, *A Business History of Britain*, p. 186.

[36]   Wilson and Thompson, *The Making of Modern Management*, p. 61.

form of governance which may be described in terms of 'charismatic authority',[37] and their entrepreneurial drive shaped the strategic direction of the organisation.

As Roy Church points out in his study of the motor car industry, 'the simple dichotomy of owner-control or control by professional managers is both deceptively inadequate and unsatisfactory for the purpose of establishing both the form and degree to which family [or individual] influence has persisted'.[38] Personal governance was a complex process and evolved over time. As firms evolved in terms of their organisational complexity, the family or entrepreneurial founders necessarily devolved responsibility to professional managerial directors, a recognition of the fact that a 'a single individual, or small group', cannot manage the functions of larger and more diverse organisations.[39]

Nevertheless, this did not necessarily undermine the degree of control by family entrepreneurs, and, as Hannah notes, even in publicly quoted companies 'recruitment' to directorships, 'where it was not confined to family, was still often by patronage of a director or senior manager rather than openly competitive'.[40] Throughout the first half of the twentieth century, administrative hierarchies in larger British companies remained, for the most part, primitive and unsophisticated, and many family owners successfully resisted losing personal control over the enterprises they had either created or inherited. They were able to do this because selection to senior executive positions depended as much on personal and private ties as on managerial competence.[41] Within business organisations, 'personal or professional networks' clearly exist, which represent the informal channels of control often based upon trust and loyalty to senior executives.[42] Thus, for example, the textile manufacturing firm of Courtaulds, despite the recruitment of professional managers to senior level 'was still run in the manner of an autocratic family business'.[43] As the case studies of Herbert and Raleigh in this book demonstrate, the founding entrepreneurs carefully selected managers to internal

---

[37]   For an examination of this idea see R. N. Langlois, 'Personal Capitalism and Charismatic Authority: The Organisational Economics of a Weberian Concept', *Industrial and Corporate Change*, Vol. 17, No. 1 (1997), pp. 195–213.

[38]   R. Church, 'Family Firms and Managerial Capitalism: The Case of the International Motor Industry', in R. Davenport-Hines (ed.), *Business in the Age of Depression and War* (London, Frank Cass, 1990), p. 311.

[39]   Wilson, *British Business History*, p. 11.

[40]   L. Hannah, *The Rise of the Corporate Economy* (London, Methuen, 1983), p. 88. See also D. C. Coleman, 'Gentlemen and Players', *Economic History Review*, Vol. 26, No. 1 (1973), pp. 92–116.

[41]   B. R. Cheffins, 'History and the Global Corporate Governance Revolution: The British Perspective', *Business History*, Vol. 43, No. 4 (2001), p. 91.

[42]   G. Boyce and S. Ville, *The Development of Modern Business* (Basingstoke, Palgrave, 2002), p. 23.

[43]   D. C. Coleman, *Courtaulds: An Economic and Social History*, Volume II (Oxford, Oxford University Press, 1980), p. 237; and Wilson, *British Business History*, p. 151.

directorships, basing their decisions on trust, long-service and loyalty, perpetuating a close association with the existing principles of the organisation. Indeed, at Hadfields, the board of directors was viewed as a collective entity, but one in which Robert Hadfield's leadership of the company would continue to dominate.

Family business and its association with personal forms of governance raised the issue of succession within the organisation. Church has noted that in the first half of the twentieth century 'the continued vigour of family influence' in British business often acted as a constraint to an effective and orderly managerial succession.[44] British business organisation still reflected its nineteenth century features, where 'the foundation for successful corporate strategies was stability of leadership through orderly succession' and this was something that 'family influence', despite the best of intentions, was often unable to supply.[45] Our case study of Herbert demonstrates the long association of the company with its founder, Sir Alfred Herbert, which created a legacy for the board of directors who eventually succeeded him in 1957, and called into question the managerial competency of the long-serving managerial elite and their ability to respond to a rapidly changing business environment.

In a number of large British companies elite non-family executives had control and power within the organisation and had a vested interest in maintaining control. Even in companies that were no longer dominated by family members personal management remained a key characteristic of the managerial style,[46] as exemplified in the case of Sir Harry McGowan, the chairman of Imperial Chemical Industries (ICI), who in 1937 successfully exerted his personal influence to challenge his directors over greater devolution of responsibility.[47] The importance of personal, vested, interests within the organisation is clearly shown in our case study of BSA, a company which by 1900 had long relinquished its family connection. After 1910, a small group of elite directors dominated governance at the company and maintained personal control over its affairs until the early 1930s. While there was no family connection, inter-personal patterns among this dominant group, reinforced by a set of business and political relationships to a former deputy-chairman of the company, Dudley Docker, established a hybrid form of personal capitalism. The emergence of a Chandler-type managerial hierarchy at BSA was suppressed by the personal power of the directorate, in particular the dominant personalities of the deputy chairman, Sir Edward Manville, and the managing director, Percy Martin, who was also a major shareholder.

---

[44]   Church, 'The Family Firm in Industrial Capitalism', p. 29.

[45]   M. B. Rose, 'Beyond Buddenbrooks: The Family Firm and the Management of Succession in Nineteenth Century Britain' (Lancaster University Management School, Discussion paper EC4/91, 1991), pp. 2–16; Church, 'Family Firms and Managerial Capitalism', p. 30.

[46]   Chandler, *Scale and Scope*, p. 239; Wilson, *British Business History*, p. 13.

[47]   Hannah, *The Rise of the Corporate Economy*, pp. 46, 85; W. J. Reader, *Imperial Chemical Industries: A History*, Volume II (Oxford, Oxford University Press, 1975), p. 245.

From the previous discussion, the 'governance' of business, which for Chandler relates to the managerial structure of organisations, may take a variety of forms, and personal capitalism is not simply reducible to the family firm. Non-family members may over time achieve overarching control of organisational strategy, or collaborating elites, as in the case of BSA, may exert executive authority during long periods of the company's history. However, the management style of companies, relating to cultural factors within organisations, which are not explicitly explored by Chandler, is more difficult to determine. As Griffiths argues, Chandler is more concerned with the 'hard' parts of organisation, the strategies they pursue and the structures they create. To the historian these are the visible manifestations of the company, but the 'soft' part of organisations, the cultural style which evolves historically, Chandler tends to relatively neglect.[48] Yet business firms are social organisations, and personal capitalism is identified with the values held by individuals within the firm. The association of personal capitalism with organisational culture involves an analysis of the shared collective values, norms, beliefs and knowledge of actors within the company, which may shape the routines and strategic direction of the organisation. A cultural approach helps us to understand the way things are done within organisations, adding a human element to the study of the business firm.[49] An emphasis upon the importance of organisational culture, what we might describe as the 'core social habits' of business organisations,[50] is an important aspect of our approach to the study of corporate governance in this book. It enables us to explore what is 'real or material

---

[48]   J. Griffiths, 'Give My Regards to "Uncle Billy": The Rites and Rituals of Company Life at Lever Brothers, c. 1900–1990', *Business History*, Vol. 37, No. 4 (1995), p. 25. See also G. Hofstede, *Cultures and Organisations. Intercultural Cooperation: Software of the Mind* (London, McGraw-Hill, 1994), pp. 180, 186, who reminds us that company culture is 'soft', and entails the use of subjective criteria which are difficult to quantify.

[49]   For an examination of cultural values within organisations see M. Alvesson, *Cultural Perspectives on Organisations* (Cambridge, Cambridge University Press, 1993), pp. 1–2; E. H. Schein, *Organisational Culture and Leadership: A Dynamic View* (San Francisco, McGraw-Hill, 1985), p. 110; M. Casson, 'Entrepreneurship and Business Culture', in J. Brown and M. B. Rose (eds), *Entrepreneurship, Networks and Modern Business* (Manchester, Manchester University Press, 1995), p. 45, and for the importance of routines within companies R. Langlois and P. L, Robertson, *Firms, Markets and Economic Change: A Dynamic Theory of Business Institutions* (London, Routledge, 1995), p. 18.

[50]   See R. Lloyd-Jones and M. J. Lewis, 'Business Networks, Social Habits and the Evolution of a Regional Industrial Cluster: Coventry, 1880s–1930s', in J. F. Wilson and A. Popp (eds), *Industrial Clusters and Regional Business Networks in England, 1750–1970* (Aldershot, Ashgate, 2003), pp. 237–40. The idea of social habits within organisations can be traced in the writings of Veblen; see G. M. Hodgson, *Economics and Evolution: Bringing Life Back to Economics* (Cambridge, Cambridge University Press, 1993), pp. 119, 125–6; G. M. Hodgson, 'On the Evolution of Thorstein Veblen's Evolutionary Economics', *Cambridge Journal of Economics*, Vol. 22 (1999), pp. 463–77.

for management',[51] and thus aids us to identify the style of executive management at the top governance level of the company. As Roy Church reminds us, leaders within an organisation shape 'not only the structure of the organisation but the character of relations among those employed, and implicitly or explicitly establish the images, symbols, and rituals associated with the firm's activities'.[52]

The case studies in this book demonstrate common patterns of culture relating to the personal capitalist form of governance, which include, for example, at the boardroom level and amongst employees of the company a high regard for loyalty, trust and longevity of service. There was a clear cultural attachment to the organisation, which transmitted itself in the governing boards in a strong personal identification with the firm, which transcended pecuniary norms. Personal capitalism, of course, implies that the ownership of companies was concentrated in a small group – often a family group – rather than dispersed across a range of personal or institutional shareholders, and unlike American corporations control of the organisation was not devolved to what Chandler called a new professional class of salaried managers, 'who had little or no equity in the firm'.[53] This divorce of ownership and control typified Chandler's idea of managerial capitalism, which found its widest expression first in the USA, but on the issue of a low dispersion of shareholding in British business organisations Chandler has not gone unchallenged.

Share ownership in the first half of the twentieth century: Hannah's challenge

When the Americans Berle and Means in 1932 identified the 'separation of ownership and control' as a key phenomenon of modern capitalism,[54] they were reflecting the location of this phenomenon, which was situated not in Britain but in America, because the dispersal of share ownership had not yet taken place in Great Britain. Such a view is taken up by Chandler, who considers that in the USA

> Such funds as were raised in the capital markets came from the sale of equity, thus increasing the company's shareholders and decreasing the influence of the founders or large investors whose families had inherited positions on boards.[55]

---

[51] K. Lipartito, 'Culture and the Practice of Business History', *Business and Economic History*, Vol. 32, No. 2 (1995), p. 2.

[52] R. Church, 'Demonstrating Nuffield: The Evolution of Managerial Culture in the British Motor Car Industry', *Economic History Review*, Vol. 49, No. 3 (1996), p. 565.

[53] Chandler, *Scale and Scope*, pp. 1, 232. See also A. D. Chandler Jnr, *The Visible Hand: The Managerial Revolution in American Business* (Cambridge, MA, Harvard University Press, 1977).

[54] A. A. Berle and G. C. Means, *The Modern Corporation and Private Property* (New York, Macmillan, 1932).

[55] Chandler, *Scale and Scope*, p. 49.

Contrasting this American perspective with that of Britain, Chandler concludes that in the British case share ownership was less dispersed, and 'personal and family control and management were still more the rule than the exception', with all the consequences this had for the limited competitive capabilities of personally managed enterprise compared to their managerial counterparts in the USA.[56] A challenge to Chandler's comparative interpretation is made by Hannah in his account of share ownership in the early twentieth century. Hannah attacks what he calls Chandler's use of the 'Whig modernization myth'[57] that managerial capitalism allowed the USA to overtake Europe late in the nineteenth century. In contrast to Chandler, Hannah claims that it was actually Britain that led the USA in the development of managerial capitalism for a number of reasons.

Hannah's arguments are based on the operation of both London and local stock markets. Initial Public Offerings (IPO) were more widely dispersed in Britain than in the USA, he suggests, because companies were required by the London Stock Exchange to issue shares with a substantial 'free float' so that at least two-thirds of any offering was taken up by the public.[58] British financial reporting, admittedly, was not well standardised, but despite 'poorly articulated disclosure laws and investor protections', securities markets could work satisfactorily: investors and their professional advisors worked on a basis of trust and shared values. In addition to the London markets, Hannah suggests, there was a strong local network of specialised markets in the industrial heartlands of Britain, which shared information and provided a welcome for local issues, so that:

> A really good thing from Glasgow, or Yorkshire, or Lancashire, or the Midlands, seldom comes to London to be floated to the public. The insiders naturally keep it to themselves and their friends.[59]

Certainly the evidence that we consider in later chapters in this book is demonstrative of the reliance of industrial concerns upon local capital markets for share distribution, and this supports a number of Hannah's claims concerning the wide dispersion of share capital, in marked contrast to the observations of Chandler. In Chapter 6, which compares shareholding at Greenwood & Batley with that of Hadfields Ltd, we suggest that small shareholders played an important role in British companies generally, and this is supported by the finding of Franks, Mayer and Rossi that dispersal of shareholdings in the sample of companies they

---

[56]   Ibid., p. 249.

[57]   L. Hannah, 'Pioneering Modern Corporate Governance: A View from London in 1900', *Enterprise & Society*, Vol. 8, No. 3 (2007), pp. 642–86.

[58]   L. Hannah, 'The "Divorce" of Ownership from Control from 1900 Onwards: Re-calibrating Imagined Global Trends", *Business History*, Vol. 49, No. 4 (2007), p. 414.

[59]   Hannah, 'Pioneering', p. 676 quoting Francis Wrigley Hirst, 1913.

consider took place rapidly between 1900 and 1940.[60] A review of the ownership structure of Raleigh in 1896, considered in Chapter 2, confirms its popularity with small investors: more than half by number (135 out of 234 investors) owned 25 or fewer shares. More than 2,000 of the 7,500 shareholders in Hadfields owned 25 or fewer shares, and a further 3,400 owned between 26 and 100. There is also evidence of strong local links. At Raleigh, more than 88 per cent of shares were held by owners in the Nottingham area where the company was based, and nearly 93 per cent in the Midlands overall. In 1916, 74 per cent of ordinary shareholders of Greenwood & Batley, a Leeds-based company, and 55 per cent of preference shareholders, were from Yorkshire, with only 10 and 13 per cent respectively from London. Hadfields showed a similar though less dramatic pattern, between 1900 and 1930, when 44 per cent of all shareholders and 55 per cent of those with 25 shares or fewer had a Sheffield address, and only 8 per cent were based in London.

It is important, though, to note a number of qualifications to Hannah's case. The examples quoted above show dispersion of ownership, but not necessarily of control. In the Raleigh case, for instance, there is a major distinction to be made between large and small shareholdings. Two-thirds of both ordinary and preference shares were in the hands of a group of six people who owned more than 1,000 of each class of shares, and half of each type of capital was held by the founder and his wife. Similarly, out of Greenwood & Batley's 1916 population of 286 ordinary shareholders, 6 individuals held 5,000 or more, compared with 167 who owned fewer than 500. Significant purchases could be made by a proprietor and his associates, often family associates, at the time of an IPO or immediately afterwards on the open market, and a variety of share types could also help in keeping control within a small group. For example, floating only a company's preference shares allowed access by outsiders to dividends but not to voting control, which as we show typified policy at Hadfields.

Furthermore, it is important to recall that a number of the companies we examine were for at least part of the period in question private companies, with fewer than 50 shareholders, and shares that were not traded on the Stock Exchange. Examples include most notably Alfred Herbert Ltd, which operated as a private company from its incorporation in 1894 until 1944, with shareholders who were linked either as managers, or members of the Herbert family or of managers' families. A comparison between the 'family gathering' atmosphere of the Herbert AGM discussed in Chapter 5, with the confrontations with dissatisfied investors that overtook BSA in the 1930s, discussed in Chapter 4, suggests that the private company regime was a potentially attractive one for many reasons. It facilitated the retention of control by a small group of the founding family and associates, and in addition it reduced pressure from both shareholders and publicity – there was

---

[60]   J. Franks, C. Mayer and S. Rossi, 'Ownership: Evolution and Regulation' (25 March 2005). ECGI – Finance Working Paper No. 09/2003; EFA 2004 Maastricht Meetings Paper No. 3205; AFA 2003 Washington, DC Meetings.

no opportunity for the press to publish reports of AGMs and/or critiques of results. Indeed, our case study of Raleigh reflects over a period of nearly 60 years the use of changes in corporate status to deal with crises and to recover personal control when it seemed advantageous. Originally a private company between 1889 and 1891, after a bumpy ride as a public company between 1889 and 1908, Raleigh was converted by its founder into a partnership and then a private company until it again made a public offering in 1934. The recovery of personal control in 1908 was worth the 10 per cent premium paid on repurchase of the shares in that year. And the study of Raleigh is also demonstrative of the parochial nature of British industrial financing, with the management's distrust of London 'speculators' and an orientation to local stock markets. Paradoxically, while Hannah might claim that the London Stock Exchange bred an environment of trust in equity dealing this was not always evident at the level of the industrial enterprise. A heavy reliance upon local capital markets in the case studies presented, especially before 1914, does suggest the parochial nature of much of British industry and its scepticism of industrial investment opportunities by the City of London, which was a centre of British foreign portfolio investment, rather than a nucleus for promoting wider investment in British industry.[61] Distrust for London investors, and a reliance on local stock markets, was typified in the views of William Edgar Allen, the founder of the Sheffield steel firm of Edgar Allen & Co. in a letter to his managing director in 1908:

> Remember the stock exchange [in London] is regarded by its members as a business concern … for their own mutual and individual profit and benefit, not to oblige you and me how to help us buy and sell, nor for the benefit of investors, nor for public or private companies, but to buy and sell exclusively for themselves.[62]

While industrial capitalism in Britain may well be construed as separated from that of the financial world of the city, Cheffins concludes that Hannah's claim that the 'two-thirds' rule was of major significance in promoting the dispersion of share ownership has some validity. Nevertheless, while it 'fostered at least some dispersion' of share ownership, the existence of the rule 'does not provide conclusive proof of a divorce between ownership and control'.[63] The case studies which follow indicate that the relations between ownership and control were

---

[61]   For a survey of these issues see M. Collins, *Banks and Industrial Finance in Britain, 1800–1939* (Basingstoke, Macmillan, 1991); M. Collins and M. Baker, *Commercial Banks and Industrial Finance in England and Wales, 1860–1913* (Oxford, Oxford University Press, 2004), pp. 1–23; Wilson, *British Business History*, pp. 121–9.

[62]   Cited in R. Lloyd-Jones and M. J. Lewis, 'British Industrial Capitalism During the Second Industrial Revolution: A Schumpeterian Approach', *Journal of Industrial History*, Vol. 1, No. 1 (1998), p. 77.

[63]   B. R. Cheffins, *Corporate Ownership and Control, British Business Transformed* (Oxford, Oxford University Press, 2009), p. 299.

perhaps more fraught than Chandler has suggested, but that the tension did not lead to outright divorce in the early part of the twentieth century. Indeed, even in American companies during this period, as Berle and Means were aware back in 1932, minority shareholders could still retain control of executive positions within the organisation.[64]

Conclusion

Case studies provide the opportunity to explore in depth the governance of a company or limited number of companies, complement works of synthesis, and enable a more nuanced history of the evolution of corporate governance and personal capitalism in twentieth-century Britain.[65] In explaining the relevance of case studies to an understanding of corporate governance, it is helpful to look at two recent examples of studies which consider Chandler's judgement on UK companies. Matthews, Boyns, Edwards and Richard consider the history of Albright & Wilson, a British chemical company with US subsidiaries, between 1892 and 1923. They highlight the extent to which Albright & Wilson used a highly developed accounting system to monitor US performance, and also its readiness to make substantial investment in research and development (R&D).[66] They argue that Chandler's suggestion that UK firms were slow to adopt modern managerial methods was based on 'reliance on a single secondary source' and that archival materials are potentially important to a better understanding of personal capitalism in Britain.[67]

Kininmonth, in her study of the Scottish thread manufacturer J. & P. Coats,[68] aims for 'a more nuanced perspective' on personal capitalism in the UK than she finds provided by Chandler.[69] Coats, she finds, was 'continuously profitable over the period 1890 to 1960,[70] 'although the company was under family control, it made extensive use of committees during the period, which took responsibility for areas including finance, manufacturing, purchasing and marketing'.[71] She

---

[64] Berle and Means, *The Modern Corporation and Private Property*, p. 156.

[65] See Cheffins, 'History and the Global Corporate Governance Revolution', pp. 87–118; and *Corporate Ownership and Control*.

[66] M. Matthews, T. Boyns, T. Edwards and J. Richard, 'Chandlerian Image or Mirror Image? Managerial and Accounting Control in the Chemical Industry: The Case of Albright & Wilson, c. 1892 to c. 1923', *Business History*, Vol. 45, No. 4, (2003), pp. 24–52.

[67] Ibid., p. 48.

[68] K. W. Kininmonth, 'The Growth, Development and Management of J. & P. Coats Ltd, c.1890–1960: An Analysis of Strategy and Structure', *Business History*, Vol. 48, No. 4 (2006), pp. 551–79.

[69] Ibid., p. 552.

[70] Ibid., p. 563.

[71] Ibid., p. 571.

argues that the company's managerial innovation is a challenge to Chandler's theory, which states that a strategy aimed at increasing managerial control over the workplace was needed for significant structural adaptation to occur. This does seem to be what happened at Coats, even though Chandler doubted that British business was capable of doing it. In her verdict on British governance in general, Kininmonth finds Chandler 'for the most part, both inaccurate and inappropriate, underestimating the firm's strategic and structural sophistication'.[72]

Both studies highlight the insights that can be offered by cases based on a close encounter with archival material – the opportunity for a close examination of an organisation and the particular characteristics of its regime of governance. This book builds on case studies drawn from a variety of industries and regions with the aim of examining the development of corporate governance in a range of different contexts. The firms considered tend to be characterised by forms of personal governance reflected often in the influence of the founders and/or a long serving group of permanent directors. It is important to note, however, that the sample of firms also displayed differences in the pattern of evolution of their governance systems. Some were clearly family-controlled firms, whilst others evolved into large, complex and diverse holding-company structures, notably BSA. They vary considerably in size, some achieving both national and international status. For example, Hadfield's was one of Sheffield's largest steel producers, employing 5,690 workers in 1914, and with subsidiary interests in the Australian, South African and American markets, while Alfred Herbert was the largest machine tool firm in Europe by the 1920s, employing 2,500 workers in 1925.

The cluster of firms making up the case studies presented here range across key industries of the second industrial revolution which entered their diffusion stage in the first half of the twentieth century. The sectors covered include specialist steels and alloys; semi-automatic and automatic machine tools; new forms of armaments; bicycles, motorcycles, car and public transport vehicles; and turbines and aero-engines. The regional clustering of the case studies, based on the well-established industrial regions of Yorkshire and Lancashire, and the more recent manufacturing activities of the Midlands, especially Coventry, reflects the decentralised control structure of personal capitalist enterprise in Britain that tended to use local sources of capital and labour. Through family ties, partnership links, contractual networking, and cross-directorships, as well as the legal devices of the private limited liability and holding company forms, manufacturing firms sought to mobilise at the regional level financial resources, to link finance to technical expertise, and to develop a close interwoven system of directorships to maintain control of their organisations.

It is not asserted that this book will provide a full understanding of the contemporary context of corporate governance, as that is not the role of historical analysis. Rather, the study will help identify those aspects of corporate governance that have undergone change, with some critical observations on the magnitude

---

[72]   Ibid., p. 572.

of change, and those which have displayed characteristics of continuity. Why have certain aspects of the governance system changed more rapidly than others, what are some of the implications of such changes, and what is their relationship to the evolution of personal capitalism on the one hand, and the market-cum technological, financial and legal environment on the other?

Hannah, in his attack on Chandler's account of the development of British capitalism in the early twentieth century, complains that Chandler asserts the relative national incidence of 'personal capitalism' on the basis of liberal – and apparently quite arbitrary – sprinkling of adjectives like 'personal', 'family', and 'professional' about his narrative.[73] Without echoing this criticism, we argue that detailed case studies have the potential to offer fresh insights into the complex and varied nature of governance, and to suggest the complexity and variety of organisation in this crucial period of industrial change. In essence we assume that organisations may well demonstrate idiosyncratic patterns, and their 'owners, managers ... and individuals' have 'the potential for affecting corporate structure and strategy in important, yet indeterminate ways'.[74] Business 'firms are generally heterogeneous even in the way they accomplish functionally similar tasks',[75] and consequently 'idiosyncratic knowledge and ways of acting are at the heart of the firm as an organisation'.[76] Understanding governance systems requires an examination of the 'personal dimension', which 'relates to the networks of power within the organisation and to the fostering of a distinctive company culture', and aids the identification of the form of governance within the company.[77] As Nelson observes, once elite groups become entrenched within organisations, the business structure and governance of the company are more difficult to change than strategy.[78] They 'tend to resist the growth of managerial hierarchies', which may threaten their power and standing, and may lead to tension with corporate stakeholders.[79] These tensions are central in many of the cases which are explored in this book.

---

[73]   Hannah, 'The "Divorce" of Ownership' p. 437.

[74]   Church, 'Demonstrating Nuffield', p. 565.

[75]   G. Dosi, R. R. Nelson and S. G. Winter, 'Introduction: The Nature and Dynamics of Organizational Capabilities', in G. Dosi, R. R. Nelson and S. G. Winter (eds), *The Nature and Dynamics of Organizational Capabilities* (Oxford, Oxford University Press, 2000), p. 12.

[76]   Langlois and Robertson, *Firms, Markets and Economic Change*, p. 13.

[77]   R. Lloyd-Jones and M. J. Lewis, '"A New Paradigm of British Business History": A Critique of Toms and Wilson', *Business History*, Vol. 49, No. 1 (2007), p. 101.

[78]   Nelson, *The Sources of Economic Growth*, p. 111.

[79]   Lloyd-Jones and Lewis, '"A New Paradigm of British Business History": A Critique of Toms and Wilson', p. 100.

.

Chapter 2
Raleigh and the Bowdens: Personal Capitalism and Business Performance, 1887–1939

Introduction

Raleigh's origins can be traced back to a Nottingham street in 1887, from where the company took its name. The name of Raleigh became synonymous with the manufacture and marketing of quality bicycles, noted for their reliability and value for money, and the company developed a reputation both in the UK and in world markets. Raleigh's system of governance and organisational culture was shaped by the entrepreneurial drive and vision of its founder, Frank Bowden, and subsequently by his son Harold. The firm was not simply a family affair; as the enterprise grew the Bowdens consolidated their control, but they also came to rely on a small, loyal and long-serving group of company directors. There is little evidence of the emergence of a managerial hierarchy, and it was under a personal capitalist form of governance that Raleigh grew, developed and prospered. Raleigh competed among some of the most illustrious names in the development of the British bicycle industry, many of which later became motor car manufacturers. Such firms included Morris, Rover, Riley, Hillman, Humber, Singer, Triumph, Sunbeam and BSA, all of which were engaged in the market for the new system of personal transport that emerged at the end of the nineteenth century. Representing one of the new industries of the second industrial revolution Raleigh was a dynamic firm; a 'first mover' in the bicycle industry.[1] For most of its history, the firm combined enterprise, innovation and a progressive business strategy, which delivered considerable financial success and earned the company a high reputation from its competitors.[2] During the period covered in this study, the company underwent a series of changes in status, starting life as a private partnership, then converting to a public company, before becoming a private family concern in 1908, and in 1934 a public holding company (see Table 2.1).

---

[1] For the idea of the 'first mover' see Chandler, *Scale and Scope*, p. 236.
[2] For the importance of 'reputation' to business success, see J. Kay, *The Business of Economics* (Oxford, Oxford University Press, 1996), p. 46.

Table 2.1   Raleigh: change in company status

Date	Event
1887	Frank Bowden enters into partnership with Angois, Woodhead and Ellis, and supplies fresh working capital.
1888	Partnership dissolved and private company formed – Raleigh Cycle Co.
1889	Company converted to a public company – Raleigh Cycle Co. Ltd.
1891	Raleigh Cycle Co. Ltd. dissolved, and 'New Raleigh Cycle Co.' registered, with a new share issue.
1896	Reconstruction – company of 1891 dissolved, new public company formed with issues of ordinary and preference shares.
1899	Another reconstruction – New Raleigh Cycle Co. voluntarily wound up and new company formed with reduced nominal capital of £120,000.
1904	New share issue of 120,000 ordinary shares.
1908	Frank Bowden buys up all shares and forms partnership with his son Harold.
1915	Raleigh becomes a private limited company.
1934	Raleigh Cycle Holdings Co. Ltd formed with public subscription of 2.25 million shares.
1946	Raleigh Cycle Holdings Co. Ltd changes name to Raleigh Industries Ltd.

To explore governance at the company, this chapter firstly explores the turbulent early years of the company's history, where it faced a uncertain market environment, financial distress, and during a series of capital reconstructions a challenge to Frank Bowden's leadership. Secondly, there is an examination of the company's business strategy during the Edwardian period, the threat to Bowden's personal control of the company, and the eventual securing of family control by the formation of a private company in 1915. Finally, the chapter assesses the leadership of Harold Bowden during the inter-war years, the devolution of authority to trusted long-serving directors, and the implications for governance of a holding company in 1934.

The early years: corporate governance and business performance

Raleigh's founder, Frank Bowden, made his fortune in property development in Hong Kong in the 1870s and supplemented his accumulating funds by marrying an American heiress in 1879. By the end of the 1880s, Bowden was a successful venture capitalist who on his return to Britain was looking to use his entrepreneurial know-how and substantial funds in a new business enterprise. The firm that he eventually acquired was the little-known Nottingham concern of Woodhead, Angois and Ellis, based in Raleigh Street. Organised as a private partnership, this firm combined the talents of a skilled mechanic, R. M. Woodhead, a technical designer, Paul Angois, and a small-time financier, William Ellis, who ran the commercial side of the business.[3] Three factors attracted Bowden to the business. First, from a purely personal aspect Bowden was attracted to cycling because he considered it a healthy activity; he remained a cycling enthusiast all his life and was a keen promoter of cycling as a sport, an increasingly popular activity in late Victorian Britain.[4] Second, Bowden had an acute business sense. He quickly recognised the potential of the newly invented safety cycle, and the attributes of Woodhead and Angois on the mechanical and design sides, but believed that they had insufficiently exploited the market opportunities for their innovative designs.[5] Finally, Bowden was confident that Woodhead and Angois had the necessary expertise to develop the product and this would allow him to focus his attention to developing the commercial and marketing side of the business.[6]

Bowden's direct involvement with the firm dates from 1887, when he entered into a partnership agreement with Woodhead, Angois and Ellis. On the condition that he gained a 'free hand' in the administration of the enterprise, Bowden injected fresh working capital into the business to expand output. His personal control was consolidated a year later when he bought out Ellis's one-third stake in the company for £1,000, and he paid an additional £1,000 each to the other partners, to ensure an equal partnership in the concern. As part of the financial restructuring the partnership was placed on a formal footing by the allocation of £10,000 in £1 ordinary shares, £5,000 distributed to Bowden and £2,500 each to Angois and Woodhead. No shares were allotted to the public and the company remained private. The dominant figure in the new organisation was Bowden, who was 'his own manager, traveller, salesman and accountant'. Bowden also provided

---

[3]   G. H. Bowden, *The Story of the Raleigh Cycle* (London, W. H. Allen, 1975), p. 13.

[4]   R. Lloyd-Jones and M. J. Lewis, *Raleigh and the British Bicycle Industry. An Economic and Business History, 1870–1960* (Aldershot, Ashgate, 2000), pp. 7–8, 47; A. B. Demaus and J. C. Tarring, *The Humber Story, 1868–1932* (Stroud, Alan Sutton, 1989), p. 4.

[5]   Lloyd-Jones and Lewis, *Raleigh*, p. 49. For the attraction of the safety cycle from the mid-1880s to a growing middle-class market see A. Millward, 'The Cycle Industry in Birmingham, c1890–1920', in B. Tilson (ed.), *Made in Birmingham 1859–1985* (Studley, Warwick and Brewin, 1989), p. 172.

[6]   Lloyd-Jones and Lewis, *Raleigh*, p. 49.

the capital investment for expansion and in 1889, in order to reduce his personal risk, the partnership agreement was dissolved and in its place the Raleigh Cycle Co. was incorporated as a public limited company. Consequently, the nominal capital of the business was doubled to £20,000, Bowden subscribing £10,000, and Woodhead and Angois a further £5,000 between them. Of the remaining allocation, £1,000 was designated as £1 founder's shares, Bowden receiving 692, and the remainder divided between Woodhead and Angois. The residual shares, totalling £4,000, were then advertised in the local press, subscriptions being invited from local businessmen and investors. Ownership remained in the hands of the original proprietors, ensured by the legal rights attached to the founder shares, and control was firmly in the hands of Frank Bowden, who was appointed chairman and managing director. To consolidate his position, Bowden purchased the majority of the publicly subscribed shares. In the division of managerial responsibilities the two other proprietors, Woodhead and Angois, concentrated on functional tasks related to the day-to-day operations of the company.[7]

The underlying factor which formed the basis of the company's early success was Bowden's conception and implementation of a business strategy which utilised and enhanced the organisation's core capabilities, and was underpinned by a capital restructuring which was intended to consolidate his control and secure a sound capital base for the firm's long-term growth and survival. Bowden's business strategy managed to bring 'faith' and 'calculation'[8] together in an optimum combination which gave strategic direction to the firm. The key strategic questions that Bowden identified were what the potential markets were that the firm could profitably enter, how the company's products were to be positioned, what type of networks were required to establish effective relations with component suppliers, dealers and distributors, and what the appropriate organisational and financial structures were that would secure the resources and capabilities the firm needed to survive and prosper.

Bowden's strategy was to enter the market for quality bicycles, positioning the company's products to meet the growing middle-class demand opened up by the advent of the safety cycle. Such a strategy required a significant increase in output but this was constrained by factory capacity, which was wholly inadequate both in scale and design. At the end of the 1880s the firm only employed 12

---

[7]   Nottinghamshire Archives, Raleigh Records, DDRN 2/7/1, Forms of Notices and Cuttings and Circulars to Shareholders, *Daily Nottingham Express*, 4 February 1896; DDRN 7/2/12, Sir Harold Bowden, Manuscript of the History of the Raleigh Company, n.d., unpublished, p. 7; DDRN 3/1/1, Company Ledger; DDRN 4/10/1/8, Frank Bowden, in The Book of the Raleigh (the company's sales catalogue) for 1904 Season, p. 4; DDRN 7/2/7, History of the Raleigh Cycle Co. Ltd. n.d.; DDRN 10/3/9/3, Prospectus of the Raleigh Cycle Co. Ltd., 1891.

[8]   See Nelson, *The Sources of Economic Growth*, p. 110, for a discussion of the idea that management commitments to a strategy are often 'as much a matter of faith … and company tradition, as they are of calculation'.

workers and a good deal of the actual work was done by Woodhead and Angois.[9] By 1891 the company was employing 200 workers, a five-storey factory was rented and production was 60 machines a week compared to just three in the mid-1880s. The capital resources to support the expansion were supplied almost exclusively by Bowden, the level of internal profits proving insufficient for self-financing. Consequently, he provided both the fixed capital for the expansion of capacity, and the working capital to sustain trading operations. To support this investment strategy, Bowden designed an advertisement and propaganda campaign to promote the reputation of Raleigh products both at home and abroad. Bowden was not simply the architect of the strategy; he played an active role in implementing it and travelled extensively abroad promoting the company's products. By the early 1890s, Raleigh had acquired some 400 agents acting for the firm all over the world and employed over 400 workers in its Nottingham plants.[10]

So rapid was the pace of expansion that Bowden accepted that a major capital reconstruction was needed and he dissolved the old company. The 'New Raleigh Cycle Co. Ltd' was registered in 1891, with a nominal capital of £100,000, divided into £99,000 in £1 ordinary shares and £1,000 in £1 founder's shares. Table 2.2

Table 2.2   Number of shares allotted on incorporation of Raleigh Cycle Co. Ltd, 1891

£1 founder's shares		£1 ordinary shares	
Frank Bowden	692	Frank Bowden	19,000
R. M. Woodhead	154	R. M. Woodhead	6,000
P. Angois	154	P. Angois	6,000
		Mrs. A. Bowden	8,000
		R. S. Gutteridge	3
		E. Strorbridge	3
		M. Bryan	3
		J. Lazonby	3
Total allocated	1,000		39,012

Source: DDRN 10/3/8 Allotment Book Register of Members and Annual Share Ledger of the Raleigh Cycle Co Ltd.

---

[9]   Bowden, Manuscript, p. 7; *Nottingham Daily Express*, 4 February 1896.
[10]   DDRN 4/10/1/8, Frank Bowden, in the Book of Raleigh for 1904, p. 4; Bowden, *The Story of the Raleigh Cycle*, pp. 16–17; DDRN 1/1/1–6, Raleigh Cycle Co. Ltd, Directors and General Meetings, Minutes 1891–1908, 4 April 1892.

shows the number of fully paid-up shares allotted to the vendors on incorporation. The flotation of 1891 was designed to ensure Bowden's position as the majority shareholder, and of the 39,000 fully paid-up shares allotted Bowden and his wife received 27,000. In addition, Bowden offered 29,988 partly paid £1 ordinary shares for public subscription and of these he applied for 10,000, Woodhead and Angois 1,000 each and the new directors of the company a total of 3,300. This left 14,688 partly paid shares for public issue, which attracted 212 subscribers, mainly from local investors who took the minimum offer of 5 shares each. The majority shareholding remained with Bowden supplemented by those with a direct engagement with the firm. Nevertheless, the strategy of expansion did lead to restructuring of the top management of the firm, and Bowden recognised the need to broaden the knowledge base of the organisation. Three new directors were appointed, two with banking connections – George Fellows, the manager of the Nottingham branch of Lloyds Bank, and Joseph Lazonby, a local banker – while the third, Sir John Turney, was a local Nottingham businessman and chairman of Turney Bros., a family firm of leather dressers. Bowden, who was installed as chairman and managing director, was the dominant figure and the new executive team was portrayed as a group of talented businessmen who would support the chairman and help him guide the company with skill and foresight.[11]

Business progress, however, proved more difficult than Bowden and the directors had anticipated. Although sales rose between 1892 and 1894, a year later on the eve of the bicycling boom Raleigh was facing financial difficulties, and in 1896 the company again underwent a financial reconstruction.[12] The immediate problem was that the company's production policy, based upon increasing output and building sufficient stock of cycles to meet rising demand, was compromised because of an over-reliance on component suppliers and market dealers. Suppliers were slow to deliver key components, notably forks and tubing, and dealers and agents, who did not sell exclusively for Raleigh, tended to push cheaper makes to customers first, rather than the higher-priced Raleigh cycles. Constrained on both the production and sales side, the company suffered a low turn-over of stock, and difficulties arose in providing the necessary revenue to meet production expenses. Added to this were considerable problems with delayed payments on goods dispatched. This all resulted in an increase in the company's bank overdraft, which by 1895 had reached £15,000, leading to the company issuing a second mortgage

---

[11]   DDRN 10/3/9/3, Prospectus of the Raleigh Cycle Co. Ltd, 1891; DDRN 1/1/1–6, Directors and General Meetings, 28 December 1891, 4 April 1892; DDRN 10/3/8, Allotment Book Register of Members and Annual Share Ledger of the Raleigh Cycle Co Ltd; DDRN 2/7/1 Forms of Notes and Cuttings and Circulars to Shareholders, Frank Bowden, Circular to shareholders, 27 June 1904.

[12]   DDRN, 3/1/2–3, Company Ledgers. For the impact of the bicycle boom on the British industry see Millward, 'The Cycle Industry', pp. 165–6; A. E. Harrison, 'The Origins and Growth of the UK Cycle Industry', *Journal of Transport History*, Vol. 6, No. 1 (1985), pp. 41–70; Lloyd-Jones and Lewis, *Raleigh*, pp. 24–31.

debenture, following the first which had been issued in 1893, as security to the bank.[13] Reliance on bank finance was unacceptable to Bowden, as it threatened his control of the company, and decisive action was called for. He believed that there was a failure of core competencies in the management of the company's factories and he laid the blame squarely on Woodhead and Angois. At a heated board meeting in October 1894, Bowden took the offensive, complaining that the two managers had failed to sufficiently meet customer demand because of inadequacies of both production and delivery. As Bowden asserted, his former partners 'had not shown the degree of initiative, enterprise and enthusiasm which was so essential if progress was to be increased'. The outcome was that both men resigned and left the company, leaving Bowden as the sole founder.[14]

It was in the context of this decisive action by Bowden that he made the decision to liquidate the old company and reconstruct a new one with an extended nominal capital base. To achieve this, he had to demonstrate considerable skills in persuading shareholders to agree to liquidation and reconstruction. In the first place, shareholder confidence had to be maintained, in terms of both the security of their existing investments in the old company and the future financial viability of the new venture. Thus, in a circular to shareholders he reassured them that the company's bank balance was now in credit, debenture mortgages had been fully repaid, and trade debts owing to the company had been fully recovered. Further, he could guarantee that existing shareholders would be paid a dividend of 3s on the ordinary shares of the old company.[15] Additionally, he staked his own reputation and his commitment to the company and to its future success. Denying press rumours that he was about to retire from active management, Bowden reminded shareholders that he was a major shareholder in the old company and no 'better assurance could be forthcoming of faith in the future … than the fact that directors of the [new] company held the majority of shares'.[16] In the public arena, Bowden affirmed that the strategic direction of the firm would remain in his capable hands, together with a new management team that included C. P. Mills, works manager, and D. W. Bassett, general manager, both personally recruited by Bowden from the rival Humber Cycle Co. Both Mills and Bassett were to take up share purchases in the new company, a fact that was communicated to shareholders in the prospectus of 1896, a signal of their long-term commitments.[17]

Personal capitalist forms of organisation, we argue, are here clearly located within the regional business networks of the Midlands industrial district. As Table 2.3 shows, the largest shareholders in the company were Nottingham based, and

[13]   DDRN 1/1/1–6, Directors and General Meetings, 10 January 1893; DDRN 3/1/2–3, Company Ledgers.

[14]   DDRN 1/1/1–6, Directors and General Meetings, 26 September, 2 October 1894; Bowden Manuscript, p. 12.

[15]   DDRN 2/7/1, Frank Bowden, Circular to Shareholders, 30 January 1896.

[16]   *Nottingham Daily Express*, 4 February 1896.

[17]   Ibid.; DDRN 2/7/1, Prospectus of the Raleigh Cycle Co. Ltd., 1896.

Table 2.3   Large shareholders holding 1,001+ ordinary and preference shares in Raleigh Cycle Co., 1896

	Location	Description	Preference	Ordinary
Frank Bowden	Nottingham	Cycle manufacturer	12,801	12,801
Amelia F. Bowden	Nottingham	Married	4,000	4,000
William Woodhouse	Nottingham	Coal merchant	1,805	1,805
Joseph F. Youngman	Nottingham	Manager, Nottingham Joint Stock Bank	1,264	1,264
Arthur J. Chamberlain	Nottingham	Solicitor	1,090	1,090
Joseph Lazonby	Nottingham	Solicitor	1,077	1,077

Source: DDRN 10/3/1/3/1, Agreement Between the Old Raleigh Cycle Co., Incorporated 1891, and the New Company, Incorporated 1896 for the Reconstruction of the Company, Supplement, 29 April 1896.

together this group represented 88.4 per cent of paid-up ordinary and preference shares in the company. Of all shareholders, 44.9 per cent were resident in the Nottingham area, as shown in Table 2.4. Large numbers of shareholders were also attracted from Birmingham and the Midlands, representing the main locality for bicycle manufacture in the late nineteenth century. Within these regions, local investor networks provided the main source of financial capital for industrial enterprise, and at Raleigh Bowden's commitment to the company, his reputation as a trustworthy businessman, acted to attract investment at the regional level.[18]

The personal style of governance at Raleigh acted as an important factor in shaping the governance of the company, and in ensuring its long-term survival. Consequently, under Bowden's guidance the new management team of Mills and Bassett were given the responsibility of running a new factory financed from the capital reconstruction of 1896. At the same time, Bowden strengthened the core competencies at the top of the company, appointing five new directors, with only Lazonby remaining from the board of the old company. Reflecting the importance of local connections to shareholder confidence, the new directors were respectable local businessmen with a legal or financial background. Table 2.5 provides a profile of the board in 1896, and clearly shows the importance of local financial interests, a factor which was prominent in the sales pitch in the 1896 prospectus, a signal to potential of trust and respectability.[19] Most important of all for shareholder trust

---

[18]   See Lloyd-Jones and Lewis, 'Business Networks', pp. 230–32.

[19]   DDRN 2/7/1, Prospectus of the Raleigh Cycle Co. Ltd., 1896.

Table 2.4   Geographic distribution of shareholders and holdings of shares in
              the Raleigh Cycle Co. Ltd, 1896

Location	% of total shareholders[a]	% of total paid-up shares[b]
Nottingham and District	44.9	88.4
Birmingham and Midlands	20.9	4.3
London and South East	8.5	1.1
Ireland	5.1	0.8
Lancashire	3.8	0.9
South West	3.8	0.9
North West	3.0	1.3
Derbyshire	3.1	0.7
Yorkshire	2.6	0.4
Scotland	1.7	0.5
Foreign	1.3	0.5
North East	1.3	0.2

Source: As Table 2.3.
Notes: a. There were a total of 234 shareholders; b. Paid-up shares totalled 33,333 preference shares and 33,333 ordinary shares, holders dividing them in equal amounts.

was their attachment to the permanency of business leadership. Thus, mindful of his governing role, Bowden was careful to inform prospective investors that the newly appointed directors were to act in an advisory capacity in the running of the enterprise.[20]

The financial reconstruction was clearly attractive to small investors (Table 2.6), with 88 per cent of the 234 investors in the company holding between 1 and 100 shares, which accounted for just 19.7 per cent of the paid-up capital in the new company. Shareholdings were widely dispersed, but large shareholders, holding more than 1,001 shares, accounted for 66.1 per cent of the paid-up share capital, and Bowden remained the dominant shareholder, holding 38 per cent of the share capital. Together with the holdings of his wife, he held 50 per cent of the share capital in the new company.[21] Bowden's financial commitment symbolised the

[20]   Ibid.; *Nottingham Daily Express*, 4 May 1896; DDRN 3/1/2/2, Raleigh Cycle Agreement for Sale or Purchase of Business upon Reconstruction, 4 March 1896.

[21]   DDRN 2/7/1, Wells & Hind (solicitors), Circular to Shareholders, 30 October 1896; DDRN 10/3/1/3/1, Agreement between Old Raleigh Co. incorporated 1891 and the new

Table 2.5   Directors of the New Raleigh Cycle Co. Ltd of 1896

Frank Bowden	Chairman and managing director, Nottingham
John Pearson Cox	Chairman of Moore & Robinsons Nottinghamshire Banking Co. Ltd
Ernest W. Enfield	Late partner in Hurst, Fellows & Co., bankers of Nottingham, and now amalgamated with Lloyds Bank
William Lambert	Director of Nottingham and Nottinghamshire Banking Co.
Joseph Lazonby	Solicitor and Manager of Cumberland Union Banking Co.
William Wright	Director of Moore & Robinsons Nottinghamshire Banking Co. Ltd
Arthur J. Chamberlain	Solicitor, Nottingham

Source: DDRN 2/7/1, Prospectus of the Raleigh Cycle Co. Ltd, 1896.

Table 2.6   Distribution of shareholders of ordinary and preference shares, Raleigh Cycle Co., 1896

Shareholding size	Shareholders no.	Shareholders %	Paid-up shares held no.	Paid-up shares %
1–25	135	57.7	4,200	6.3
26–100	71	31.2	8,904	13.4
101–500	21	8.1	8,738	13.1
501–1,000	1	0.4	750	1.1
1,001+	6	2.6	44,074	66.1
Totals	234	100.0	66,666	100.0

Source: as Table 2.3.

independence of the company, allaying shareholder fears that Raleigh would be absorbed into the speculative ventures which characterised the bicycle boom.[22]

---

company incorporated 1896, Supplement, 29 April 1896.

[22]   For the speculative nature of the bicycle boom see A. E. Harrison, 'Growth, Entrepreneurship and Capital Formation in the United Kingdom's Cycle and Related Industries, 1870–1914', University of York, unpublished PhD thesis (1977), pp. 360–62;

During the build-up to the 1896 reconstruction, prominent in the minds of shareholders were the activities of an outsider, the company promoter E. T. Hooley, a former Nottingham lace manufacturer turned stockbroker. In 1895, Hooley had proposed the buy-out of Raleigh's rival in cycle manufacture, the Humber Co., and its public flotation, which caused general consternation in the trade press as well as leading to considerable turmoil in the governance of that company. Hooley was one of the leading industrial promoters of his time, and one of the most notorious, and his association at Humber with its general manager, Martin D. Rucker, created deep suspicions among investors generally.[23] At Raleigh, Hooley had acted in negotiations with Lloyds Bank in 1895 for the extension of the company's overdraft, and was described as 'a mutual friend' of Bowden. Hooley's association with Bowden created deep suspicion among shareholders, and undoubtedly was a key factor in Bowden's constant reassurances to shareholders of his own continued association with the company. Thus, Bowden informed shareholders in February 1896, of the 'erroneous' statements in the press that he had conspired with outside agencies and that Raleigh was, with Humber, 'controlled by a syndicate'.[24] Although the company had a wide spread of shareholders, Bowden nevertheless was well aware that they carried a voice, and that ethical conduct was important in the governance relationship with stakeholders.

Despite Bowden's considerable skill in managing the reconstruction of 1896, an achievement made easier by the high confidence engendered by the bicycle boom, the new company proved even less reliable than its predecessor. The new management team did not provide the harmony and efficiency Bowden expected, leading to yet another reconstruction in 1899, and a relationship between management and shareholders which was hardly harmonious. Disputes in the board room rumbled on into the new century, at times causing a serious challenge to Bowden's leadership, as he became embroiled in a battle for control. While turmoil reigned in the board, Bowden nevertheless was able to guide the company through the difficult economic climate of the late 1890s, and maintain the company's reputation as a high-quality maker of bicycles that served national and international markets.

Long-run business success, however, was no foregone conclusion, despite Bowden's optimistic overtones to shareholders on the reconstruction of the company in 1896. Swayed by the high expectations of the bicycle boom in 1896, Bowden could confidently predict high future profits to shareholders, but the boom collapsed in the summer of 1897.[25] Prior to this, Bowden had been forced to relinquish control over the business affairs of the company through ill health,

A. E. Harrison, 'Joint Stock Company Floatation in the Cycle, Motor Vehicle and Related Industries 1882–1914', *Business History*, Vol. 23, No. 2 (1981), pp. 165–90.

[23]   Lloyd-Jones and Lewis, *Raleigh*, pp. 28–31.

[24]   *Nottingham Daily Express*, 4 May 1896.

[25]   See Lloyd-Jones and Lewis, *Raleigh*, pp. 68–83.

and in December 1896 Bassett was elevated to temporary managing director.[26] After recuperating in Australia, Bowden returned in July 1897, to confront a precarious financial situation. Surveying the company's performance, he was 'much astonished and upset … that during the past five months the expenses of the company had been exceedingly great, and that there was now an enormously heavy stock of raw materials, cycles and parts, whilst the output in comparison with the large outgoings could only be described as trivial'.[27] While Bowden held Bassett directly responsible, he also accused other directors who had not monitored 'the great discrepancy between the output and the expenses'.[28] Quick to recognise that a growing crisis was brewing, Bowden addressed the financial problems of the company. Attempts were made to re-position the company's product range by offering cheaper machines, notably the 'Gazelle' brand, which was privately owned by Bowden, but the chairman was wary of undermining Raleigh's reputation as a maker of quality bicycles.[29] On the financial side, however, the company faced a deepening crisis, which threatened to undermine shareholder confidence. Directing his displeasure at Bassett's incompetent management, Bowden argued that this was primarily responsible for the financial difficulties, with an unacceptable rise in the company's bank overdraft. In 1898, Raleigh recorded a trading loss of £24,000 'and the view of the [Lloyds] Bank was that the Raleigh … trade creditors have been paid at the bank's expense'.[30]

With Raleigh facing a rising liquidity problem, Lloyds Bank now played a direct role in determining governance relations at the company. Although the bank was prepared to service Raleigh's overdraft, it would only do so after another reconstruction of the company, and with the understanding that Bowden would return as managing director in place of Bassett.[31] Not surprisingly, Bowden accepted the bank's proposal and in this he was supported by a shareholders committee formed in January 1898. Chaired by Edward Harlow, a Nottingham solicitor and stocks and shares broker, the committee comprised Sir John Turney, the former Raleigh director, and two local yarn merchants, A. Schmidt and S. Morley.[32] The shareholder committee formed the basis for stakeholder support for Bowden, but was also consistent with his conception of governance and his

[26]   DDRN 1/1/1–6, Directors and General Meetings, 28 October 1896; DDRN 2/7/1, Frank Bowden, Circular to Shareholders, 27 January 1897.

[27]   DDRN/1/1–6, Directors and General Meetings, 13 July 1897.

[28]   DDRN 1/1/1–6, Directors and General Meetings, 30 March 1897.

[29]   DDRN 1/1/1–6, Directors and General Meetings, 18 January, 29 March, 26 April, 10, 24 May 1898.

[30]   DDRN 1/1/1–6, Directors and General Meetings, 7 June, 19 July, 29 August, 19 October 1898.

[31]   DDRN 1/1/1–6, Directors and General Meetings, 19, 25, 28 October 1898.

[32]   DDRN 1/1/1–6, Directors and General Meetings, 11 November 1898; DDRN 10/3/4/6/1, Memorandum and Articles of Association of the Raleigh Cycle Co., incorporated 15 February 1899.

principle that the company should be held accountable to shareholders. It has to be acknowledged, of course, that this belief may have been premised on the fact that he and his family were the majority shareholders, but it is reasonable to suggest that Bowden did bring an ethical dimension to the company's governance. For example, in 1897 when he returned to Nottingham he accused Bassett of not paying enough attention to shareholders or customers in relation to proposals to form an associate company, the Kestrel Cycle Co., to manufacture cheaper models.[33] 'It was not fair' to Raleigh shareholders for a rival concern to be started, and it could not be 'considered straight dealing'.[34] While boardroom tensions rose, of course, the financial difficulties of the company continued, and the shareholders committee formed under Harlow played its part in the company's affairs.

At a meeting of the committee with the Raleigh board in November 1898, Bassett's role as managing director and his possible replacement by Bowden were top of the agenda. Bowden was absent from the meeting, but he had prepared a letter which was read out proposing Bassett's removal in order to restore shareholder confidence in a reconstructed company. Denying any personal ambition, Bowden suggested that the board might take the major role in the reconstruction and 'he need not figure' or could play 'only a minor part' in any scheme.[35] He knew perfectly well, of course, that both the board and the shareholder committee recognised that his role was central to gaining bank approval for the reconstruction. Negotiations with the bank proceeded and Bowden consented to a scheme on the condition that 'arrangements satisfactory to him were made with regard to management'.[36] The new 'arrangements' required changes in the company's system of governance that sanctioned Bassett's removal, Bowden's return as managing director and a strong representation on the Raleigh board from the shareholder committee. Indeed, in the newly appointed board Turney became chairman and Harlow a director, a move which the latter considered as essential to address the problem of a 'want of harmony *between the members of the board*', and a 'weak financial policy'. The new regime, Harlow promised, would ensure 'a sounder and more economical business policy'.[37] In late 1898 another reconstruction scheme was undertaken by Bowden, with the backing of Harlow. Essentially, this involved the formation of yet another new company, in which shareholders paid the full cost of the share conversion. Existing shareholders were offered the option of converting their shares in the new company at 2s 6d per share, plus an additional 2s 6d for each share. Shareholders, as Harlow acknowledged, lost out as the scheme involved a

---

[33]   DDRN 1/1/1–6, Directors and General Meetings, 12 January 1897.

[34]   DDRN 1/1/1–6, Directors and General Meetings, 15 January, 16 February 1897.

[35]   DDRN 1/1/1–6, Directors and General Meetings, 15, 24 November 1898, and Letter from Bowden to Wells and Hind, 22 November 1898.

[36]   DDRN 1/1/1–6, Directors and General Meetings, 29 November, 2 December 1898; DDRN 2/7/1, Bowden, Circular to Shareholders, 23 November 1903.

[37]   DDRN 2/7/1, Harlow, Circular to Shareholders, 17 December 1899; *Economist*, 10 December 1898, pp. 260–62.

considerable reduction of capital. Assets in the balance sheet were written down from £90,000 to £50,000, and the amount of £132,000 representing patents and good will 'wiped out'.[38] In January 1899, a majority of shareholders voted for the 'voluntary winding up' of the company, and accepted yet another reconstruction by the creation of a new company with a reduced nominal capital of £120,000.[39]

With Bowden seemingly back in charge the new executive faced the challenge of the collapse of the bicycle boom, but the problem of governance was not yet resolved. Within two years of the newly reconstituted company a split once again opened up in the board over the appropriate strategic direction that Raleigh should pursue. This time, the outcome of the conflict was that Bowden was to reassert his authority on the company once and for all, and in so doing lay the foundations for a family dynasty and its long-term ownership and control of the enterprise.

Strategy, control and personal capitalism at Raleigh

Following the reconstruction of 1899, Bowden remained determined to expand production, while at the same time maintaining financial security through the use of internal profits to finance growth. His policy of expansion was adventurous, involving not only the growth in cycle production but also diversification into the market for motorised transport. Bowden's reasons for diversification met immediate resistance in 1901 from Turney, the company's chairman, who cautioned against Bowden's plans, and on this he was supported by Harlow.[40] Turney and Harlow were not in principle against diversification but they felt that motorised transport was still 'in its infancy' and they strongly objected to Bowden's proposal that the appropriate means of financing diversification was using the company's un-issued share capital. Instead, the two directors believed that if diversification was to go ahead, Raleigh should continue to rely on bank finance. This raised the issue of control over strategic decision-making and the role of external funding, which obviously affected the business independence of the concern. For his part, Bowden was determined not to tie Raleigh too closely to the bank,[41] and on this point the split over the policy of diversification spilled over into a direct personal confrontation over who really controlled the company.

The split became public at the AGM of November 1903, when Frank Bowden proposed that his son Harold should be elected to the board in place of Harlow,

[38]   DDRN 2/7/1, Harlow, Circular to Shareholders, 17 December 1899.

[39]   DDRN 2/7/1, Edward Farrow, Cicular to Shareholders, 19 January 1899; DDRN 1/1/1–6, Directors and General Meetings, 18 February 1899; DDRN 10/3/4/6/1, Memorandum and Articles of Association of the Raleigh Cycle Company Ltd, incorporated 15 February 1899.

[40]   DDRN 1/1/1–6, Directors and General Meetings, 28 February, 7 March, 22 August, 14, 30 October 1901.

[41]   DDRN 2/7/1, Frank Bowden, Circular to Shareholders, 23 November 1903.

a matter that became a personal crusade as he sought the proxy votes of non-attending shareholders. At the same time, Frank Bowden publicly criticised Turney and Harlow, who were 'sailing too close to the wind financially through their rejection of an additional subscription of share capital, which Bowden had personally guaranteed would be subscribed for.[42] Despite both Turney and Harlow threatening to resign, the Bowdens' aggressive style continued, and a month later Harold proposed that his father should be appointed chairman in place of Turney. Raleigh's embattled chairman threatened legal action, but there was to be no compromise, Frank Bowden throwing down the challenge that a law suit would be 'at your own expense'.[43] Nevertheless, such disputes within the internal governance of the company threatened to damage its business reputation, its trust with shareholders and its relationship with its bank.

On the business front, the dispute negatively affected the company's reputation with agents and customers, leading to falling sales and profits. In December 1903, Frank reported 'serious losses', which he related to the fact that the governance dispute had prevented him and the company secretary from attending the National Cycle Show in November. The result was that vital information concerning Raleigh prices had not been communicated to their travellers and agents, who 'did not know how to act without instructions', and who feared that Raleigh would follow the lead of their competitors and drastically reduce prices in the face of adverse trading conditions.[44] Given the internal turmoil at the company, 'mistaken impressions gained ground at the show that the management intended to adopt a policy antagonistic to agents', and in May 1904 Raleigh was forced to maintain prices, despite falling sales, to retain the confidence of its sales agencies.[45]

Shareholder confidence was also seriously affected, as Turney and Harlow attempted to organise the voice of stakeholders against Bowden. The forum for this organised action was the unelected shareholder committee, formed by Turney and Harlow in 1898. Initially the committee had provided crucial support to Bowden during the reconstruction negotiations of 1899, but it now became a vehicle to promote shareholder agitation against the Bowdens' influence in the company. A circular by the committee to shareholders in November publicly denounced Bowden's management, alleging that he had played little role in the success of the organisation, and that his one aim was to gain complete 'control' over the company.[46] Such action clearly represented an attempt to undermine shareholder confidence in the company, and in particular Bowden's managerial competence. Bowden perceived the committee's circular as a deliberate attempt 'to prevent shareholders from subscribing' to a call for £15,000 of new capital, and the result

---

[42]   DDRN 1/1/1–6, Directors and General Meetings, 16 November 1903.

[43]   DDRN 1/1/1–6, Directors and General Meetings, 3 December 1903.

[44]   Ibid.

[45]   DDRN 2/7/1, Report of Directors, 5 December 1904.

[46]   The circular was referred to in Frank Bowden, DDRN 2/7/1, Circular to Shareholders, 27 January 1904.

of this was that by January 1904 only £2,047 of the new issue had been taken up, and only £247 of this by 'Nottingham shareholders'.[47] Attacking Bowden's policy of product diversification as a 'dangerous strategy of expansion', in January 1904 the Turney and Harlow committee further attempted to block a resolution for the offer of 120,000 ordinary shares of 2s 6d each, part of unissued share capital, on a pro rata basis to existing shareholders.[48] As Bowden acknowledged, Turney and Harlow were sowing the seeds of distrust amongst shareholders. Their persistent circulars publicly alleged that Bowden received an excessive salary, that he exacted high interest payments on personal loans to the company, and that his ultimate aim was 'to gain control over the company'.[49] While Bowden discounted these claims as 'gross perversions of the truth',[50] it was nevertheless clear that the two directors still carried some weight, not least in organising shareholder voice and denting shareholder confidence in a Bowden-led board.

As tensions mounted in the company, the relationship between Bowden and Lloyds Bank became vital to the governance of the company. Central to this relationship was the issue of the bank overdraft, a topic which Bowden used to his advantage, with constant references to the financial mismanagement by Turney and Harlow, who had exceeded bank guidelines. As Bowden reminded shareholders, the Bank was reluctant to accede to a higher overdraft limit, and confidence was only maintained by Bowden providing a personal guarantee for the overdraft and by a commitment by the company to reduce it by raising more share capital.[51] Ultimately, the preservation of Bowden's governance of the company was determined by the trust of the Bank, and by the fact that his financial policy was geared towards maintaining financial stability free from the reliance on overdraft funding. Thus, at a board meeting in December 1903, Bowden reaffirmed his commitment to ensuring financial stability, and providing additional capital for expansion, while at the same time condemning the shareholder committee as a 'clique' which 'has from first to last' been only concerned with causing 'great injury' to 'the business of the company'.[52] Indeed, as Bowden made clear, they represented not a committee of 'large shareholders', but a group of 13 whose total shareholding in the company was a mere £1,300.[53]

Rallying local shareholder support Bowden emphasised the importance of prudence in financial accounting, skilfully drawing out his distinction between shareholders as 'investors' and shareholders as 'speculators'.[54] At the AGM of

[47]   Ibid.

[48]   DDRN 2/7/1, E. C. Farrow (Secretary), Circular to Shareholders, 7 January 1904.

[49]   DDRN 2/7/1, Frank Bowden, Circular to Shareholders, 23 November 1903.

[50]   Ibid.

[51]   Ibid.

[52]   DDRN 1/1/1–6, Directors and General Meetings, 3 December 1903.

[53]   DDRN 2/7/1, E. C. Farrow, Circular to Shareholders, 7 January 1904; Frank Bowden, Circular to Shareholders, 27 January 1904.

[54]   DDRN 2/7/1, Frank Bowden, Circular to Shareholders, 24 January 1904.

1896 he had urged shareholders to accept lower dividends in the interest of long-term expansion, distinguishing between 'investment shareholders' who 'heartily approve the board's policy in building up a large fund – and the speculators [who] oppose it and desire a large dividend'.[55] Again in 1901, Bowden urged caution, and considered it prudent to limit the dividend on ordinary shares to 10 per cent, pay no dividend on the deferred shares and transfer £12,000 of disposable profit to reserves as a sign of the need for additional capital for modernisation.[56] In Bowden's assessment, Turney and Harlow represented a group of London 'speculators', while he aligned himself to local Nottingham investors who he maintained were concerned with the long-term prosperity of the company. When, in February 1904, Turney supported by a minority of London shareholders attempted to secure Harlow's re-election to the board, Bowden was quick to inform shareholders that the 'Turney and Harlow clique of my enemies ... have no real interest in the Raleigh company [beyond making] fees for their nominees, and at the same time harass and annoy me'.[57] This distinction between short-term speculators and long-term investors was a common one amongst businessmen and accountants in the late nineteenth and early twentieth centuries. Speculators were concerned only to make a quick profit, and cared only for dividends but investors focused their expectations on the long-term survival of the company, and were prepared to defer to the directors' judgement.[58]

Bowden's distinction between speculators and investors raised in the minds of shareholders the ethical behaviour of those in charge of the governance of a company. By labelling Turney as a speculator, Bowden was able to regain the moral high ground with shareholders. A return to Turney's rule, Bowden charged, would be at the expense of the shareholder interest because

> If you want management by Directors, who have as much knowledge of the cycle trade as Messrs. Turney and Harlow, look at Humber Ltd., where the Directors apparently think a practical Managing Director or General Manager unnecessary, and note the result. That firm has twice our turnover, and yet made only half our profit during 1903.[59]

Continuing the assault, Bowden reminded shareholders that Harlow would be better advised to 'utilize his abilities in his special business, that of a stockbroker',

---

[55]   DDRN 2/7/1, Frank Bowden, Circular to Shareholders, 22 October 1896.

[56]   DDRN 1/1/1–6, Directors and General Meetings, 5 December 1901; Raleigh AGM 16 November 1901, 11 November 1902.

[57]   DDRN 2/7/1, Frank Bowden, Circular to Shareholders, 27 January 1904.

[58]   See J. Maltby, '"A sort of Guide, Philosopher and Friend": The Rise of the Professional Auditor in Britain', *Accounting, Business & Financial History*, Vol. 9, No. 1 (1999), pp. 40–41.

[59]   DDRN 2/7/1, Frank Bowden, Circular to Shareholders, 27 January 1904.

leaving the long-term strategy of Raleigh to those who knew the cycle business.[60] In effect Bowden was arguing that the distinctive capabilities of the Raleigh Company lay in his knowledge of and expertise in the cycle business and it would be in the long-term interest of shareholders to place their trust in him. Further, speculators such as Harlow were not to be trusted in providing accountability to shareholders. Referring to Turney's chairmanship of his own company, Turney Bros., leather dressers, Bowden asserted that 'Although [it is] a public company, no reports or accounts of meetings ... are I believe allowed to be published', while Turney himself drew a annual salary equal to one-quarter of the entire profits of his company, 'and half as much again as my salary'.[61]

A war of incrimination and innuendo, carried out through contradictory circulars to shareholders, is perhaps an apt description of governance at Raleigh in 1903 and 1904. However, by the end of 1904 Bowden's control of the board was ensured, when the additional shares offered in the company were finally subscribed to, a victory that Bowden related to his commitment to devote personal investment funds to the company, and the regaining of shareholder trust through his efforts to persuade local investors to subscribe for the share allocation.[62] His control was not to be challenged again, but at the time of his triumph he changed track and abandoned the strategy of diversification into motorised transport. At the end of 1904 the company ended the production of its three-wheeled motorised cycle, the 'Raleighette', and postponed its development work on motor cycles until the First World War.[63] In rejecting diversification Bowden steered Raleigh along a path different from most other bicycle companies. Quite why he decided to reverse the policy that he had fought the Turney and Harlow 'clique' over is not easy to discern given the lack of any recorded discussion on the matter at board meetings. Three factors probably swayed Bowden to focus Raleigh on its core business. First, he became increasingly concerned over his financial security and personal commitment to Raleigh and the immediate priority was survival. Second, the Raleighette venture had not proved successful. It demonstrated the risks of entering a new market, and paradoxically vindicated the reservations of Turney and Harlow concerning the wisdom of the diversification strategy. Finally, the increasingly competitive nature of the bicycle industry led Bowden to believe that scarce financial resources were best used to expand capacity and capture a larger size of the market.[64]

At an Extraordinary General Meeting in February 1904, following a poll of shareholders, the outcome of which was largely determined by his father's

---

[60]   Ibid.

[61]   Ibid.

[62]   DDRN 1/39/6, Report of Directors, 1904.

[63]   DDRN 1/1/1–6, Directors and General Meetings, 28 February, 7 March, 22 April, 4, 30 October 1901; Raleigh AGM, 7 November 1903; Bowden, *The Story of the Raleigh Cycle Co.*, p. 28.

[64]   Lloyd-Jones and Lewis, *Raleigh*, p. 93.

shareholding, Harold Bowden was elected a director of Raleigh. As a result, Turney resigned and Frank Bowden was officially appointed the company chairman. The new board, clearly dominated by Frank and Harold Bowden, also consisted of Joseph Lazonby, E. C. Farrow, the long-serving company secretary, and Ernest Jardine, a Nottingham machine maker.[65] Under their direction, cycle output was substantially expanded (Table 2.7), and from 1905 profits recovered, and escalated after 1908 in the pre-war boom (Table 2.8).

Table 2.7   Output of cycles, Raleigh Cycle Co., 1904–14

1904	9,865
1905	16,555
1906	25,689
1907	28,156
1908	32,577
1909	33,434
1910	38,890
1911	46,075
1912	51,805
1913	57,675
1914	59,219

Source: DDRN 4/10/1/19, Book of the Raleigh for 1915.

With Frank and Harold Bowden in control, and with a significant amount of personal capital tied up in the business, the immediate objective of the management was prudence when it came to dividend policy. In the precarious financial situation of 1904, no dividend was paid, and between 1905 and 1908 dividends on ordinary shares stood at 5 per cent, compared to 10 per cent during the period 1899 to 1903 (Table 2.8). The chairman acknowledged that Raleigh's 5 per cent payment was well below the 10 and 20 per cent paid in other comparable companies, but he made it clear to shareholders this was 'principally because we have been working on borrowed capital', and that he was the guarantor of most of that borrowing. For example, in March 1908 he had provided his own personal guarantee for a bank overdraft of £40,000, but by July he was not prepared to advance any further commitments. Indeed, as he made clear to shareholders, he would withdraw his guarantee to the bank 'unless some arrangement was come to whereby he became the purchaser of the Company's business, or could be in some form compensated

---

[65]   DDRN 2/7/1 Frank Bowden, Circular to Shareholders, 23 November 1903; DDRN 1/1/1–6, Directors and General Meetings, 5, 8, February 1904.

Table 2.8   Profits of the Raleigh Cycle Co., 1899–1908 and 1912–14

	Net profit (£)	Dividend on ordinary shares (%)	Dividend on deferred ordinary shares (%)	To reserve (£)
1899	11,661	10	0	8,000
1900	11,632	10	0	2,000
1901	8,312	10	0	12,000
1902	9,479	10	0	6,000
1903	10,069	10	0	6,000
1904	1,301	0	0	0
1905	6,988	5	0	3,265
1906	16,206	5	0	8,000
1907	18,811	5	0	8,000
1908	15,246	5	0	8,000
1912	36,415			
1913	41,191			
1914	49,512			

Source: DDRN 3/1/1–3, Company Ledgers; DDRN 2/7/1, AGM Raleigh Bicycle Co. 1899–1914.

for the risks he was taking'. In other words, Bowden wanted total ownership of Raleigh and he offered shareholders a 10 per cent premium on their ordinary shares.[66] Shareholders unanimously agreed to wind up the company in July 1908, which they then sold to Frank Bowden for £69,733 by a deed of transfer in February 1909. In 1913, Frank established a formal partnership with his son Harold, and this set the agenda for the governance of the company down to the 1930s.[67]

The inter-war years: succession and business performance

In 1915, Frank prepared the way to the succession of his son in the company when he registered Raleigh as a private limited company, the newly incorporated

---

[66]   DDRN 1/1/1–6, Directors and General Meetings, 18 July 1908; DDRN 2/7/1, Frank Bowden, Circular to Shareholders, 4 June 1908.

[67]   DDRN 2/7/1, Frank Bowden, Circular to Shareholders, 4 June 1908; DDRN 10/3/4/13–15, Agreements between Frank Bowden and the Raleigh Cycle Co., 18 July, 17 August 1908; DDRN 1/1/1–6, Directors and General Meetings, 30 July 1908; Bowden, *The Story of the Raleigh Cycle Co.*, p. 33.

business having a nominal capital of £240,000 divided into £1 shares and equally distributed between father and son. To ensure the long-term pattern of family control, the agreement of 1915 stipulated that Harold would have the right to purchase the shares held by Frank in the company for a nominal payment of £50,000, but that Harold would have no authorisation to transfer shares without the prior consent of his father.[68] Even within a tightly knit family partnership, such as that defined by the Bowdens, legal frameworks were essential to secure the future family succession and commitment of Harold to the running of the business. Part of the process of succession involved the devolution of managerial authority, with Harold's appointment as joint managing director in 1916, and when Frank retired from that position in 1918 Harold was appointed sole managing director, although Frank retained the chairmanship of the company until his death in 1921. Underpinning the succession process at Raleigh was the high level of profits made during the war, net profits rising from £49,512 in 1914 to a peak of £251,740 in 1917. Consequently, the Bowdens took their full share of the profits, and between 1916 and 1918 received dividend payments totalling £212,000, approximately £12 to £15 million in present-day values, as well as accumulating large sums in capital reserves.[69] How did governance and business performance evolve under Harold's leadership from 1921? To examine this question requires an understanding of the broad trends that shaped the development of the bicycle industry during the inter-war years.

Three key factors shaped the external environment facing the bicycle industry in the period. First, as for all manufacturing firms, the inter-war years were challenging ones for bicycle firms, but it is important to stress that it was by no means a period of continuous gloom. Following the brief post-war boom there were two periods of sharp depression between 1920 and 1924 and again between 1929 and 1932, and two periods of recovery between 1925 and 1929 and 1932 to 1937. The years from 1932, in particular, witnessed a relatively robust recovery in the British economy, despite the persistence of high unemployment, and firms such as Raleigh experienced rising profits and prosperity.[70] Second, there were important changes in the structure of demand for bicycles during the period, and 1932 marked a revival in both empire and domestic markets. Finally, there was a trend in the bicycle industry towards increased concentration, a pattern that

---

[68] DDRN 1/2/1–6, Raleigh Cycle Co. Ltd., Board and General Meetings, Minutes with Fortnightly Reports, 29 January, 4 February 1915.

[69] DDRN 1/40/6, Auditors Reports and Balance Sheets, 1916; DDRN 1/1/1–6, Board and General Meetings, 12 December1916, 20 September 1917, 16 December 1918.

[70] For an examination of the cyclical trends facing bicycle manufacturers during the inter-war years see Lloyd-Jones and Lewis, *Raleigh*, pp. 109–115. For an exploration of the main macro-economic trends and their impact on British industry over the inter-war decades see S. Bowden and D. Higgins, 'British Industry in the Inter-War Years', in R. Floud and P. Johnson (eds), *The Cambridge Economic History of Modern Britain*, Vol. 11 *Economic Maturity, 1860–1939* (Cambridge, Cambridge University Press, 2004).

mirrored that of British manufacturing generally.[71] By the end of the inter-war period the industry was dominated by a few large firms, notably Hercules, the largest British producer, New Hudson, Raleigh and two subsidiaries of large holding companies, J. A. Phillips, acquired by Tube Investment in 1919, and the bicycle division of BSA. In 1935, the three large firms of Hercules, Raleigh and BSA Cycles employed 70 per cent of all workers in the industry, and the first two in this group accounted for approximately one-half of the total sales of British bicycles in that year.[72] Despite this increase in industrial concentration, it is important to note that bicycle firms grew predominantly via internal expansion rather than by merger and vertical integration. Further, managerial organisation remained much the same, with a close association between ownership and control, and personal capitalist forms of control continued to predominate.[73] A 'widespread individualism' prevailed amongst businessmen in the bicycle industry which 'militated against a general merger movement'.[74] Harold Bowden, for example, endorsed a philosophy of individualism, in 1934, when he praised the virtues of individual leadership in industry asserting that 'Any industry was the creation of the mind. Some men remained employees all their lives, others like Lord Nuffield, the late Lord Leverhulme or Sir Herbert Austin, created work for thousands'.[75]

When Harold Bowden took over the helm of the company in 1921, he did so in the face of an acute depression, but remained steadfast in his belief that his individual leadership 'would be able to steer the company safely through the storm of depression which is now passing over the country'.[76] His knowledge of the company specifically, and of the industry generally, enabled him to define a set of distinctive capabilities which came to be identified with Raleigh and gave it a competitive advantage over its main rivals. Bowden's belief in his own ability to lead the business, together with an historical commitment to the values of the company based upon personal control of the organisation, enabled him to set a progressive business strategy directed towards a modernisation programme as an

[71]   See Hannah, *The Rise of the Corporate Economy*, pp. 88–99; Wilson, *British Business History*, pp. 165–7.

[72]   P. Sargent Florence, *The Logic of British and American Industry: A Realistic Analysis of Economic Structure and Government* (London, Routledge and Kegan Paul, 1933), pp. 24, 87–9, 116; *Economist*, 30 November 1935, p. 1,060.

[73]   Millward, 'The Cycle Industry in Birmingham', p. 175. See also S. Beeley, *A History of Bicycles: From Hobby Horse to Mountain Bike* (London, Studio Editions, 1992), p. 99; *Bicycling News*, 9 September 1937.

[74]   Millward, 'The Cycle Industry', p. 175.

[75]   H. Bowden, 'The Four "Ms" of Industry: Men, Management, Machines and Money', address to Birmingham Rotary Club reported in *Birmingham Gazette*, 16 October 1934, pp. 21–4.

[76]   DDRN 1/2/1–6, Board and General Meetings of the Raleigh Cycle Co. with Fortnightly Reports, 13 January, 5 May 1921; Bowden, *The Story of the Raleigh Cycle Co.*, pp. 45–6.

antidote to the depression. In addition, Harold insisted that the company could increase output and modernise without sacrificing quality, to maintain its long-standing reputation as a producer of quality machines.[77] Harold articulated his deep attachment to the norms of a personal capitalist enterprise, in a speech he delivered in 1922 to the British Cycle and Motor Cycle Manufacturers Traders Union, the industry's main trade organisation:

> In the great cities of the Midlands and the North of England there are many manufacturing houses where the business has been handed down from father to son, where there is a family pride in the family products, where the reputation of the house stands before profit or anything else. It is by these firms that the reputation of British industry has been, and will be maintained, and as long as this spirit exists in Britain we need fear no challenge to our commercial pre-eminence.[78]

British business leaders, it was assumed, with the co-operation of the skilled British worker, had the capabilities to produce those quality products that could compete effectively with foreign makers. Bowden was determined that his own company would guarantee quality, but he was well aware that a major obstacle to commercial success was the requirement to cut costs and prices. To achieve these desired outcomes and to remain consistent with his belief in personal control, Bowden needed the cooperation of the workforce. Embedded in the core company values celebrated by Bowden was a commitment to an ideology of industrial welfarism, which promoted co-operation between management and labour. The creation of a Raleigh Welfare Department, the introduction of bonus schemes and profit sharing for workers, all represented the practical implementation of Bowden's belief in fostering a culture of co-operation.[79] Reflecting on his leadership of Raleigh and the historical tradition of co-operation, Bowden observed that 'The founder of the business always desired to foster that personal contact and sympathy between those who stood in authority, and those who bore the heat and burden of the day, and this was instilled in his son at an early age'.[80] This is illustrative too of the idiosyncratic nature of personal capitalism, with the Raleigh management taking a very different approach to its workforce from that of the machine-tool firm of Alfred Herbert Ltd, discussed in Chapter 5. The leading personality in that company, Sir Alfred Herbert took a pro-active role in the engineering lockout of 1922, and was a strong supporter of the Engineering Employers Federation (EEF), while Raleigh, under Harold's leadership, gave only tacit support to the EEF, and refused to become directly involved with the dispute.[81] Similarly, during

---

[77] Lloyd-Jones and Lewis, *Raleigh*, pp. 147–50.
[78] *Motor Export Trader*, July 1922.
[79] Lloyd-Jones and Lewis, *Raleigh*, pp. 152–3.
[80] Bowden, Manuscript, p. 16.
[81] DDRN 1/2/1–6, Board and General Meetings, 21 June 1922.

the General Strike of 1926 Raleigh could report that 'with few exceptions none of [its] workers are affected', and they were 'carrying on as usual'.[82]

Raleigh's distinctive approach to its workforce dovetailed with three other strategies that Harold pursued, from the time that he took full control to the conversion to a public limited holding company in 1934. These constituted a production programme involving the modernisation of plant, a determination to increase volume sales and market share of quality cycles, and a diversification policy that would take the company into the market for motorised transport and components.[83]

In 1922, Raleigh brought into operation a new factory extension designed to accommodate diversification into motor cycle production and countershaft gears, the latter to be produced under the Sturmey-Archer trade mark. Raleigh had been associated with the Sturmey-Archer business, a high-quality producer of bicycle gears, since 1902, and formally acquired it as a valuable complementary subsidiary to its bicycle manufacture in 1910.[84] There were four main reasons why Bowden and his managerial advisors pursued a strategy of diversification. First, they expected that motor cycles would provide a niche market, which could act as a counter to the depressed market for bicycles. The aim was to produce a range of quality light-weight motor cycles trading on Raleigh's reputation as a quality maker. Second, the company could reap economies of scale and scope as the new factory, utilising flexible technology, had the capability of producing bicycles and motor cycles as well as gears, and they could exploit the technical capabilities of both Raleigh and Sturmey-Archer engineers. Third, Bowden saw the opportunity of extending the company's product base to meet the rising demand both home and abroad for light-weight motor cycles, for recreational purposes, and for countershaft gears by other manufacturers. Indeed, during 1923 the factory could not keep pace with the rush for orders. Finally, Raleigh could exploit the company's existing capabilities in marketing by using their extensive agency networks to push an extended range of products.[85]

If Harold's strategy had been successful, it would have radically transformed the nature of the Raleigh organisation, but the company's entry into the motor-cycle market was fraught with difficulties, which were not fully anticipated by the chairman and his top management team. Raleigh had entered a market of some 400 makers in 1922 and while it met with some initial success with its light-weight machine, the industry was subject to ruthless price-cutting.[86] Between

[82]   DDRN 1/2/1–6, Board and General Meetings, 6 May, 26 May 1926.

[83]   See Lloyd-Jones and Lewis, *Raleigh*, pp. 156–67.

[84]   DDRN 1/1/1–6, Directors and General Meetings, 27 March, 28 April, 1 May, 30 October 1902; DDRN 1/23/1, Sturmey-Archer Gears, Minutes, 27 February, 10 March 1903, 20 July 1910; Bowden, Manuscript, pp. 17–18.

[85]   DDRN 1/2/1–6, Board and General Meetings, 20 December 1922, 4 January, 17 May 1923; Bowden, Manuscript, p. 27; Bowden, *The Story of the Raleigh Cycle*, pp. 48–9.

[86]   *Motor Cycle and Cycle Trader*, 30 November 1922; DDRN 1/2/1–6, Board and General Meetings, 26 July 1923, 18, 25 February 1925.

1922 and 1928, the contribution of motor cycles to the company's net profit was marginal, and in 1928 steps were taken to limit the range of machines to just three standard models.[87] Bowden, however, remained reluctant to abandon the business and supported by a loyal group of directors he sought in 1931 to launch a motorised delivery van, followed two years later by a light three-wheeled car.[88] Unfortunately, neither venture proved profitable,[89] despite Raleigh's claim that their three-wheeler was 'The cheapest car in the world to run'.[90]

Raleigh's venture into the motor trade demonstrated that the organisation did not possess the managerial capabilities that were necessary to combine successfully the production of motorised vehicles with its core business of bicycle making. For example, the contribution of flexible technology to production was less beneficial than Bowden had hoped and there were mounting problems associated with co-ordinating the flow of components required for different products and model types. In tackling these organisational deficiencies, Bowden did not take action until 1928, when he appointed a 'first class' production engineer, J. M. Lees, who quickly identified a new set of organisational capabilities necessary to overhaul existing systems. He recommended, in particular, the formation of a planning department, to facilitate a more co-ordinated system for the movement of stocks, work in progress and finished parts. Despite Lee's endeavours problems persisted, and planned targets fell short of expectations.[91] Sustaining diversity would have required a complete organisational restructuring, requiring 'separate staff for manufacturing, selling and distribution', and this Bowden was not willing to sanction. By 1932, the demand for bicycles was beginning to pick up strongly, and within two years Bowden had decided to withdraw Raleigh from motorised products. He premised this decision on a belief that 'better financial results might be obtained by concentrating the entire resources and energy of the works to one product only – the bicycle and its accessories'.[92] The decision to abandon diversity was a bold step by Bowden, as one estimate suggested that it might reduce the company's annual turnover by as much as £1 million. Nevertheless, the firm could now re-focus its core competencies on what it did best and Bowden was convinced that the increased demand for bicycles was 'no passing phase'.[93] Correctly anticipating a 'boom in bicycles', Bowden

---

[87]   DDRN 1/2/1–6, Board and General Meetings, 1 May, 13 July 1928.

[88]   Bowden, Manuscript, pp. 31–2; Bowden, *The Story of the Raleigh Cycle*, p. 61; DDRN 1/13/1, Promotional Material sent to LDV Agents, October 1932.

[89]   *Motor Cycle and Cycle Trader*, 18 May 1934.

[90]   DDRN 1/19, Promotional Material sent to Agents, 1935.

[91]   DDRN 1/2/1–6, Board and General Meetings, 2 February, 14 March, 17 April, 13 June, 28 August, 10 October 1928, 12 February 1929; DDRN 3/11/11, Auditors Reports and Accounts, 1929.

[92]   Bowden, Manuscript, p. 35; Bowden, *The Story of the Raleigh Cycle*, pp. 65–6.

[93]   Bowden Manuscript, p. 35; Bowden, *The Story of the Raleigh Cycle*, pp. 65–6; *Financial News*, 14 May 1934.

sanctioned a £80,000 investment in new plant in 1933 and this 'forward policy' ran parallel to his decision, backed by the board, to convert Raleigh to a public holding company, a seemingly radical change in the pattern of long-established personal ownership and control in the company.

Going public: the formation of the Raleigh Cycle Holdings Co. Ltd

Owning and controlling a substantial-sized company was clearly not without its stresses and strains and, even before the onset of the major depression of 1929, Harold had contemplated selling the firm. During the summer and autumn of 1928 there was an attempt by an American consortium to purchase the company, but just after Christmas the *Nottingham Guardian* reported that negotiations had been broken off, and Harold announced that 'The business would continue for the time being as a family concern'. Harold's justification for his decision, at least in the public arena, owed much to a patriotic fervour, and he claimed that 'There was no question of the company going to a United States firm. I would rather see it, if the ownership does change, taken over by British interests and I hope that it will always remain in British hands'.[94] There was, however, no rejection of a possible future sale and the company moving outside the ownership of the Bowden family. Disengagement from the company remained a serious option for Harold Bowden, but the form this should take, and the extent to which this would dilute his personal control of the company, remained paramount in any final decision. Nevertheless, what influenced the decision on the future organisational form of the company were events both external and internal to the firm. Harold retained control to ensure that the company had firm leadership during the sharp business downturn of 1930 to 1931. A robust recovery led the management to embark on a policy of expansion, which involved investment in new plant and the acquisition of the bicycle interests of Humber in 1932.[95]

As the scale of the company's activities increased, Harold announced record profits at Raleigh's 1933 AGM, and intimated that the time might be right to consider a public flotation. To achieve this, the Raleigh management offered 2.25 million shares to the public on 13 February 1934 in a newly created Raleigh Cycle Holdings Co. Ltd. The holding company was the vehicle by which shares were sold to the public, investors in the holding company essentially acquiring the share capital of the main subsidiary, the Raleigh Cycle Co. and its various subsidiaries, which included well-known brands such as Rudge-Whitworth, Robin Hood Cycle and Humber Cycles. At the same time, the Holdings Co. also acquired 90 per cent of the share capital in Sturmey-Archer.[96] Brokering this new venture was the Suffolk Trust Co. and its chairman Sir Connup Guthrie, who acquired the

---

[94]   Bowden, *The Story of the Raleigh Cycle*, p. 54.
[95]   Ibid., p. 64.
[96]   DDRN 5/1/6, Press Cuttings 1931–34, *The Star*, 13 February 1934.

490,350 ordinary shares in the Raleigh Cycle Co. for 49s 9d each in cash, and the 14,490 shares of Sturmey-Archer at £3 per share in cash. Acting as vendors, the Suffolk Trust then sold these shares to the Raleigh Cycle Holding Co. Ltd in consideration of the allotment of 1 million 5 per cent cumulative preference shares, with an additional 1 per cent dividend depending on profits, and 1.25 million ordinary shares. To provide an inducement to subscribers the ordinary shares were allocated to applicants in the ratio of one ordinary share for every two preference shares subscribed to.[97] Such was the public demand for the shares that the subscription list was closed after four days, and applicants were not deterred by the *Economist*'s observation that 'The existence of two separate companies – an operating and holding concern – would appear to serve, at the moment, no concrete purpose'.[98] So what implications did the holding company have for governance at Raleigh? To answer this question, two key issues require consideration: first, the style of management that evolved in the new holding company structure, and, second, the degree of financial disclosure between executive management and shareholders at Raleigh.

In terms of managerial style, the formation of the public company did not appear to lessen the Bowden family commitment to the firm. In 1934, Harold was re-appointed chairman and managing director at the first meeting of the holding company board, and his executive team was appointed on the basis of loyalty, trust and a knowledge of the Raleigh business. Consequently, George Wilson, a former Sturmey-Archer manager, who had joined the board of the Raleigh Cycle Co. in 1931, became a director of the holding company. Frederick Bush, an employee who had served Raleigh for over 40 years, and had been general manager of the Raleigh Cycle Co. since 1920, joined Wilson on the holding company board, forming a small group of trusted and loyal managers to direct the holding company.[99] The elevation of Wilson, however, served a further purpose for Harold Bowden, in that it provided him with the means to groom his successor. Wilson epitomised Harold's concept of the 'Raleigh man', and in 1936, when Bush retired as general manager of the Raleigh Cycle Co., Wilson succeeded him, assuming 'executive authority' in the management of the main operating company. In 1938, Harold Bowden retired as managing director of the Raleigh Cycle Co., aged 58, and Wilson succeeded him, forming a managerial partnership with Harold retaining the chairmanship of the company. At Raleigh, the devolution of strategic decision-making was based upon a planned succession, which involved a partnership in the running of the operating company, and the continuation of Bowden's active role in executive management.

Changes at the executive level were complemented by a general strengthening of the managerial capabilities of the company, with Bowden and Wilson

---

[97]   *Economist*, 17 February 1934, p. 366.

[98]   *Economist*, 17 February 1934, p. 1,109; 24 February 1934, p. 422.

[99]   DDRN, 1/3/1, Minute Book of the Raleigh Cycle Holding Co. Ltd, 13 February 1934; DDRN 7/2/27, Raleigh Company Executives, 1887–1962.

promoting managers to the status of 'working director'. These included R. L. Jones, the new works manager, A. E. Simpson, sales manager, and the long-serving W. H. Raven, who had joined Raleigh in 1908, as the head of the cycle department.[100] The title of 'working director' said much about the personal style of management at Raleigh, with its demarcation between executive management, associated with the strategic decision-making of Bowden and Wilson, and the functional management concerned with the direct running of the business. There is no evidence of the formation of a managerial hierarchy at Raleigh, and Bowden was unwilling to relinquish 'his final say in the running of the company'.[101] Indeed, it was not until 1946 that Bowden devolved further responsibilities to Wilson, when the latter was appointed joint chairman of the Raleigh Cycle Co., and also now granted the status of deputy chairman and deputy managing director of the holding company. Finally, in 1955, Harold, then aged 75, relinquished all executive titles to Wilson, assuming the role of life President until his death in 1960.[102]

The formation of a holding company in 1934 did little to disturb the existing style of personal management. Further, the holding company, as *The Economist* had observed, seemed 'to serve no concrete purpose'. Strategic decision-making rested within the board of the Raleigh Cycle Co., which was the operating company which co-ordinated the various subsidiary companies. The holding company itself was no more than a ghost-like creature, a vehicle for executives to deal with the transfer of shares within the company. The substantial minute books of the holding company contain nothing more than volumes of records relating to share dealings, while it was within the boardroom at the Raleigh Cycle Co. that the real business of cycle manufacture was conducted, and where crucial issues such as dividend payments were discussed. Yet in terms of shareholder relations, and the transparency of financial disclosure and business policy, the holding company was the public personification of the Raleigh organisation. The reputation and responsibility of the company to its shareholders could not be ignored, as demonstrated by the inclusion of Sir Connup Guthrie, representing the Suffolk Trust, which had brokered the public subscription, as a director of the Raleigh Cycle Co. in an 'executive capacity'.[103] However, Guthrie, with the interests of shareholders to represent, was not averse to challenging Bowden's authority. At a board meeting in November 1934, for example, there were clear differences over the level of dividend that should be set. Bowden 'was definitely of the opinion that it should not exceed 7 per cent ... Guthrie pressed on behalf of the interests he represented, for a minimum final payment of 8 per cent, a request which was subsequently acceded

---

[100] DDRN 1/2/1–6, Board and General Meetings, 31 May, 29 June 1938; Bowden, *The Story of the Raleigh Cycle*, p. 66.

[101] Bowden, Manuscript, p. 38; Bowden, *The Story of the Raleigh Cycle*, p. 61.

[102] Lloyd-Jones and Lewis, *Raleigh*, p. 223.

[103] DDRN 1/2/1–6, Board and General Meetings, 13 February 1934.

to'.[104] Guthrie did not confine his activities to dividend policy but ventured into other areas of the company's business, including its lending requirements from the financial sector. Between 1932 and 1937 Raleigh had benefited from rapidly rising sales, but a sharp, albeit short, recession in 1938 caused deterioration in Raleigh's financial position, worsened by delayed payments by the War Office for a large contract on fuses. Consequently, by February 1938 the overdraft with the bank stood at £190,000, and Bowden and Wilson considered raising £50,000 on bills at 1.75 per cent through a London discount house. Opposing this strategy, in the interests of shareholders, Guthrie argued that the use of bills for raising cash was financially unsafe, and he pointed to the fact that the company had already arranged an overdraft with Lloyds Bank at a favourable rate of 3 per cent. The bank 'was totally opposed to business financing by bills and they would be sure to get to know', and this 'might undermine their reputation for financial stability by the spread of rumour'.[105] No further reference to this matter was made in the minutes of the board, and it would seem that Guthrie got his way. Nevertheless, it is ironic that Bowden was being cautioned not to compromise the 'reputation' of the company in the eyes of its shareholders, and that it took an outside interest to remind him of his responsibilities.

From the evidence available, the creation of a public holding company hardly ushered in an era of greater accountability for shareholders of the company. In 1934, *The Economist* had perceived that the holding company could only be justified by the fact that it would enable the publication of a consolidated balance sheet, providing disclosure of the overall profits of the holding company's 'chief assets', the Raleigh Cycle Co. and Sturmey-Archer.[106] Such optimism, however, was unfounded, and the personalised style of management at Raleigh created a limited policy of public disclosure. At the time of the passing of the 1947 Company Act, for example, *The Accountant* reported on the speech made by Sir Harold Bowden at the AGM of Raleigh Industries Ltd, the new title assigned to the holding company in 1946. Facing shareholder disquiet, over the level of financial reporting, and the uncertainties of the future strategy of the company in the highly competitive post-war business environment, Bowden announced his intention to fulfil 'his last year's promise to issue more informative accounts', publishing 'a consolidated balance sheet and profit and loss account'. This, he finally admitted, was 'obviously necessary', given that 'Raleigh Industries was 'solely a holding company, its sole source of income being its holding of 490,350 shares in the Raleigh Cycle Co. Ltd', totalling £2.2 million. In turn, the Raleigh Cycle Co. had its own subsidiaries (Rudge-Whitworth, acquired in 1943, Robin Hood Cycle, Gazelle Cycle, Sturmey-Archer Gears, and Gradual Payments (Nottingham)). The loose relationship to Raleigh Cycles, and thus to its subsidiaries, was remarked upon by Bowden when he observed that

---

[104] DDRN 1/2/1–6, Board and General Meetings, 14 November 1934.

[105] DDRN 1/2/1–6, Board and General Meetings, 24 February 1938.

[106] *Economist*, 17 February 1934, p. 1,109.

Raleigh Industries 'is not even treasurer for the combine. It is in effect, the channel through which shareholders receive their dividends, all profits which the directors see fit to retain being held in the subsidiaries' accounts'. In a frank public admission, and as a testimony to the low transparency of financial disclosure in some British companies even in 1947, Bowden accepted that without consolidated accounts there had been 'no proper view of the undertaking'.[107] Despite this public admission, the words as 'the directors see fit' were typical of the company's relationship to shareholders, and the building of reserves from profits remained a key priority of executive management. Consequently, in 1950 the company's 'special reserve' was £954,000, and by 1951 this had risen to £2.7 million, which Bowden and the directors considered a vital financial resource to account for future capital investment in new and replacement plant. Despite facing shareholder pressure for increased dividends, and calls for more transparent accounts on the operations of subsidiaries, Bowden was insistent that the large reserve was 'the result of the wise and conservative policy adopted by us in the years gone by in retaining in the business what no doubt at the time seemed excessive amounts'.[108] A strong attachment to internal financing rather than large dividend payments was well and truly entrenched at Raleigh even in the early 1950s, at the cost of course of low transparency in accountability to shareholders.

Conclusion

Raleigh's history in some respects typifies personal capitalism as a regime of family control. The Bowdens, father and son, held key roles in the company between 1895 and 1955. The succession was secured despite opposition in 1903, one of a number of occasions of conflict between Frank Bowden and directors or shareholders. The Bowdens' uneasy relationship with shareholders seems likely to have been the reason for the 1908 decision to buy back the company's shares. It may also have underlain the structure of the public company that was floated in 1934, with a holding company form, and a lack of transparency in reporting, keeping shareholders at a distance from strategic decision-making. The Bowdens' regime was, however, successful, as measured by the sales growth and profitability that they achieved. Both father and son demonstrated that 'family pride in family products' could result in continuing engineering and product innovation. A key feature of their regime was the reinvestment of profits, coupled with reluctance to declare large dividends at the expense of capital growth, and their own substantial shareholdings did not motivate them to take out profits as excessive dividends. The Bowdens' success is a challenge to the view of personal capitalism as likely to damage company performance in

---

[107]   *Accountant*, 5 April 1947, p. 258.
[108]   *Accountant*, 19 January 1952, pp. 64–5.

the long run. Raleigh demonstrates a style of governance which combined over a long period of time a strong commitment to the enterprise with identification and deployment of the company's core capabilities.

Chapter 3
Hadfields Ltd: Personal Capitalism, Boardroom Culture and Corporate Governance

Introduction

Individual business leaders can have a profound effect on how institutions work, how they change over time, and how they create a particular form of organisational governance. Hadfields Ltd of Sheffield, a major British manufacturer of steel castings, specialist alloy steels, large machinery and armaments, clearly demonstrates this personal element in organisations. In 1876 the company was founded by Robert Hadfield Senior, who was succeeded by his son Robert Abbott Hadfield in 1888. From this time onwards, his influence permeated all corners of organisational life until his death in 1940. The firm demonstrated classic features of the personally controlled enterprise, with Hadfield presiding over a small but close-knit group of loyal directors, many of them of long standing. What emerged was a boardroom culture that celebrated the virtues of strong leadership and collective responsibility. While Robert Hadfield did devolve responsibility to senior directors, especially in the 1920s, he remained throughout his time in office the dominant figure within the company. Founders and successors may well 'explicitly or implicitly' shape the culture of organisation, 'the character of relations among those employed' and the establishment of 'the images, symbols and rituals associated with the firm's activities'.[1] Leadership of this type, within a public company, shaped a style of governance that was autocratic. To study governance at Hadfields, this chapter first will explore the personal control of the company in the boardroom, at the AGM and in relations with shareholders. Second, it will examine the dominant style of governance exercised by Robert Abbot Hadfield and the board during the period of business turbulence in the 1920s and early 1930s when the company faced diminished profits, falling dividends and shareholder discontent concerning its strategy of diversification, notably into car manufacture through its association with Bean Cars. Finally, the chapter explores changes in management in the 1930s, when the board, under the direction of a long-established executive, attempted to create a more structured hierarchy of middle management through the formation of a local board of directors. As will be demonstrated, such devolution of responsibility did little to reduce the importance of the elite board

---

[1]   Church, 'Demonstrating Nuffield', p. 565.

of directors, who were slow to introduce organisational changes, despite the fact that they employed management consultants to review the company's operations and systems.

Personal control, dominant leadership and boardroom culture

Robert Abbot Hadfield was 29 in 1888, when he assumed control, following his father's death, of the Hadfields Steel Foundry Co. Ltd, later (in 1913) to be renamed Hadfields Ltd. He had originally joined the company in 1877, and was groomed by his father in the various aspects of steelmaking, and the marketing of the company's products. By 1888 Robert had made a significant reputation for himself as a metallurgist, and he was to become one of Britain's leading figures in the field. Robert Hadfield was an expert in the complex business of steelmaking technology, and consequently what the firm made, how it made it, and the value placed on the product range were a source of individual pride. The reputation of his firm and the pride that customers and shareholders took in the maintenance of an engineering tradition were issues that mattered a great deal to Robert Hadfield throughout his career. Hence, as shown below, Hadfield was quick to justify the company's role as a leading armaments producer during the First World War, and the reputation it had created for itself at both a local and national level.

On succeeding to control, Robert Hadfield inherited a private company which, under the directions of his father's will, was to convert to a public one, with a nominal capital of £110,000, divided into £10 shares, a decision designed to raise capital for expansion.[2] Hadfield, nevertheless, retained the controlling interest in the new public company, acquiring £63,750 of the nominal share capital.[3] During the 1890s, production expanded, and in 1897 the company opened a second works, the East Hecla Works at Tinsley, Sheffield. Between 1900 and 1914, output expanded rapidly, both in Britain and abroad. The company's patented manganese steel, which owed much to the inventive talents of Hadfield himself, found receptive markets, especially for track-work. Alloy steels, developed to manufacture shells, for both the British army and navy, as well as for America and Japan, proved a lucrative business. Hadfields also branched out into mining equipment, which was in heavy demand in South Africa.[4]

Expansion brought with it considerable financial success; profits soared between 1900 and 1914, and dividends averaged a remarkable 25 per cent per annum (Table 3.1). Crucial to the success of the company were Robert Hadfield's

[2]   G. Tweedale, *Giants of Sheffield Steel: The Men who made Sheffield the Steel Capital of the World* (Sheffield, Sheffield City Libraries, 1986), pp. 41–4.

[3]   Sheffield Archives, Hadfields Records, Volume 7, Ordinary, Extraordinary and AGM Minutes 1889–1919, 17 August 1888.

[4]   G. Tweedale, *Steel City: Entrepreneurship, Strategy and Technology in Sheffield 1743–1993* (Oxford, Clarendon Press, 1995), pp. 129, 259.

Table 3.1   Net profits and dividends: Hadfields 1890–1918

	Profit (£)	Dividend (%)
1890	20,534	7.5
1891	26,067	7.5
1892	12,102	7.5
1893	9,637	6.5
1894	7,792	5.5
1895	7,845	5.0
1896	19,008	6.5
1897	19,377	7.0
1898	18,080	8.0
1899	17,368	9.0
1900	39,500	20.0
1901	82,818	25.0
1902	86,121	25.0
1903	84,051	30.0
1904	76,866	30.0
1905	86,733	30.0
1906	101,497	35.0
1907	66,170	17.5
1908	72,554	17.5
1909	68,234	17.5
1910	69,995	17.5
1911	79,477	17.5
1912	116,297	20.0
1913	109,512	20.0
1914	139,301	22.5
1915	265,403	25.0
1916	252,126	30.0
1917	257,509	30.0
1918	202,895	30.0

Source: Tweedale, *Steel City*, pp. 124–5.

dedication to the business and his extensive knowledge of metallurgy. Through a heavy expenditure on research, which developed a series of innovative and patented steel products, coupled with Hadfield's assiduous cultivation of both commercial and military business, the company was a success story prior to the First World War. Military orders accounted for about 18 per cent of turnover before the war, but the company became a major supplier of shells during the conflict, and by 1918 it was the largest and most profitable arms machine in the city, employing 5,000 people.[5] *The Statist*, in its report of the 1919 AGM, observed that

> Hadfields has a reputation second to none for the manufacture of steel castings and forgings for every branch of engineering and constructional equipment. Its pre-eminence in efficiency was very clearly demonstrated in 1917 when it beat all the leading American munitions manufacturers by obtaining a contract for 14-inch and 16-inch shells from the US Government worth $3,141,000. Its prices were 30% under the nearest American tender, and it undertook to deliver in half the time.[6]

Preceding the depression of the 1920s, the company's business success owed much to the enterprise of its executive management, led by the dominant personality of Robert Hadfield. A strong company culture emerged that embodied as core values the high quality of the steel goods produced, the technological innovations in manufacture, and the importance of the company to the national interest, especially during the war. During a visit by dignitaries of the Iron and Steel Institute, in 1911, Hadfield articulated the core values and traditions of his company. Business success depended upon the quality of skilled workers, 'the long experience' of the company in experimenting with and making 'high quality material', and a consideration for meeting the requirements of customers.[7] He perceived the company as a unitary organisation, in which there was a 'fine spirit of co-operation' between directors, managers, foremen and workers.[8] Workers were described as stakeholders in the governance of the company, and Hadfield, a frequent champion of industrial co-operation, advocated that 'colleagues', as he often referred to his employees, 'should share in any prosperity that the firm shared'.[9] During the war, the company produced 'enormous quantities of various products ... nearly all demanding the highest expert knowledge'.[10] The company's contribution to the war effort led Hadfield at the 1917 AGM to justify the board's policy of paying high dividends, and to defend its reputation against public

---

[5]   Ibid.

[6]   *The Statist*, 5 April 1919, Report on Hadfields AGM.

[7]   Sheffield Central Library (SCL), 623.4 SSTQ, *The Hadfield System as Applied to War Material* (n.d., most probably 1911).

[8]   Hadfields AGM, 1912, reported in *Sheffield Independent*, 12 March 1912.

[9]   Hadfields AGM, 1907, reported in *Sheffield Independent*, 22 March 1907.

[10]   SCL, 338.4SQ, Hadfields Ltd, Report of AGM, 28 March 1919.

criticism that they were 'warmongers'. Hadfield reminded the AGM that there was nothing excessive about returns to shareholders in 1917; the board 'had paid the same dividents five times before'. Dividends were a just reward for 'the work we are doing [which] constitutes a necessary and honourable service to the nation'. At the same time, business firms had a social responsibility, and Hadfield assured shareholders that they paid Excess Profit Duty 'cheerfully'.[11]

Collective action lay at the heart of Hadfield's perception of an effective business organisation, a culture based upon a strong team spirit. The development of collective authority rested in the hands of an executive board, which consisted of hand-picked directors, many of whom had been promoted through long service to the company. Peter B. Brown, who had served the company since 1888, emphasised to shareholders the values attached to internal promotion. Proposing the re-election to the board in 1915 of J. P. Crosbie, works manager, and W. B. Pickering, commercial manager, he announced:

> In our Company, which is now getting a fairly old one, we have a tradition that every man should have the opportunity to rise from the lowest position to the very highest. We have already on the board a number of men who have climbed up the ladder, and in these two gentlemen before you we have conspicuous examples of this type.[12]

A strong team ethos, based upon managers who knew the business of steelmaking, was how Hadfield projected the governance of the company to shareholders. At the 1917 AGM, for example, he informed them that:

> Any little differences that must from time to time exist among a body of active, hard working men, with original ideas of their own, have been microscopic. Each and all have worked together hand and glove, first for the common good of our Empire, and next for this company. I am indeed happy to be the captain of such a team.[13]

Hadfield equated governance with collective responsibility, and he appointed himself a captain of industry, leading a team that had one function, to act in the best interests of the company and its stakeholders. Within the confines of the board room, Hadfield's ethos was based upon collective responsibility, while at the same time he remained a commanding figure in strategic decision-making. Company culture is reflected at the level of the executive board in terms of the 'training and recruitment of directors', the 'responsibilities' and collective authority of senior managers, the remuneration of directors, and the processes for succession

---

[11]   Hadfields Records, Box 124, AGM, 26 March 1917.

[12]   Hadfields Records, Box 9, AGM, 22 March 1915.

[13]   Box 124, AGM, 26 March 1917.

to chairmanship and managing director.[14] Hadfield was typical of founders or their successors in British business who 'recruited salaried managers but continued to be influential shareholders, held executive managerial positions, and exercised decisive influence on company policy'.[15]

The governance and style of Hadfield's management was evident from the outset. On his succeeding his father in 1888, the ideal of personal control, with the devolution of authority to a collective team of trusted directors, was central to Hadfield's vision of the company. Just a week after the death of his 'dear father', he wrote to John Mallaband, a metallurgist[16] who and had been a close, influential and loyal director to his father for 20 years, making clear his intentions on family succession. Referring to the fact that Mallaband had been bequeathed £5,000 of shares in the new public company, a 'Christmas present' to a loyal servant, Hadfield assured him that 'With an interest of this kind, and a seat as a Director on the Board ... you will feel secure'. Such touching loyalty, however, came with a stark reminder that he was a servant of the company. Repeating a conversation with his father, Hadfield reminded Mallaband that he 'asked you not to act in any way in the future detrimentally to his or his family's interests in the new company, he still retaining seven-tenths or more of the interest therein'. As heir apparent, 'this is all I too ask'. Mallaband represented a potential threat to the continuation of family control, compounded by the fact that Hadfield had reluctantly conceded to his father's wishes to convert to public liability. Although he accepted that the company faced serious shortages of working capital for expansion, Hadfield confided to Mallaband that the conversion was arranged 'entirely' by his father, and 'in my opinion it would have been better to keep the company entirely a private one to ourselves'.[17] Consequently, it was this which persuaded Hadfield to invest £63,750 out of a total new share subscription of £110,000, 'much more of my own money than intended'. To all intents and purposes, public conversion was a disguise for the continuation of family control: a private concern under the umbrella of a public corporation. Together with his father's 'seven-tenths interest' in the company, Hadfield was overwhelmingly the controlling shareholder; his investment in new stock was 'principally for the purpose of being able to have matters so that you [Mallaband] and I with my father's interest can control affairs and not be interfered with by anyone'.[18]

Non-interference extended to his perspective of the public shareholder, whom Hadfield viewed as being satisfied simply with the reward of satisfactory

---

[14]   Jeremy, *A Business History of Britain*, p. 504.

[15]   Church, 'The Family Firm in Industrial Capitalism', p. 18.

[16]   Mallaband's reputation had been forged at the leading Sheffield firm of Vickers. G. Tweedale, *Sheffield Steel and America: A Century of Commercial and Technological Interdependence 1830–1939* (Cambridge, Cambridge University Press, 1987), p. 231, note 3.

[17]   Hadfields Records, Box 103, R. A. Hadfield to J. Mallaband, 7 April 1888.

[18]   Ibid. See also Tweedale, *Steel City*, p. 140.

dividends, 'of say over 7%', and he believed that 'there is not much doubt' that the company could deliver this.[19] Shareholders, Hadfield assumed, were passive rather than entitled to engagement with the strategic direction of the company. Strategy was the remit of a governing board of directors, a group of hand-picked and trusted executives, supported by a general manager and selected departmental managers. Hadfield informed Mallaband, 'we must be free from routine work', as in his position as chairman and managing director, as well as his 'experimental work', he could not provide 'more than a general superintendence' of operations. Consequently, Hadfield devolved responsibility for general management to his board of trusted directors, which assumed direct control over strategic planning.[20] Such a managerial philosophy was central to the evolution of management in the company from 1888, shaped the culture of the board, and retained Hadfield's personal control of the concern. At the first meeting of the board in April 1888, Hadfield signalled his intentions, and his style of boardroom governance. Executive management was to be a collective activity, his co-directors acting to support him 'to carry on the business along the same honourable and upright lines which characterised it in the past'. On behalf of the directors, Benjamin Freeborough, another long-serving director well versed in the art of steelmaking, acknowledged that 'in Mr Hadfield they had an excellent chairman and managing director, one in whom they would at all times be ready and willing to cooperate'.[21]

Table 3.2 gives the directors of the company from 1888 to 1940. Hadfield judged directors on three important criteria: loyalty and commitment to the company, knowledge of the business, and reputation, especially in relation to the development of the company's armaments manufacture. Prior to the 1920s, there was fluidity to the board, but during the inter-war years a long-established directorate conducted the operational management of the company. In the event of death or retirement, internal promotions provided a means of recruitment, and Hadfield appointed new directors to deal with works management.

Alexander M. Jack, the works manager, joined the board in 1897, and in 1905 was appointed managing director with direct responsibility for the everyday running of the works, together with Henry Cooper, a long-serving engineer who had worked under Hadfield's father. Two other important directors, responsible for works management, were Major Augustus B. H. Clerke and Peter Brown. The former had gained a reputation at the Royal Arsenal, before his appointment to the board in 1913, while Brown had joined Hadfields as an assistant manager and draughtsman in 1888, headed the London office in 1903, succeeded Jack as works manager in 1905, and in 1910 became a director.[22] When Jack became deputy

---

[19]   Box 103, R. A. Hadfield to J. Mallaband, 7 April 1888.

[20]   Ibid.

[21]   Hadfields Records, Volume 94, Hadfields Steel Foundry Co. Ltd, Board Minutes, 1888–1904, 27 April 1888.

[22]   Tweedale, *Steel City*, p. 261; Hadfields Records, Volume 7, 14 March 1905, 17 March 1910.

Table 3.2   Directors of Hadfields Ltd 1888–1940, and directors who continued after 1940

	Appointed to board	Office	Left board
Robert A. Hadfield	1888	Chairman to 1940, MD to 1920	Died 1940
George Curzon, MP	1888	Director	Retired 1897
Horatio Marsden	1888	Director	Retired 1893
John Mallaband	1888	Director	Retired 1897
Benjamin Freeborough	1888	Director	Died 1915
Alexander M. Jack	1897	Works Manager, then MD 1905, Deputy Chair 1920	Retired 1922
Colonel Sir Howard Vincent	1903	Director	Dies 1910
General, the Rt Hon. Sir Henry Brackenbury	1904	Director	Retired 1914
William Henry Dixon	1905	Director	Retired 1917
Henry Cooper	1905	Director	Retired 1919
Admiral Sir Archibald L. Douglas	1907	Director	Retired 1914
Lord John Claude Hamilton	1909	Director	Died 1923
P. B. Brown	1910	MD from 1921, deputy chairman 1930 and succeeded Robert Hadfield in 1941	Continued
Major A. B. H. Clerke	1913	MD from 1921	Continued
I. B. Milne	1914	Director – Head Metallurgist	Retired 1926
J. P. Crosbie	1915	Works manager – Director	Retired 1933
W. B. Pickering	1915	Commercial manager – Director	Continued
Commander E. H. M. Nicholson	1917	Director	Continued
Henry B. Sandford	1921	Director	Retired 1930
William E. Parker	1929	Local Director	Continued
A. Roebuck	1931	Director	Continued
W. J. Dawson	1920	Director	Continued
J. B. Thomas	1936	Finance Director	Continued

Source: Compiled from Hadfields Records, Volume 7, Volume 93.

chairman in 1920, Clerke and Brown became joint managing directors, directly responsible for running the works. Brown was later to be promoted to deputy chairman in 1930 and eventually to succeed Robert Hadfield in 1940. Hadfield also made a number of external appointments, especially in connection with the company's government business in armaments. George Curzon, a Conservative MP, and an imperial enthusiast, became Viceroy of India in 1897 when he retired from the board. Colonel Sir Howard Vincent, appointed in 1905, was a Sheffield Conservative MP and supporter of Joseph Chamberlain's tariff reform campaign. As a shareholder in Hadfields, Vincent had 'taken a great interest in its well being'. Over the years, a number of naval commanders joined the board, which inserted the company into contractual networks, and at AGMs these prominent personalities were paraded in front of shareholders.[23] Above all, Hadfield expected loyalty and a dedication to the business of the company, and in 1894 a special resolution was passed incorporating into the articles of association the stipulation that directors with external business interests 'must disclose' these facts 'at the meeting of directors'.[24]

Two factors determined Hadfield's decision to delegate responsibility for the general management of the works to trusted internal directors. First, he could not effectively supervise the operations of an expanding company without devolution.[25] Second, he moved from Sheffield to the 'fashionable' surroundings of London before the First World War, to come closer to the 'scientific milieu of the technical societies, which he relished so much', and to be 'on the doorstep of the supply ministries for armament orders'.[26]

With Hadfield having less time to devote to the running of the company, day-to-day management passed to carefully selected mangers, and Hadfield facilitated internal promotion, and distinguished between strategic and operational management. At the outset, he had replaced half of his father's senior staff with his own handpicked men,[27] and in 1896 he created the status of 'official director'. The term defined the subservient role of professional managers within the organisation. Official directors owed their appointment to the discretion of the board, and consisted of employees designated as 'managers or officers of the

---

[23]   Sir Archibald Douglas, for example, appointed in 1907, had connections with Armstrong Whitworth, one of Britain's largest armaments firms, and together with Vincent had approached that company on behalf of Hadfields regarding a proposed amalgamation. Although this was 'dropped' by the Armstrong Whitworth directors in 1908, Douglas brokered contracts with the Admiralty between 1908 and 1910, and secured contracts with the Japanese Imperial Navy in 1911. Hadfields Records, Volume 93, Hadfields Steel Foundry Co. Ltd, Board Minutes No. 2, 1904–36, 18 November 1907, 6 March 1908, 8 November 1910, 9 May 1911.

[24]   Hadfields Records, Volume 7, 10 March 1894.

[25]   Box 103, R. A. Hadfield to J. Mallaband, 7 April 1888.

[26]   Tweedale, *Steel City*, p. 261.

[27]   Tweedale, *Giants of Sheffield Steel*, p. 44.

company'. To distinguish them from 'managing directors', whose remit was to deal with strategic decision-making, official directors were responsible for works management, their remuneration being determined 'as other directors see fit'.[28] At AGMs, shareholders voted for resolutions that entitled Hadfield to distribute 'at his discretion' bonus payments to managers and directors.[29] These procedures enabled Hadfield to devolve responsibility and groom trusted managers for full director status, while ensuring that he maintained control over strategic decision-making. Leading directors, such as Jack, Brown, Crosbie and Pickering, had first become official directors, before final promotion to full directorships.[30] Hadfield's control over recruitment was confirmed in 1904 when he was authorised to 'enter into any provisional arrangement that he may consider desirable to appoint anyone as a director'. To implement this, it was the duty of directors, 'by their votes ... and by their influence with the shareholders to endeavour to procure such persons to be duly elected'.[31]

A strong attachment to loyalty amongst staff and directors epitomised Hadfield's style of governance both within the boardroom and in the company generally.[32] Such an approach to management was vital to his control over strategic decision-making but Hadfield continued to keep 'a strong hold over his directors, who rarely appeared to have questioned his decisions', and he was a constant visitor to Sheffield, where he demanded a strong work ethic.[33] Writing in the 1950s, a former manager of the crushing machine department between 1903 and 1905, William F. Kett, described Hadfield's intervention into the day-to-day life of the company:

> Mr R. A. Hadfield, Managing Director of the ... Company ... was dedicated almost solely to his business and he never spared himself. His energy was phenomenal. He had two secretaries who were alternately in attendance from early morning till late at night. One or other of these secretaries travelled with him wherever he went, making notes of any thoughts that occurred to him. Hardly a day passed that I did not remember one of these suggestions, usually covering some subject with which I was fully cognizant.

---

[28]   Hadfields Records, Volume 7, 28 March 1896.

[29]   See, for example, Box 9, AGM, 22 March 1915, where one shareholder commented that 'the shareholders have no hesitation in saying that you deserve this'.

[30]   See Hadfields Records, Volume 7, 17 March 1910, 16 March 1915; Hadfields Records, Volume 93, 8 September 1913.

[31]   Hadfields Records, Volume 51, Directors' Private Minute Book, 1904, 1918–47, 14 March 1904. Additional directors were accommodated on the board by periodic changes to the articles of association of the company, which increased the size of membership. No fewer than three but to a maximum of six in 1894, a maximum of nine in 1905 and eleven in 1909. Hadfields Records, Volume 7, 14 March 1905, 22 March 1909.

[32]   Tweedale, *Giants of Sheffield Steel*, p. 45.

[33]   Tweedale, *Steel City*, p. 261.

Life at the company, according to Kett, was a constant routine of dicta, relayed by the company secretary, William Dixon, who became a director in 1905. At the daily 'conference', between 9am and 12pm, presided over by the works manager, Alexander Jack, 'who was closely associated with Mr Hadfield', departmental managers were subjected to details on customer enquiries, technical aspects of orders, and via Dixon a barrage of questions raised by Hadfield.[34]

Even after 1921, when Hadfield suffered a serious illness, he remained the key figurehead of the organisation, being usually present at AGMs. 'All policy decisions were referred to him', and he insisted upon being kept regularly informed of company business through a constant stream of telegram and telephone communications.[35] A personal secretary of Hadfield recalled that 'Things would start to liven up after the London message had been passed that "the old man's coming up for a few days"'.[36] The Hadfield archive contains a stream of red-lined memorandums, containing Hadfield's reflections on the operation of the business, and which were duly received by various works directors. They represent a testimony to his prodigious work ethic, but also reveal a determination to control key decisions, to be kept regularly informed, and to use trusted directors to get things done. For example, in late 1920 Hadfield established an inner circle of directors under the title of a 'Financial Advisory Committee', consisting of Jack, Clerke and Brown, to sanction all capital expenditure decisions.[37] Although these directors were given a free hand, they could not avoid the watchful eye of Hadfield. In 1921 he wrote to Brown and Clerke berating them for what he considered their imprudent decision to sanction further capital expenditure for the East Hecla Works, which were in the present depressed conditions of demand operating at under-capacity. Enforcing his authority, he warned them that 'It is very easy to draw a cheque on the account, that is to say this will be accounted for at the end of the year. That is too late, we must have it watched, as I say, month by month'.[38] When dissatisfied he would exert his authority, often referring to long past association to force home the point. In 1917, for example, he wrote to I. B. Milne, the chief metallurgist, who had joined the board in 1913, concerning the limited co-ordination between his department and Clerke, who was the director in charge of armaments production. Referring to a long association and 'friendship' with Milne, Hadfield reminded Milne of his responsibility to ensure that Clerke 'is kept regularly informed', as 'if you are away, or if Mr Jack and I were away, he will be a sheep without a shepherd'. To solve the problem Hadfield suggested 'a

---

[34]   Hadfields Records, Box 53, Extract from Autobiography of W. F. Kett, written in the 1950s.

[35]   Tweedale, *Steel City*, pp. 260, 261–2.

[36]   Cited in Ibid., p. 261.

[37]   Hadfields Records, Volume 93, 15 November 1920.

[38]   Hadfields Records, Box 58, Memo by R. H. Hadfield to P. B. Brown and A. B. H. Clerke, 13 January 1921.

little dinner at … the club, and a full and frank discussion to gather 'the collective wisdom of you all'.[39]

Hadfield's continued control of the board, of course, owed much to the fact that he remained the largest shareholder, and this shaped his governance of the company and relations to shareholders generally. Despite the expansion of the shareholding base, as discussed in Chapter 6, Robert Hadfield still held 237,500 of the 1.8 million £1 ordinary shares in 1935, with no other shareholder owning more than 22,000. While he held 30,000 shares or more, Hadfield was automatically managing director and chairman; he could be neither rotated nor retired due to his voting powers at board level and at the AGM.[40] In a public company, owners are often vulnerable to a loss of control, through potential takeovers, especially when shareholding widens to meet the needs for business expansion. To circumvent this, Hadfield utilised preference shares to expand capital between 1898 and 1906 (see Table 6.3). Holders in 1898 had 'no right to attend or vote at the meetings of the company unless and until the company makes default in paying interest on these shares'. A year later, to meet an expansion in capacity, further preference shares were issued, each to convey one vote, but only in the event of a decision to reduce capital or to wind up the company. In all other matters, preference shareholders were to have no 'right to attend [the AGM], or to vote either in person or proxy'. In 1904, the directors reported that steps were being taken to obtain a quotation for its shares on the London Stock Exchange, but with a business which was continuing to expand decided instead to increase capital by issuing £1 ordinary shares, which were 'to be offered to present holders' only. This ensured that the board secured the voting rights of such shares.[41] Hadfield, through such financial devices, could maintain a direct relationship between ownership and control, and at the same time expand the capital base of the enterprise.

The issue of shares, which lay with the discretion of the board, conferred on Hadfield significant power in the general governance of the company. At the 1915 AGM, Hadfield announced the creation of £500,000 of new shares, of which only £400,000 were to be issued in 1916, the remainder held 'under the control of the directors, to be issued as and when the occasion requires'. In the event, the company did not distribute any of these shares until 1919. New capital issues received board approval only when required to meet exceptional increases in capital expenditure for expansion, as was the case in 1915 with the increasing demands of the war.[42] As Hadfield reminded shareholders in 1917, this was consistent with a 'conservative' financial policy, 'pursued by your directors in the past', of 'keeping down the capital account to a very low figure – far below the assets employed in

---

[39] Box 58, Memo by R. H. Hadfield to I. B. Milne, 13 August 1917.

[40] Tweedale, *Steel City*, pp. 140, note 80, p. 141.

[41] Hadfields Records, Volume 7, 23 February 1897, 12 October 1898, 3 July 1900, 14 March 1904.

[42] Box 9, AGM, 22 March 1915.

the business.'[43] The ability to reduce the capital account, Hadfield acknowledged at the 1915 AGM, related to the accumulation of 'substantial reserves with a view to meeting any contingency which may arise', which were employed as capital in the business.[44]

For shareholders, this raised two fundamental issues: their expectations that the board should distribute the reserves in dividends and that they should be eventually capitalised and distributed as bonus issues. On the dividend, Hadfield immediately quelled complaints that the bonus paid on top of the ordinary dividend was too low. At the 1917 AGM he reminded shareholders that a bonus of 1s on ordinary shares, 'free of income tax', was the result of keeping the capital account low, and the bonus, 'having regard to the small amount of our working capital, absorbs only £20,000 more'. Demonstrating his autocratic style of governance, he insisted that shareholders had received their due reward, an average 25 per cent dividend over the previous four years. Dismissing any dissenting voices, he concluded:

> if anyone questions our policy and dividend, they evidently do not know what they are talking about. They must be unaware of the comparatively small figures to which we have got down our capital account. Such 'doubting Thomases' deserve reprimanding if they question the small extra bonus we are paying.[45]

On rights issues, and the 'conservative' policy of building large reserves, however, Hadfield had to pursue a more cautious approach. In 1915, he acknowledged that

> you have for a long time expected that these reserves should be capitalised and distributed ... your directors have come to the conclusion that it is only fair and reasonable that the ordinary capital should be increased by the capitalisation of £800,000 of the company's resources which have, in fact, hitherto, been employed as capital in the business, although not so designated in the company's accounts.[46]

Reserves, therefore, rather than share capital, had provided the basis for the expansion of output during the war, but despite Hadfield's promise to capitalise the reserve, and distribute as ordinary shares, a promise reiterated in 1917, he did not finally approve it until 1919.[47]

Summing up Hadfield's relationship with shareholders, we might refer back to his earlier comments to Mallaband in 1888, that shareholders were passive, content with a satisfactory and, during the war, quite remarkable dividend payment.

---

[43] Box 124, AGM, 26 March 1917.

[44] Box 9, AGM, 22 March 1915.

[45] Box 124, AGM, 26 March 1917.

[46] Box 9, AGM, 22 March 1915.

[47] Box 124, AGM, 26 March 1917; 338.4SQ, Hadfields Ltd, Report of AGM, 28 March 1919.

He commanded the AGM in an autocratic manner, as he did the board, with a determination that echoed his words to Mallaband that he should not 'be interfered with by anyone'. Shareholders should demonstrate loyalty to the company name, take pride in the reputation of its products and its technological achievements, and be content with the receipt of dividends. In this, they could rely on a team of directors to deliver business success. During the inter-war years, however, the company faced the winds of change. Led by an aging chairman and board of directors, it felt the full blast of the depression, and the problems of managing a diversified organisation through decisions to acquire subsidiary companies.

Failure born out of optimism: diversification at Hadfields in the inter-war years

Amongst the history of Sheffield's largest steel manufacturers during the inter-war years, Hadfields stands out in one important respect. Unlike many of Sheffield's largest firms, which rationalised through merger, symbolised by the absorption of a number of prominent makers into the English Steel Corporation from 1927,[48] Hadfields remained an independent concern.[49] At the end of the war, Hadfield and his directors set a tone of optimism, backed up by a major reorganisation, to convert the works to meet the demands of peace-time production.[50] Hadfield urged 'produce, produce, produce', and in the immediate post-war period the company converted its works from shell production, installing a modern electric rolling mill.[51] Reconstruction was supported by an expansive capital outlay policy, and in 1919 Hadfield finally announced the raising of capital. Ordinary share capital increased from £400,000 to £1,600,000. Reserves, totalling £800,000, were capitalised in a bonus issue and there was a rights issue of £400,000.[52] Both these decisions, as noted earlier, had been on the agenda since 1915 but, as *The Statist* observed, it was now inevitable given the need to 'cover large extensions already made ... to adapt the works to post-war conditions, and to provide further money ... in the development and extension of the various departments'. The conservative financial policy of the company, to keep the capital account low, had clearly resulted in undercapitalisation in 1919, its issued capital of £700,000 compared with stocks of £2,021,167, which inevitably called for an increase in capital 'for further expansion'.[53] Between 1918 and 1920 issued capital rose from £700,000 to £2,889,746 and at the latter date the company issued £1 million

---

48   Tweedale, *Steel City*, pp. 246–53.
49   Ibid., p. 259.
50   Ibid., pp. 259–60.
51   Ibid., p. 260.
52   338.4SQ, Hadfields Ltd, Report of AGM, 28 March 1919.
53   *The Statist*, 5 April 1919, Report on Hadfields AGM.

7.5 per cent, 10-year first mortgage debenture stock at 9s each, raising £744,962 by April 1921.[54]

Yet as the brief post-war boom turned to slump, Hadfields faced considerable constraints. These included escalating labour disputes, shortages of skilled workers and rising overhead charges, with the increase in supervisors and technical staff during the war. A report by Brown and Clerke in 1920 took six days to complete, the managing directors frustrated by the fact that departmental managers did not compile their own data on wages and costs. It concluded that overheads had increased by 50 per cent compared to pre-war costs, and to compensate would require an increase of prices by 25 per cent, which would render the company uncompetitive in most classes of work.[55] During the war, costing practices had become inefficient, and despite Hadfield's constant berating of his managers to produce reliable figures, and reduce overheads in the face of falling turnover, by 1923 problems of internal costing persisted.[56] Two reports by the company accountant in 1924 and 1925 found similar discrepancies in accounting procedure and continued rises in overhead costs; despite recommendations to introduce modern accounting procedures,[57] the problems persisted into the 1930s. The introduction of budgeting controls proved difficult to enforce and, as Hadfield admitted, 'a budget ... a sort of forecast is not altogether an easy matter ... and necessarily very approximate'.[58]

Most urgent, however, was the necessity of meeting rising competition, given that Hadfield's original patents for alloy steels had expired, and there was a changing structure of demand, notably a decline for its traditional steel castings. On the demand side there was a switch from castings to rolled steel and 'newer heat-resisting and stainless steels for cars and aircraft',[59] and in 1923 the company was well aware that business reconstruction 'can only be accomplished when the demand for our products matures'.[60] Hadfield was 60 in 1918, his health deteriorating, but he remained acutely aware of the need to develop new lines of business. Reluctant to enter into formal mergers, Hadfield pursued a policy of diversification through investments in allied trading companies.[61] Hadfield's strategy owed much to commercial logic, but as Tweedale argues the form that it took also represented his determination to remain 'independent', refusing 'to ally the firm with any of its rivals'. Consequently, his policy of diversification

---

[54]   *The Statist*, 9 April 1921, Report on Hadfields AGM.

[55]   Hadfields Records, Box 64, Report by P. B Brown and A. H. B. Clerke, 18 August 1920.

[56]   Tweedale, *Steel City*, p. 260.

[57]   Hadfield Records, Box 135, Reports on Wages and Costing Systems', Jeffrey's Reports, 1924 and 1925.

[58]   Box 64, R. A. Hadfield to Jeffrey, 7 April 1924.

[59]   Tweedale, *Steel City*, p. 260.

[60]   Box 58, AGM, 3 April 1922, speech by P. B. Brown.

[61]   Tweedale, *Steel City*, pp. 260–61.

involved devising 'his own schemes'.[62] This resulted in three key decisions. First, technological innovations in stainless steel production, building on Hadfields' development of heat-resistant steel for aero-engine production during the war were made in the 1920s in collaboration with the French firm Commentry-Fourchambault et Decazeville. Second, under Hadfield's guidance, the company developed its core capabilities in projectile production. A partnership with the American Clay Machinery Co. led to the formation of the Hadfield-Penfield Co., a realisation of 'Hadfield's long-standing dream' to enter the American market and exploit the potential for their technological lead in alloy steel castings and the production of armour-piercing projectiles.[63] Hadfield's investment in the new company totalled $1,166,700 to acquire a 40 per cent share of the common stock, the remaining 60 per cent being acquired by R. C. Penfield, the proprietor of the Machinery Co.[64]

While these two initiatives were in line with the company's managerial and technological capabilities in steelmaking, the third decision involved branching out into the manufacture of cars to provide an 'outlet for surplus alloy steel'. Diversification into the car market 'was popular amongst the steel and engineering firms', with BSA, Vickers, Armstrong-Whitworth and Beardmores 'all attracted, for better or worse, into car production'. In 1919, Robert Hadfield made the move into car production when he acquired an interest in Harper Son & Bean, the car subsidiary of Harper Bean Ltd, a West Midlands holding company.[65] Given the lack of managerial and engineering knowledge of the business, this was the most ambitious of all the schemes. To acquire the interest, Hadfields issued 166,600 of its ordinary shares to Harper Bean Ltd, in exchange for 166,600 shares in Harper, Son & Bean, an investment that initially cost Hadfields £250,000.[66] Forward integration into car manufacture offered the opportunity to utilise Hadfields' high-grade steel capacity, the company capable of producing 170,000 tons per annum, and, as they informed shareholders in 1923, the alliance had secured a market for a large proportion of its output.[67] To secure a voice in the management of the car company, Clerke was appointed as a nominee director of the Harper Bean board, together with Henry B. Sandford, and J. P. Crosbie.[68]

Carried by Robert Hadfield's optimism during the post-war boom, the schemes all ultimately proved disappointing. Experiments with heat-resistant and non-corrosive alloys proved costly in research and development, and found only limited

---

[62]   Ibid., p. 262.

[63]   Ibid., pp. 263–3. See also *The Statist*, 9 April 1921.

[64]   Tweedale, *Sheffield Steel and America*, p. 121.

[65]   Tweedale, *Steel City*, p. 262.

[66]   G. Tweedale, 'Business and Investment Strategies in the Inter-War British Steel Industry: A Case Study of Hadfields Ltd and Bean Cars', *Business History*, Volume 29 (1987), p. 52; *The Statist*, 14 April 1923, Report on Hadfield AGM.

[67]   Box 124, AGM, 12 April 1923.

[68]   Box 58, AGM, 3 April 1922.

markets. Ambitions to develop the market in the USA, via Hadfield-Penfield, proved over-optimistic; orders from the American government for projectiles did not materialise, and in the saturated American market for steel castings of the 1920s the result was substantial over-capacity. Market trends were not favourable to the venture, a fact not available to Hadfields' management in 1919, but they must bear some of the blame nevertheless. They proved 'incapable of organising a business', located across the Atlantic, despite regular trips by senior executives.[69]

At home, the car venture turned into a fiasco. In 1923 the Harper Bean holding company collapsed, after making consistent losses in 1921 and 1922.[70] Summing up the situation in 1923, *The Statist* concluded that the business had 'proved almost worthless'.[71] Influenced by Hadfield, and supported by a £50,000 investment to take up debenture shares, Harper, Son & Bean purchased from the defunct holding company 55 per cent of its shares. Removed from the shackles of the holding company, it performed little better than under its predecessor. Clerke, as the main Hadfield representative on the board, supported by the managing director Jack Bean, lacked knowledge of mechanical engineering. Stretched by his managerial commitments at Sheffield, he had problems in finding a suitable works manager, which led to serious technical problems in car design and engineering efficiency. In 1926 Hadfields acquired the controlling interest, renamed the company Bean Cars, and after 1929 reduced its commitment to the car market to concentrate on commercial vehicles, especially for empire markets. By 1927, Hadfields' total holding in Bean represented an investment of £626,000, and when it entered into liquidation in 1931, a casualty of the depression, Hadfields' total losses stood at £552,000. Nevertheless, Robert Hadfield persisted with the venture and in 1933 he formed a new company, Bean Industries, which in turn acquired Bean Cars, discontinued car production and concentrated on profitable operations at its stamping works at Smethwick and a foundry at Tipton. This proved short-lived, and although Bean Industries returned to profits by 1935, the following year Riley Motors purchased it for £625,000. Tweedale puts the venture cost of Hadfield's association with Bean at £1.1 million, 'which included shares purchased, cash advanced, [and] goods not paid for'. The sale to Riley partly offset the loss, but this still left a net loss of £192,820, excluding the original share exchange, valued at £250,000, or the £50,000 in debentures that Hadfield took up in 1922.[72] In addition, this estimate makes no allowances for lost dividends or the return on a more astute investment. In other words, the opportunity cost to Hadfield of the diversification into Bean was that it deprived the former company of much-needed investment capital, which they might have employed better elsewhere.

---

[69]   Tweedale, *Steel City*, p. 263.

[70]   Tweedale, 'Business and Investment Strategies', p. 52.

[71]   *The Statist*, 14 April 1923, Report on Hadfields AGM.

[72]   Tweedale, 'Business and Investment Strategies', pp. 52, 63–4; Box 124, AGM, 28 March 1924.

Table 3.3   Profits and dividends: Hadfields 1919–39

	Profit (£)	Dividend on ordinary shares (%)
1919	203,194	10.0
1920	107,857	5.0
1921	158,157	5.0
1922	187,250	5.0
1923	106,510	4.0
1924	80,622	2.5
1925	117,660	3.0
1926	68,876	2.5
1927	187,223	5.0
1928	112,053	2.5
1929	109,572	2.5
1930	40,560	0
1931	21,000	0
1932	15,242	0
1933	36,553	0
1934	130,000	0
1935	117,000	0
1936	219,400	7.5
1937	269,040	17.5
1938	279,000	22.5
1939	264,000	22.5

Source: The Statist, 1921–39.

The failure of these ventures reflected the dismal overall profit record of Hadfields (Table 3.3), and for shareholders a low return on investments, with no dividend accruing between 1930 and 1935. Tweedale concludes that depressed market conditions acted as a major constraint on the company's operations, but he also observes that Hadfield and the board should also accept responsibility.[73] Management practices, as shown by the reports on costing and budgeting

---

[73] Tweedale, *Steel City*, p. 264.

procedures in the 1920s, remained archaic. Hadfield's attempts to run the company outside Sheffield proved ineffective, leading to exasperation with his trusted directors, Brown and Clerke. The management were clearly stretched, but Hadfield complained that 'I am led from pillar to post, constantly misled ... until I do not know what to believe'.[74] Hadfield's governance of the board, and his personal control, became more fragile in the 1920s, but if Hadfield felt 'misled' by his own executive team, what did this say for relations with shareholders in which the board had an obligation to the investing public? To explore these issues of governance, the next section examines the transparency of disclosure in the company, and the actions of the board in stifling shareholder voice, especially in relation to growing concerns over the Bean fiasco.

Shareholders and governance at Hadfields: the Bean fiasco

Addressing the 1932 AGM, at the request of the chairman, the managing director Peter B. Brown justified the association with Bean. It had 'promised an extensive outlet for our special steel', but 'Unfortunately the historic slump of the following year [1920–21] destroyed all hopes of the success of that concern'. No details were provided on the accounts of the company, and Brown concluded with the announcement that receivers had been appointed. Shareholders had to make do with a potted history of the Bean association, a reiteration of 'facts' which were 'reported to you from time to time ... and received your approval'.[75] Bland 'facts', however, hardly represented an explanation of the true state of affairs, nor did they reflect with credit on the company's previous disclosure policy. A study of the reports presented by Hadfield and his directors at successive AGMs between 1921 and 1931, analysed by *The Statist*, reveals the paucity of detailed information disclosed.

At the 1921 AGM Hadfield informed shareholders that the Bean venture had 'proved to be very unfortunate', the expected advantages of increased demand for steel not forthcoming. He reassured shareholders, however, that under the arrangements negotiated there would be 'no immediate cash contribution' and no 'further issue of capital by the company'.[76] A year later, in Hadfield's absence, Brown informed the AGM that the venture was 'in the best interests of this company', and under the managerial supervision of Clerke, 'we all trust that it will be crowned with glory'.[77] What he did not disclose, of course, was the serious financial predicament of Bean, and the fact that negotiations were proceeding to take up the 55 per cent share allocation from the holding company.[78] *The Statist* observed that shareholders were given scant information in the balance sheet relating to the

---

[74]   Cited in Ibid.

[75]   Box 124, AGM, 31 March 1932.

[76]   *The Statist*, 9 April 1921, Report on Hadfields AGM.

[77]   Box 58, AGM, 3 April 1922.

[78]   Box 64, A. H. B. Clerke to C. Sinclair, 31 March 1923.

book value of outside investments, which still recorded the investment in Bean, at the original purchase price of £250,000, while at prevailing market prices in 1922 'the market value … is less than £15,000'.[79] At the 1923 AGM the reserve account was debited with a sum of £137,000 representing the depreciation of investment holdings, notably in Bean, although no separate items were recorded in the balance sheet.[80] During 1923, Hadfields increased its investment in Bean through a £50,000 investment to guarantee the purchase from Harper Bean in the car concern, but there was no separate item shown in the balance sheet. *The Statist* considered the report for 1923 'a very disappointing document'. A decline in overall profits had accrued despite the fact that the company 'was, unlike 1922, immune from serious labour disputes', and 'all the more unsatisfactory in view of the recovery in earning reported by other steel manufacturers, who had to contend with almost equally keen competition from abroad'. Given the paucity of financial disclosure, *The Statist* speculated that declining profits were the result of 'very large permanent investments in outside companies, or [Hadfields] had accounted for very large future investment in new plant'. The latter, it considered, unlikely, as its post-war 'adaptation' programme had reached the stage of being practically completed.[81]

The views of *The Statist* clearly contained a warning to shareholders that the Bean venture was a drain on the company's resources but that the Hadfield board had not fully communicated to shareholders the full extent of the motor company's problems. *The Statist* tempered its veiled criticisms of financial reporting in 1926, when it received with some optimism the announcement by the Hadfields board of the purchase of the controlling interest in Bean, and the intention to strengthen the management. Based upon the chairman's up-beat address to shareholders, *The Statist* ventured to predict that 'The outlook' for Hadfields 'is better than for some years, and if the … motor subsidiary comes up to expectations it should be possible to pay a considerably larger dividend next year'.[82] Dividends doubled in 1927 to 5 per cent, a result of growing profits (Table 3.3), but the high expectations for the company and its venture into commercial vehicle manufacture did not materialise. Profits fell sharply thereafter, dividends fell to 2.5 percent in 1928 and 1929, and between 1930 and 1935 no dividend was paid. In 1928 and 1929, *The Statist* returned to its criticism of the company's financial disclosure policy, asserting that 'it must be considered defective' on two counts. First, the accounts did not show the allowance for depreciation, and, second, they did not disclose the 'earnings' of 'allied firms', notably the substantial investments made in Bean and the Hadfield-Penfield Steel Co. While *The Statist* did recognise the guarantee of the auditors that the company's reserves accounted for losses sustained by subsidiary investments, the journal nevertheless condemned the accounts, which did not provide separate information to shareholders on valuation of stock or profits

[79]   *The Statist*, 8 April 1922, Report on Hadfields AGM.
[80]   *The Statist*, 14 April 1923, Report on Hadfields AGM.
[81]   *The Statist*, 26 April 1924, Report on Hadfields AGM.
[82]   *The Statist*, 1 May 1926, Report on Hadfields AGM.

and dividend accruing.[83] Following the Companies Act of 1929, which introduced a minimum legal requirement for the disclosure of profit and loss in subsidiary companies, separate valuations of the holdings in Bean and Hadfield-Penfield were included in the accounts. Despite this, *The Statist* concluded with dismay that 'No information is offered as to the profits and dividend payment of the subsidiaries, or as to the character of the investments which are included in one composite item with debtors and cash'. Although the auditors expressed the opinion that the company's reserves were adequate to cover any depreciation on the investments, the balance sheet 'should of course, be much more informative in this connection'.[84]

In the opinion of *The Statist*, Hadfields represented a company with a low level of transparency, especially in relation to the performance of its subsidiary undertakings. Given this, and the increasing problems of Bean, how did shareholders react? The available evidence suggests that shareholders were largely silent, but the board remained deeply concerned over the possibility of organised shareholder dissent, and exit. Robert Hadfield and his managing directors acted to stifle the potential for organised voice.

A Birmingham shareholder in Hadfields, Charles Sinclair, proposed in March 1932 to raise awkward questions at the AGM, notably over the involvement of Hadfields in Hadfield-Penfield and in Bean, which prompted the directors to act to circumvent open discussion. On the request of Hadfield, and 'at a loss to understand [Sinclair's] object', Clerke sought information on Sinclair through Ansell & Sherwin, a prominent firm of Birmingham solicitors.[85] Their reply represented Sinclair as a well-informed critic, a client of stockbrokers who were themselves clients of Ansell & Sherwin. An Irish American, he was retired from active business, but was 'fairly wealthy, holding considerable interests in stocks and shares'.[86] Clerke could not ignore Sinclair; he wrote to him explaining the financial deal underpinning the acquisition of the controlling interest in Bean, and inviting him to a meeting at the Bean works. 'I would be glad to show you what we are doing, and explain a little more fully the relationship between the companies', and 'We could perhaps also have an interchange of views on the American position, in which you have displayed so much interest'.[87]

At this meeting, reported by Clerke to Hadfield, Sinclair was fully prepared with detailed financial information on the American business, as well as an informed series of questions concerning the financial deal with Bean. Faced with 'a series of questions which were not easy to deal with', Clerke conceded that there was a need for a private disclosure 'of the entire knowledge of the facts, which could not appear on the balance sheets'. Clerke consequently proceeded to reassure Sinclair that the Hadfield-Penfield business was now completely under

[83] *The Statist*, 24 March 1928, 23 March 1929, Report on Hadfields AGMs.

[84] *The Statist*, 15 March 1930, Report on Hadfields AGM. A similar condemnation was made by *The Statist*, 18 April 1931, Report on Hadfields AGM.

[85] Box 64, A. H. B. Clerke to Ansell & Sherwin, 22 March 1923.

[86] Box 64, Ansell & Sherwin to A. H. B. Clerke, 26 March 1923.

[87] Box 64, A. H. B. Clerke to C. Sinclair, 31 March 1923.

the direction of Hadfields, that the Bean venture offered an opportunity to diversify into car production, and that its financial control rested firmly with the Hadfield board. That Clerke wanted to keep the level of disclosure in-house he made clear; 'the information I was giving him was entirely confidential and constituted matters that could not be discussed at an open meeting'. Clerke's diplomatic style proved effective, and Sinclair, 'entirely relieved of the anxiety which he had felt', assured him that he would not disclose any information he had been privy to in the meeting.[88] To 'flatter his vanity', and to avoid any 'unpleasant' questions, Clerke invited Sinclair to second the vote of thanks to Robert Hadfield at the next AGM.[89] Clerke turned Sinclair from a potential liability at the AGM into a potential ally. 'It occurs to me', Clerke wrote to Sinclair, 'that it would be of great interest to a large number of shareholders to hear … any impressions you may have formed of the present state of our investment in Harper Sons & Bean Ltd.'[90] Such diplomacy paid dividends. Sinclair accepted the invitation, and Clerke informed Hadfield that 'that I am applying to him the principle of Balaam's Ass'.[91]

Sinclair, however, did not simply become a voice for the directors, and continued to inundate Clerke with letters relating to both the financial management of the American business and the marketing policy of the Bean concern.[92] By February 1924, Sinclair's continual interference had tested the patience of Robert Hadfield and Clerke to the full, and revealed their personal style of governance when it came to shareholder voice. By this stage, Sinclair's persistence was an irritant, rather than a direct threat to the reputation of the board. Sinclair, as a holder of 680 shares in the company, purchased originally for £1,400, clearly had an interest in the affairs of the company, but also was using his voice to barter for a position in the company, notably in the financial management of Hadfield-Penfield.[93] Clerke informed Hadfield:

> I am sorry to see that Mr Sinclair is again getting active. We have at the same time a clue as to the reason of his activity in his suggestion that he should go out and take charge of our interests. This would of course be wildly impossible but we want to turn him down in a diplomatic way, having regard to the prospects of the [AGM]. Of course the figures he gives are quite wrong and I do not propose to tell him where they are wrong but give him just enough to disturb his confidence.[94]

---

[88] Box 64, A. H. B. Clerke to R. A. Hadfield, 6 April 1923.

[89] Box 64, A. H. B. Clerke to R. A. Hadfield, 11 April 1923.

[90] Box 64, A. H. B. Clerke to C. Sinclair, 11 April 1923.

[91] Box 64, C. Sinclair to A. H. B. Clerke, 12 April 1923; A. H. B. Clerke to R. A. Hadfield, 11 April 1923.

[92] See, for example, Box 64, C. Sinclair to A. H. B. Clerke, 23 April 1923; 11 May 1923; 4 September 1923.

[93] Box 64, C. Sinclair to A. H. B. Clerke, 29 February 1923.

[94] Box 64, Memorandum from A. H. B. Clerke to R. A. Hadfield, 29 February 1924.

While Clerke was still prepared to play a diplomatic game, Hadfield himself displayed his usual impatient and autocratic manner. Writing to Brown, he provided his personal view of governance relations. 'I see our old friend [Sinclair] has turned up again … What a tiresome individual he is. Whilst a shareholder has a right to communicate, surely the company is in no way bound to give him details.'[95] Such a statement from a chairman of a public company demonstrated a view prevalent amongst personal owners of British companies, that shareholders should place their trust in the reputation of the board to manage the affairs of the concern. Indeed, such was Hadfield's determination to silence Sinclair that he proposed to buy his shares 'privately'.[96] Although Clerke viewed this as a dangerous precedent, 'laying our self open to blackmail indefinitely',[97] Hadfield was prepared to push the matter. He wrote to Clerke:

> one cannot begin to promise to buy up every dissatisfied shareholder. Still the man is such an intolerable nuisance that one would really pay something to get rid of him. If he were a big shareholder one could understand, but his is a trumpery investment and I really think he has no right to be so tiresome.[98]

Under Hadfield's persuasion, Clerke brokered a deal with Sinclair in March 1924 in which Hadfield bought out his holding in the company.[99]

The inference drawn from the Sinclair affair was that governance was a personalised affair, and that the business of the company should remain outside the public domain of the AGM. In his treatment of Sinclair, Hadfield remained dismissive of the voice of small shareholders. The question of the Bean investment, however, remained a contentious issue for management from the late 1920s, coupled with growing shareholder disquiet concerning the low dividend accruing. At the 1927 AGM, for example, Hadfield was forced to respond to pressure from a Bournemouth car dealer, who was critical of the chairman's 'over optimistic speech', and suggested that Bean was 'sadly in need of a strong man with brains', especially in design. He added that the sales policy should be under the control of 'your most able Sales Director and his organisation'.[100] In his usual abrupt style, Hadfield simply dismissed the critique,[101] but in 1928 he clearly recognised that the board would have to adopt a more pragmatic stance. What concerned him was a growing number of letters requiring information on the performance of Bean, and a significant increase in the transactions in ordinary shares during 1927

---

[95] Box 64, Memorandum from R. A. Hadfield to P. B. Brown, 3 March 1924.

[96] Box 64, Telegram from R. A. Hadfield to A. H. B. Clerke and P. B. Brown, 3 March 1924.

[97] Box 64, A. H. B. Clerke to R. A. Hadfield, 5 March 1924.

[98] Box 64, R. A. Hadfield to A. H. B. Clerke, 10 March 1924.

[99] Box 64, C. Sinclair to A. H. B. Clerke, 12 March 1924.

[100] Cited in Tweedale, 'Business and Investment Strategies', p. 54.

[101] Box 9, Abstract from 1927 AGM.

(Table 3.4). Responding to this trend, Hadfield wrote to his two managing directors and the company auditor J. B. Thomas: 'This influx of new shares, some of them at comparatively high prices, may mean more consideration and attention being paid to what I say at our AGM.' The fear of shareholder exit, coupled with an influx of new and larger shareholders, might threaten the authority of the board, and required more thought. Thus, Hadfield was particularly concerned about the proposed dividend, the business prospects for 1928, and 'what is to be said about Bean Car matters, we are sure to be asked'.[102] In this sense the AGM became a vehicle to affect the views of shareholders, in which the directors were fully prepared to meet any challenge that they faced, as demonstrated by the volumes of letters and memorandums that flowed between Hadfield, the managing directors and the auditor, J. B. Thomas, prior to the AGM.

Table 3.4   Number of ordinary shares in Hadfields Ltd transferred each month June–December 1927

	No. transferred
June	3,930
July	5,015
August	4,248
September	5,889
October	6,842
November	71,407
December	68,678

Source: Box 66, R. A. Hadfield to A. H. B. Clerke, P. B. Brown and R. B. Thomas, 23 February 1928.

At the same time, Hadfield kept information to shareholders at a minimum, especially concerning the affairs of the trading companies. This is not to suggest that he deliberately misled, but rather that he believed that public disclosure was detrimental to the interests of the company, and that shareholders should trust the decision of the board.Addressing the 1927 AGM, Hadfield referred to the ideas of the statistician and public servant Sir Josiah Stamp on accountability in public companies. According to Hadfield, Stamp perceived the 'obscurant' nature of 'the present method of accounting in public companies', but saw in this 'two great advantages', which Hadfield proceeded to articulate to shareholders. First, limited

---

[102]   SA, Hadfields Records, Box 66, R. A. Hadfield to P. B. Brown, A. B. H. Clerke and J. B. Thomas, 23 February 1928.

disclosure was a deterrent against shareholders as speculators, who 'often only have a passing interest and would secure any point they could by selling. Their interest in the business is not a vital one.' Second, 'you cannot possibly show in published accounts the exact state of your business, because you would expose its strengths and weakness to business rivals, and that would be very unfortunate, as they would be able to judge of your future action.' Having outlined Stamp's basic principles, Hadfield then equated these with his own vision of shareholder trust in the reputation and conduct of the board of directors. 'Whilst it is always quite easy to give fuller information, if the shareholders of a limited company are satisfied with their chairman and their board', nevertheless, Hadfield argued, 'they must take their report and explanation to some extent upon trust.' Trust was central to the governance of organisations, and in the presentation of financial information he reassured shareholders that they could rely on 'the ability and integrity' of the company auditors, Camm, Metcalf & Co., whose head, J.B. Thomas, 'has enabled us to surmount many a difficulty in accountancy in these parlous times'.[103]

A strong assertion of the trust factor in governance, of course, rested uneasily with the growing concerns of the accounting profession in the 1920s over the limited disclosure in public companies, but in the hands of Hadfield it became a key instrument at successive AGMs. In 1928, for example, two shareholders wrote to the company secretary suggesting that in the light of the revival of trade a higher dividend would have been appropriate, and requested more information in the balance sheet concerning investment in 'allied' companies.[104] Forewarned, Hadfield responded at the AGM, with a reminder to shareholders that the release of detailed knowledge was playing into the hands of their competitors, while at the same time a low dividend was premised upon a 'prudent policy', a response to the past fall in profits.[105] The following year, responding to the same questions at the AGM, Hadfield remained consistent: 'I don't believe in giving competitors a great deal of information … We are doing our very best, and you must trust us', and to reinforce a prudent financial policy he stressed the fact that as the largest shareholder 'this has my entire approval'.[106] By 1930, limited financial disclosure of the Bean venture had taken on the status of a 'policy', Hadfield responding to questions by reminding shareholders that:

> There was a very good reason for preparing the balance sheet in the form it was prepared. The cash was there and represented the largest proportion of the item.

[103] Box 9, Abstract from 1927 AGM.

[104] The memorandum contained Robert Hadfield's annotation – 'one had only 90 shares and the other was not yet on the share register'. Box 66, Memorandum by Secretary to R. A. Hadfield, 21 March 1928.

[105] Hadfields Records, Box 116, AGM, March 1928.

[106] Box 124, AGM, 27 March 1929.

> It had been their custom to work on these lines ... and as the largest shareholder the procedure met with his entire approval.[107]

AGMs became managed affairs, and the financial dealings of the Bean investment remained a mystery to many shareholders, compounded by the resilience of Hadfield and Brown in dealing in public with what had become an embarrassing fiasco. At the 1932 AGM, when a number of shareholders raised the issue, they were cordially invited 'to leave matters as they are', seek a private audience with the managing director, and avoid 'asking questions in public that do not carry us any further'.[108]

Shareholders remained in the dark, but in the boardroom there was growing concern over the viability of the Bean concern and the capability of the existing management to manage operations, and a mounting realisation of the financial cost to Hadfields. A series of reports conducted in 1927 and 1928 for Clerke and Brown provided damning reading. The first, conducted by the auditors Camm, Metcalf in 1927 identified serious deficiencies in the system of design of new models, 'low staff morale', and a 'state of confusion' in the production process resulting in excessive overhead costs. Equally damning was their assessment of financial management, which suggested that there was a loose relationship between the management of Bean by Hadfields, with few or no controls in place. Modern accounting procedures were non-existent, and the report advocated 'the adoption of ... budgetary control' and the preparation of realistic costing estimates, 'and once the policy of the company has been framed on the basis of these estimates it should be the function of the financial director to exercise close control on expenditure'.[109] A follow-up report in 1928, conducted personally by J. B. Thomas, remained 'very disturbed at the manner in which the works were managed and that substantial losses were being sustained through negligence and mismanagement'. Bean's cost accountant, S. H. L. Greaves, and sales manager, Noel Martin, both inferred that 'unless drastic changes were made in the works management and the control thereof, it would be impossible ... to realise any of the programmes which had been, or were being prepared'.[110] Another report in 1928, this time by Sir Harold Peat, a partner in the Birmingham firm of accountants Peat, Marwick, Mitchell & Co., showed that between December 1927 and September 1928 Bean had become a serious financial drain. It had run up a 'huge increase in the amount of the loan and current account with Hadfields Ltd'. The estimated cash loss was 'roughly £10,000 a month', and Peat concluded that if the business

---

[107] Box 124, AGM, 17 March 1930.

[108] Box 124, AGM, 31 March 1932.

[109] Hadfields Records, Box 47, Report on Investigation into the Bean Car Organisation by Camm, Metcalf, 1927.

[110] Hadfields Records, Box 70, Report by J. B. Thomas on Bean Cars, 12 November 1928.

were to continue Hadfields would have to provide additional finance amounting to between £85,000 and £90,000.[111]

None of these findings were recorded in the proceedings of the AGM, but for the chairman and managing directors, notably Clerke who had been directly involved in the Bean management, they could have not made easy reading. The reports, however, sparked off an attempt by Hadfields to extricate itself from the business. The Peat report had recommended three main strategies for dealing with Bean. First, and 'infinitely the best way out of the situation', was to merge Bean with a stronger company in the motor trade, which 'would mean that expert supervision of the factory would probably be forthcoming'. Failing this, Peat's second recommendation advocated the sale of the business as a going concern, and, third, 'if there was no prospect of this and no brighter prospects for [the] company – cut losses'. The final option, Peat made clear, would result in a substantial loss, which he estimated at £471,000 on Hadfields' holdings of debenture shares in Bean, plus a further cash loss of £349,000 representing the liabilities on the loan account, current account and bank overdraft.[112] Faced with this reality, the directors had little option but to opt for exit, and under the direction of Clerke and Brown attempts were made to negotiate a sale, preferably attached to amalgamation in the motor car industry. At a meeting of directors in December 1929, it was noted that 'negotiations have been going on for some time now with regard to the sale of [Bean] and it was hoped that these negotiations would be successfully carried through within the next few months'.[113] Such optimism Hadfield communicated to the AGM in 1930 when he referred shareholders to newspaper reports of a proposed National Motor Co., a move towards rationalisation crucial for 'the prosperity of this country'. To facilitate negotiations, the directors passed the financial information on Bean to 'a well known firm of chartered accountants', with the intention of the sale of Bean to the National Motor Co. Hadfield concluded by informing shareholders that negotiations were proceeding, and that they would be informed in due course.[114] Amongst the firms involved in the proposed merger were Arrol-Astor, Rover, Lanchester, Swift, Acedes and Crossleys. After two years of negotiations, the merger came to nothing.[115]

Nevertheless, hopes of a sale explain the reluctance of the board to disclose detailed financial information to shareholders in the AGMs that followed the passing of the 1929 Companies Act, despite the stipulations of the Act that companies should produce separate items for subsidiaries in the balance sheet.

---

[111] Hadfields Records, Box 45, Draft Report on Bean Cars Ltd by Sir Harold Peat, 1928.

[112] Box 45, Draft Report on Bean Cars Ltd by Sir Harold Peat, 1928.

[113] Hadfields Records, Box 122, Extract of Minutes of Directors' Meeting, 6 December 1929.

[114] Box 124, AGM, 17 March 1930.

[115] See Hadfields Records, Box 46, Bundle of Documents on National Motor Co. Merger.

Consistent with the policy that such disclosure would be an advantage to competitors, the directors in Decembers 1929 discussed the implications of the Act for the disclosure of financial information on Bean. The meeting provides a remarkable testimony to the status of Bean in the minds of the leading directors, the company viewed not as a permanent part of the organisation, but as an outside investment, which the directors described as a trading investment designed with the purpose of promoting the sales of Hadfields' products. As Brown concluded, 'The position in regard to Bean Cars was that the board never intended to incorporate that Company with Hadfields'. Given this, and with the intention of disposing of the concern, 'it was considered that it was not in the best interests of Hadfields Ltd that the Bean Company be shown as a subsidiary Company in the balance sheet as it might prove prejudicial to such negotiations'. To circumvent the 1929 Act, it became necessary for Hadfields to dispose of their controlling interest in Bean, 'so far as ordinary and preference shares are concerned'. Consequently, the chairman offered to purchase the 1,600 ordinary shares and 120,000 preference shares of Bean, at a price of £7,500. The controlling interest in Bean was transferred from Hadfields to the chairman. In the opinion of their legal advisor, Mr Preston KC,

> The transaction is not only a perfectly fair, proper and reasonable bargain, at any rate from the company's point of view, but is also clearly in the interests of the Company. Further I see no grounds on which the transaction could be successfully challenged or impeached.[116]

Armed with this legal advice, Hadfield explained the balance sheet at the 1930 AGM. Two small companies, the Manganese Steel Co. Ltd and Hadfield's (South Africa) Proprietary Ltd were included as separate items, and described 'as permanent parts of our organisation', having been formed 'to facilitate our trading operations and we hold all the shares, and particulars are given in accordance with section 125 of the new act'. Hadfield acknowledged that the Act 'had been framed ... to safeguard the interests of the investing public', but 'It is bristling with new conditions, and has been the subject of a great deal of criticisms by experts. Numerous papers have been issued in an endeavour to explain what the Act really means.' Consequently, in the interests of facilitating negotiations for a sale, shareholders were given the news that, although Hadfields had

> recently held sufficient shares in Bean Cars Ltd to make that company a subsidiary within the meaning of the Act, our shareholding has been reduced by the sale of preference and ordinary shares. The sale has ... been made to your chairman at a price which the board, acting independently of the chairman, consider very beneficial to the company.[117]

---

[116] Box 122, Extract of Minutes of Directors' Meeting, 6 December 1929.
[117] Box 124, AGM, 17 March 1930.

In the minds of the directors, Bean no longer constituted a permanent part of the organisation, it was on the market for sale, and Hadfield justified the non-disclosure of information in terms of providing an advantage to competitors as negotiations continued. At the same time, Bean had to be reorganised to make it an attractive proposition for a buy-out, and in 1929 the decision was made to switch production entirely towards commercial vehicles, with a realisation that it could no longer compete against larger producers in the highly competitive market for 'pleasure cars'. Reorganisation at Bean involved changes in management personnel,[118] in sales distribution channels, and in plant and machinery to economise on production.[119] Hopes of disposing of a going concern, however, proved unfounded. Demand for commercial vehicles stagnated, 'price competition' intensified, and in June 1931 Bean was placed into receivership, the board forced 'to decide between making further financial commitments and cutting our loss'.[120] While market factors go a long way to explain this decision, another interested party, the Manchester bank of William Deacon, who provided overdraft facilities for both Hadfields and Bean, had an influence in forcing the directors' hand.

William Deacon had become involved with Bean in 1926, at the time of Robert Hadfield's buy-out of the controlling interest in that company. Hindley, the general manager of the bank, reminded Brown that it was not their policy to become 'partners in a business', and subsequently refused requests to take up debenture stock in Bean, held by the National Provincial Bank, as a guarantee of an extended overdraft of £100,000. The bank would only advance with firm guarantees from Hadfields.[121] Hadfields thus became guarantors of the Bean overdraft, which the bank increased by £100,000 in 1926.[122] Hindley continued to remain aloof from direct involvement, and in 1928, following reports in the financial press that Hadfields were acquiring additional debenture stock in Bean, he provided a stark warning that 'Hadfields hold themselves responsible to us for any and all overdrafts upon the account of Bean Cars'.[123] The growing overdraft and debt burden on Hadfields were a central aspect of the Peat report on Bean in 1928, which warned of 'the huge increase in the amount of the loan and current account with Hadfield's.'[124] By 1930 the bank overdraft had exceeded a limit of £215,000 by £40,000, bringing forth a terse reminder from Hindley that the bank required repayment, and held little faith in the promises of the Hadfield board of a proposed merger into a National Motor Co.:

---

[118] Notably the appointment of Brown to assist Clerke, and Noel Martin as Works manager. Tweedale, 'Business and Investment Strategies', pp. 55, 63.

[119] Box 124, AGM, 17 March 1930.

[120] Box 124, AGM, 31 March 1932.

[121] Box 122, Note of meeting at William Deacons Bank, 10 September 1926.

[122] Box 122, Note of meeting at William Deacons Bank, 26 October 1926.

[123] Box 122, Hindley to P. B. Brown, 31 January 1928.

[124] Box 45, Draft Report on Bean Cars Ltd by Sir Harold Peat, 1928.

when rationalisation schemes come along we find generally they mean that those who are in remain in – only receiving paper for their debts ... if and when anything happens with Bean we shall require to be repaid in cash the whole of our advance ... the matter has gone on so long that ... I do now ask you (as I have suggested many times) to begin making transfers in reduction of the £215,000 limit.[125]

The bank had no long-term commitment to Bean, except to ensure the repayment of debts. Following the receivership of Bean in July 1931, Hindley pushed the Hadfields directors in August to accept offers for Bean at prevailing market prices, to 'substantially reduce' the overdraft account. At the same time, it extracted further guarantees from Hadfields in the form of gilt-edged investments held by the bank on Hadfields' account.[126] A month later, Hindley requested a repayment of £178,663 from Hadfields 'in substantiation of the guarantees given by you to us on behalf of Bean Cars Ltd'.[127] That the bank held more power than shareholders in governance at Hadfields was demonstrated by their insistence that Hadfields forwarded their balance sheet, and 'amplify the information it contains by giving details of a more intimate character than is necessary for the shareholders of the principal items which appear in it'.[128]

By 1931, under mounting pressure from the bank, the board had little option but to cut its losses, but receivership dragged Hadfields further into the financial mire, bringing with it considerable risks for the company and its shareholders. Receivership, Brown informed shareholders in 1932, was aimed to protect 'the interests of the debenture holders and other parties concerned', the latter a veiled reference to Bean's creditors and the bank. The majority holding in Bean rested with Hadfields. In addition to the ordinary shares held personally by Robert Hadfield, 'Hadfields Ltd' held the whole of the 'A Debenture' stock in Bean, while outside investors held the remaining 'First Debenture' stock. As Brown admitted, this placed the company in a predicament, with only limited control over the policy to dispose of Bean. While outside debenture holders 'were interested only in the realisation up to the extent of their Debentures in as short a time as possible, we as holders of the A Debentures were interested in a realisation of the greatest possible value, the time element being of secondary consideration'. A 'forced sale', therefore, would entail substantial losses to Hadfields. With this in mind, the two receivers, J. B. Thomas and Sir Harold Peat, themselves intricately connected to Hadfields, recommended acquiring the 'First Debentures to control effectively ... the realisation of the assets to the best advantage of all concerned'. At the same time, they disposed of stock and work in progress, totalling £70,000 by March

---

[125] Box 122, Hindley to P. B. Brown, 30 August 1930. Hadfields promptly repaid £20,000, followed by a further sum in early 1931.

[126] Hadfields Records, Box 55, Hindley to P. B. Brown, 11 August 1931.

[127] Box 55, Hindley to P. B. Brown, 23 September 1931.

[128] Box 55, Hindley to P. B. Brown, 11 August 1931.

1932. As this proceeded, shareholders were left with the scant reassurance that 'it is estimated that our reserves will be adequate to cover any deficiency'. Shareholders received no 'detailed account', as it 'would not serve any useful purpose … and might militate against the advantageous realisation of the assets'.[129]

Shareholders were expected to play a waiting game, and at the 1933 AGM Hadfield justified the policy. 'Trading investments', representing 'arrangements … for the purpose of promoting the sale of our products', totalled £400,000, and chief among these was Bean, which was not considered as a subsidiary. Hadfield announced the acquisition of all 'First Debenture' stock, which enabled them to buy in order to sell, and thus control the process of asset disposal at Bean. 'Under the prevailing industrial conditions' of 1931 to 1932, he asserted, 'a forced sale' would have resulted in disposal at prices well below their real value. The alternative strategy of the receivers had been to maintain operations at Bean in profit-making departments, and complete stock for sale. The objective was to maintain Bean as a going concern, enhancing its future market potential for sale at a price that would redeem the sum paid for the 'First Debenture [stock], without touching any of the fixed assets'. During 1932 Bean had made a small trading profit 'so that while waiting for a more propitious time for dealing with the whole position the prospects of the ultimate realisation are improving from day to day'. Patience was the ultimate message given to shareholders, together with trust in the board to reduce losses.[130] Optimism soon vanished, and at the 1934 AGM Hadfield announced that 'unfavourable conditions' had negated the disposal 'of the business as a whole at an acceptable figure'. Despite the fact that the working departments were expanding trade contacts, and operating at a small profit, the stigma of receivership did little to enhance its market potential, while at the same time the expenses involved rose appreciably. Consequently in August 1933 Hadfields, as sole debenture holders, purchased the fixed assets, plant and machinery for the sum of £213,000, paid for by the issue of £163,000 debenture stock and £50,00 ordinary shares, representing the whole of the issued capital, and in December formed a new company, Bean Industries, under the directorship of Brown, Clerke and Thomas. Commercial vehicle production was discontinued, the new company concentring on metal stamping at Smethwick and general engineering at Tipton. The reassurance to shareholders was that there was 'no intention of merging these assets as such into those of our own company, but rather to maintain as a separate entity the conditions of working which were proving so beneficial'.[131]

In many ways, the Bean affair was a fiasco. Despite the fact that market trends were adverse to the venture, the failure to manage it effectively, notably through the incapability of Hadfield's two managing directors, showed the limited managerial resources of the company. Hadfield and his directors acted in good faith in their attempts to sell the business, and realise the highest value on its

---

[129] Box 124, AGM, 31 March 1932.
[130] Box 124, AGM, 20 April 1933.
[131] Box 124, AGM, 28 March 1934.

disposal, but the fact remains that before Riley Motors acquired Bean Industries in 1936, the estimated loss to Hadfields stood at £1.1 million. At the same time, shareholders remained in the dark, asked to trust the board and remain patient. As Tweedale concludes, the managing directors should shoulder the blame, while a largely absent chairman became increasingly frustrated 'with his lack of personal control'.[132] Nevertheless, in the Bean affair, Robert Hadfield was well aware of the extent of the problems existing in that company, and this became a central issue between him and his managing directors in 1935.

The year 1935 witnessed the writing down of capital, an 'unthinkable event', in one of Sheffield's most prestigious firms.[133] The capital reconstruction scheme put before shareholders was premised upon the fact that overall 'trading profits' had 'not been sufficient to permit any depreciation of the company's fixed assets' for the five years between 1929 and 1934, a deficiency in accounting practice, which as noted earlier had been commented on by *The Statist* on numerous occasions. In addition, no dividend had accrued to shareholders, including the 4.5 per cent preference holders, since 1930. The board proposed writing off, or lowering to present utility use, the book value of building and plant which were 'redundant or which cannot be fully employed', in the hope that in future it would result in a 'much smaller charge for depreciation' and bring nearer the resumption of dividend payments for shareholders. Consequently, fixed asset valuations fell from £3,762,800 to £2,791,000, while ordinary shareholders felt the pain; the ordinary share capital of Hadfields was reduced from £1,859,800 to £929,400, by the conversion of £1 ordinary shares into 10s shares.[134] The Hadfield directors faced a barrage of complaints from small ordinary shareholders at the March 1935 AGM concerning the depreciation of their shareholdings, although many conceded that there was no alternative to reconstruction, and the resolutions for the scheme duly passed.[135] What shareholders did not know was the chaotic circumstances leading up to the AGM, the unreliability of financial accounting procedures, and total confusion between Hadfield and his directors over the status of Bean Industries in the reconstruction scheme. Adding to the confusion was a voluminous correspondence, which passed between the directors in Sheffield and Hadfield in France, where he had retired to on health grounds.

In a telegram to Brown and Clerke in February 1935, Hadfield, who was ploughing through the financial balance sheet prepared by the auditors, berated his managing directors for not sending an accompanying explanation detailing the report of the accounts for the AGM. This, he insisted, should 'have been prepared weeks ago as I suggested', in particular information concerning Bean Industries

---

[132] Tweedale, *Steel City*, p. 264.

[133] Ibid.

[134] Hadfields Records, Box 6, Circular to Shareholders, 13 March 1935; Notice of AGM, 13 March 1935; Memorandum by P. B. Brown on Capital Reconstruction Scheme, 12 February 1935.

[135] Box 124, Extracts from Questions Received at AGM, 1935.

'must be out forward and made perfectly clear to me'.[136] Brown duly dispatched the explanatory notes the following day, with a reminder to Hadfield that 'it contains only information which must be given to obtain the necessary support',[137] which was consistent with the minimal nature of the company's disclosure policy. Hadfield's reply was prompt, and in his usual style he produced a detailed set of questions, consisting of seven pages and 50 separate queries, a number of which referred to the status of Bean within the overall reconstruction scheme.

A priority for Hadfield was to represent Bean in the accounts in the best possible light to shareholders. As he insisted, 'We naturally want in some way to show whether openly and outwardly in the balance sheet or in the private reserve that the capital and income producing value of Bean Industries has increased literally wonderfully and have seen this to benefit Hadfields' ... accounts and balance sheet'. As Hadfield recognised, the formation of Bean Industries had created a legal and accounting dilemma; no longer could it be included as an item under trading investments, but now it constituted a subsidiary, and 'this is the first time that it will be brought in properly into the balance sheet'. Hadfield proceeded to admonish his managing directors that 'far too much has been settled without my being fully advised'. In particular, the role of Brown, Clerke and Thomas as directors on the board of Bean Industries raised suspicions that they were acting independently and possibly against the general interests of the main Hadfields board. 'I do want it to be fully ... understood', Hadfield insisted, that Bean Industries 'is absolutely under the direction of Hadfields Ltd's board. They [Brown, Clerke and Thomas] must not go and settle the balance and dispose of results without Hadfields Ltd fully approving and acquiescing'.[138] Fearing the loss of control, he made it clear that it was the responsibility of Brown and Clerke to represent 'Hadfields Ltd not the Bean Industries Board'. Referring to the fact that Bean Industries had recorded a small profit of £20,000 for the financial year, Hadfield was insistent that this should be visible to shareholders:

> We must specifically think about Hadfields Ltd getting any possible benefit from Bean Industries. Never mind Bean Industries so to speak, we helped them and they must help us in every way possible. I sometimes think Mr Thomas writes as if in paying us amounts due they are granting us a favour – nothing of the kind.[139]

Robert Hadfield's conclusion on the affair was certainly not one he would want to reach the ears of shareholders. As he reminded his managing directors, 'Bean Cars milked us every penny they could and now we must do this reasonably with them

---

[136] Box 6, R. A. Hadfield to P. B. Brown and A. B. H. Clerke, 11 February 1935.

[137] Box 6, Memorandum by P. B. Brown on Capital Reconstruction Scheme, 12 February 1935.

[138] Box 6, Memorandum by R. A. Hadfield to Board, 13 February 1935.

[139] Ibid.

as far as ever possible, it is either that or Bean Industries finding some capital to relieve us'.[140] Rather than a set of working governance procedures, the Bean affair had degenerated into utter confusion, and as Hadfield informed his managing directors, concerning the profit of £20,000, 'Here is another poser, … neither I nor apparently anyone else knows just what we are going to get from Bean Industries. It is high time this investment was dealt with quite separately on all accounts … it should not be brought into our statement except as shown in the Bean Industries balance sheet. Surely this can be done.'[141]

Brown's reply demonstrated the relations of power within the board, and that Hadfield had not lost his grip on control. 'What we must have … is your approval, first with regard to the manner in which we propose to deal with Bean Industry's affairs, second your approval of Hadfields Ltd accounts for 1934, and third your general approval of the actions we are taking with regard to the reorganisation.' On the issue of Bean, Brown informed Hadfield that the accountants could not allocate the profit of £20,000 fully to the Hadfield accounts. Bean had insufficient cash funds to do so, and could only pay in instalments in the future. While Brown agreed with Hadfield that Bean Industries required to be seen as a 'separate entity', he rebuked his chairman: 'The policy we have pursued was determined after the most careful consideration by the Major [Clerke] and myself and was not influenced by any other parties, and we think it is a fair and reasonable arrangement as between the two companies.' Moving onto the attack, Brown admonished Hadfield to the effect that 'All you say regarding our balance sheet and Bean Industry's relationship to Hadfields Ltd are thoroughly appreciated by everyone and it should be quite unnecessary for you to write as you have done on this subject'.[142] Brown defended the integrity of the decision-making in Sheffield and appeared to have little truck with Hadfield interfering in matters that he considered to be well in hand.

Hadfield and his managing directors came out of the Bean affair with their reputations intact; they certainly did not receive the battering from shareholders experienced by the directors at BSA, discussed later in Chapter 4. Nevertheless, the sorry story of Bean exposed personal tensions between the absentee chairman, determined still to keep his hands on the tiller, and Brown and Clerke in Sheffield, charged with both the day-to-day operations and steering the company towards its strategic objectives. Nevertheless, by the 1930s an ageing managerial elite faced acute problems and, Tweedale argues, were desperately in need of an injection of new managerial blood.[143] Internal, and quite unknown to shareholders, were the problems of the quality of management in the 1930s. Despite the attempts by the executive directors to create a platform for internal management promotion, via the creation of a local board of directors, the conservative nature of management,

[140] Ibid.

[141] Ibid.

[142] Box 6, Memorandum by P. B. Brown to R. A. Hadfield, 15 February 1935.

[143] Tweedale, *Steel City*, p. 265.

notably to Hadfield and his two managing directors, clinging on to their personal control, remained resistant to change.

Personal capitalism at work: the local board of directors and managerial change

At the March 1929 AGM, Hadfield informed shareholders that the company was to establish a new management tier, consisting of selected managerial staff to be designated as 'special and routine director' on fixed-term contracts. Hadfield's motives echoed his earlier pronouncements concerning the virtues of internal promotion and the ethic of collective activity. Eight local directors were promoted 'in recognition of the valuable services rendered, and with a view to extend the scope of their activities'. They all had 'long-standing experience in the company's affairs' and were able to offer 'assistance of the most valuable character and nature'. Brown also addressed the meeting, but was more sanguine in his explanation of the appointments, admitting that 'Hadfield's had done nothing in the way of rationalization, except internally, and the appointment of local directors was a step in that direction'. Bringing new blood into the organisation was central to this decision. As Hadfield informed a shareholder, who questioned the cost implications of the local board, and their exact remit, the cost represented 'a nominal amount', and 'We are all getting older, and we want to have a picking-up by the younger division'.[144] The formation of the local board might be seen as a positive step, consistent with an attempt to nurture talent from within the organisation and promote a culture of growing its own timber, develop a managerial hierarchy, and groom a new generation for succession.

The remit of the local board, as originally outlined by Brown and Clerke, seemed to be wide ranging. After a detailed scrutiny of all the departmental returns, and an explanation of their duties to provide accurate information, Brown informed the local directors that they had 'full powers to investigate the workings of any department and to make recommendations in regard thereto'.[145] Outside the local board, however, Brown was more circumspect. He intimated to Hadfield that his managing directors did not intend to instigate regular prolonged meetings with the local board. Rather, it would be possible 'to earmark certain responsibilities to certain individuals in such a manner that they may be helpful, and I think ultimately they may be able to relieve the directors of a great deal of work which now takes up so much time, but of course that will have to work itself out as things develop'.[146] For Brown, the local board was a group of useful company servants, rather than a cohesive tier of management that would establish an effective line of communication with the main board. Nevertheless, the local

---

[144] Box 124, AGM, 27 March 1929.

[145] Hadfields Records, Box 130, Minutes of Local Directors, November 1929.

[146] Box 130, Memorandum from P. B. Brown to R. A. Hadfield, 21 January 1929.

board did develop a number of lines of investigation, which focussed on the investigation of production costs and overhead charges. Within the first two years of its operation, the local board had suggested the establishment sub-committees and six were eventually formed – to investigate and report on cost of patterns, overhead charges, advertising methods, the recording and fixing of piece rates, long and late delivery dates, suggestion schemes and stock carrying.

On the face of it, this represented an impressive managerial endeavour, but from the outset the sub-committees ran into interference from the main board. The sub-committee on overheads, for example, formed in September 1929, was considered essential if the firm was to economise its production methods and remain competitive, and it recommended a scheme of centralisation of work and modernisation of plant. In addition, the sub-committee suggested the appointment of a committee of investigation under the chairmanship of a 'full director' to be appointed by the board.[147] The latter, in the view of the managing directors went well beyond the remit of a local board, and they vetoed the suggestion. Brown, while acknowledging the importance of local directors 'taking a real and wider interest in the general affairs of the company', and assuring them that their recommendations 'would be valued and given serious consideration', dismissed any idea of a 'full director' chairing a committee of investigation. Such a remit, he argued, was too broad, and he reminded the local directors that they needed to be more specific if the main board was to make a 'clear decision'.[148] Brown effectively stymied the formation of an investigating committee on centralisation until 1934,[149] and this was symptomatic of his intolerance of junior managers who delved into strategic matters, which Brown considered the prerogative of the executive board.

In the meantime, Brown simply by-passed the local board, and in 1930 appointed an economy committee of the main board, to examine the lowering of production costs, while effectively sidestepping the issue of centralisation and modernisation. The main board was not prepared to devolve downwards strategic control; in reality, the local board was to deal mainly with operational and departmental issues. Nevertheless, in 1931 the local board discussed a number of interesting initiatives, including accounting procedures for cost estimation, which it considered 'a matter worthy of further inquiry'.[150] Brown, however, deferred any further discussion of the formation of a sub-committee to investigate this matter, and reported that the main board were themselves making a study with a view to appointing an official works estimator.[151] During 1932, the local board considered the marketing policy of the company, in relation to the technical capabilities of sales representatives,[152] and in a related initiative in 1935 they instigated meetings

---

[147] Box 130, Minutes of Local Directors, September 1929.
[148] Box 130, Minutes of Local Directors, November 1929.
[149] See Box 130, Minutes of Local Directors, March 1934.
[150] Box 130, Minutes of Local Directors, November 1931.
[151] Box 130, Minutes of Local Directors, December 1931.
[152] Box 130, Minutes of Local Directors, January 1932.

between production and sales staff, 'to strengthen and improve understanding', which was greeted by Hadfield with some disdain, when he reminded his local directors of the expenses involved.[153]

Nevertheless, with rising trade after 1934, especially for armaments products, there was a growing recognition at an executive level of the need to enhance the company's competitive capabilities. In March, discussions about the centralisation of the steel plant, originally raised in 1929, returned to the agenda of the local board, which formed a sub-committee to investigate. The sub-committee's report in August provided a damning indictment, observing antiquated methods of production and a failure to centralise operations between the various departments of steelmaking and armaments.[154] The implications of the report for economical working were subsequently taken up by a main board director, A. Roebuck, who had until 1931 been a member of the local board, before being promoted a full director. In October 1935, with Roebuck in attendance, the local board considered the causes of unprofitable orders for steel castings, and concluded that 'In recent years many orders have been taken at unremunerative prices', especially for foundry work. The works were generally disorganised and congested, and most damning of all was a condemnation of works management, which, given the increase in throughput since 1934, had been incapable of adequately supervising operations. Consequently, the local board recommended to 'strengthen the executive work staff'.[155] This entailed no more than minor modifications to the works management, but following the discussion in October, Roebuck, together with Jenkins-Gibson, a member of the local board, recommended to the main board the services of Wallace Clarke, a leading management consultant.[156] Wallace Clark's preliminary report on management problems at Hadfields identified the need for radical changes, and implied a failure of the executive management:

> The importance of high quality ... requires that the best technical knowledge existing in your company be methodically applied to your product throughout its manufacture. The more aggressive competition makes it necessary to have cost information which will show your directors (a) in what parts of the works money is being made and where it is being lost (b) the cost of idleness of your £750,000 investment in plant and the exact point to which it is wise to reduce prices in the face of competitive bidding and (c) where you can reduce costs and overhead expenses.[157]

---

[153] Box 130, Minutes of Local Directors, March 1935; Memorandum from R. A. Hadfield to Parker, 3 April 1935.

[154] Box 130, Minutes of Local Directors, March 1934; August 1934.

[155] Box 130, Minutes of Local Directors, October 1935.

[156] Hadfields Records, Box 135, Report on Wallace Clark Methods by A. Roebuck.

[157] Box 135, Report of Wallace Clark.

With an estimated cost of £10,500 and taking a year to complete, the final report by Wallace Clarke recommended a thorough reorganisation of works management.[158] Under the guidance of consultants this would mean the installation of new management methods, in 'Planning and progressing; Production recording; Stores-keeping; Cost keeping; Budgeting; and Executive direction'.[159]

These recommendations went well beyond the original reforms proposed by the local directors in October 1935, but Roebuck was determined to see the consultants implement change. During his assessment of the methods employed by Wallace Clarke, Roebuck, sanctioned by Brown and Clerke, visited two French steel firms, which had successfully installed these methods. Roebuck's assessment of the Wallace Clark methods demonstrated that he possessed a thorough knowledge of prevailing management methods. After a full 'consideration of the proposals', which included an assessment of the alternative Bedaux system of management, Roebuck was convinced that the Wallace Clarke methods represented best practice and that 'nothing but good and improvement would arise from a thorough overhaul of our present methods'. Roebuck, however, was well aware of the potential for the main managerial board to resist change. In his summing up of the Wallace Clark methods, Roebuck attempted to forestall the objections of Brown and Clerke. He raised two potential objections and offered solutions. First, he acknowledged that although the introduction of new management methods would result in a considerable disruption of work, involving the need to train personnel 'to operate the new methods', this difficult 'problem' could be overcome by a planned phasing in of the new procedures. Second, the use of consultants raised the issue of business confidentiality, the leaking of commercial and technical information, which, as we have seen, was a sensitive matter for the executive directors. Roebuck therefore assured the directors that the consultants had guaranteed that they would not 'deal with any competitor for at least five years'.[160]

Roebuck's carefully laid plans were of no avail, and in June 1936 J. B. Thomas, on behalf of Brown and Clerke, informed Wallace Clarke that after full consideration, and taking into account the cost of the consultancy,

> the changes suggested in your report would raise such complications as might seriously affect production during the period of installation of the scheme. The position is that the company is unable at present to take any risk that might necessitate the slowing down of production. Therefore, the directors have decided that under the circumstances they do not deem it advisable at present to proceed with the scheme outlined by you.[161]

---

[158] Box 135, Wallace Clarke to P. B. Brown, 18 May 1936.
[159] Box 135, Report of Wallace Clark.
[160] Box 135, Report on Wallace Clark Methods by A. Roebuck.
[161] Box 135, J. B. Thomas to Wallace Clark, 26 June 1936.

After 1936, the company did indeed face rapidly rising orders, an outcome of the government's drive to rearmament, and this necessitated a focus upon maintaining production at full capacity levels. In his last address to shareholders in 1937, before his deterioration in health made it impossible for him to attend, Robert Hadfield committed the company to the 'national defence programme', which involved increasing capital expenditure for the modernisation of plant. That Brown saw rearmament as a short-term factor, he made plain at the 1938 AGM. While acknowledging that the company had extended the armament works and introduced modern electric arc capacity, Brown nevertheless viewed rearmament as temporary, and pledged a policy of ensuring that the company was equipped to increase output for commercial work when government orders fell.[162] Although the decision to reject managerial change may well have been rational in the short run, it nevertheless disguised an inherent conservatism that failed to see the benefits of managerial efficiency for long-run productivity. At the same time, Brown and his co-directors were uncertain about the effects of the growth of new managerial roles on their own authority. Brown was an engineer, not a managerialist, and although he could celebrate in 1938 Hadfield's technical contribution to the national interest, he knew little about modern management practices.

Brown's conservatism towards managerial innovation showed in 1938 when he dismissed initiatives by the local board to introduce standard schedules of practice for commercial work, a procedure that Roebuck had witnessed operating successfully in France as part of the Wallace Clarke method of management. Via Gibson-Jenkins, the chairman of the sub-committee on standard schedules of the local board, Roebuck attempted to promote change. The sub-committee, under Roebuck's guidance, viewed the issue as a central step in gradually introducing modern managerial practices. Standard schedules involved the formulation of statements for 'each separate process applicable to the manufacture of certain classes of product' and of the technical specifications of the product, which would facilitate increasing standardisation. The schedules were a blueprint, enabling a working instruction for manufacture, providing a check on deviations from standard specification, a device to analyse cost, and 'assist towards standardisation of related types of product'.[163] Brown's response to these managerial initiatives was largely non-committal. Clearly not understanding the implications for cost efficiency that these managerial practices entailed, he objected on a series of technical issues relating to the diverse range of work carried out by the company, which required consideration of 'the quality of the steel; the process by which it is manufactured'. Standard schedules, therefore, were not appropriate to 'the infinite variety of shapes and sizes' of Hadfields' commercial work.[164] A status quo in management was central to Brown's technical perspective on operations, and:

---

[162]   Box 124, AGM, 14 April 1937; 12 April 1938.
[163]   Box 130, Minutes of Local Directors, June 1938.
[164]   Box 130, P. B. Brown, Notes, 23 July 1938.

in a factory such as ours any such records would have to be subject to constant adaptation and amendment day by day, by those in charge of various departments. It is for that reason we have highly competent men in charge of the various departments and sections to whom we entrust a discretionary power. If our work could be properly standardised the supervision would be largely a matter of routine.[165]

The directors of the local board did not accept the conservative attitude of Brown to managerial reforms meekly, and to forestall collective discussion he cordially invited the local directors to discuss their concerns in 'private' with Brown.[166] At a meeting conducted by Brown and Roebuck with three local directors in November 1938, to discuss schedules, a compromise proposal met Brown's approval, which involved reducing the content of the schedules substantially, producing concise schedules for educating managers, and suitably tailoring them to avoid the disclosure of secretive technical information.[167] Change, when it did receive sanction, was minimal and piecemeal. The conservatism of the 1930s, however, left a permanent legacy of inadequate management, which an investigation by the consultants Urwick, Orr & Partners in 1944 and 1945 made evident.

Despite the initial reluctance of Brown, who succeeded Hadfield as chairman in 1940,[168] under Roebuck's initiative Urwick, Orr were invited to undertake preliminary investigations in May 1944.[169] Their initial view of management practices were that they considerably lagged behind the high standards established by the company in the technology of steelmaking.[170] The preliminary report of the consultants in March 1945 identified two major flaws in management techniques. First, the growth of the business since the mid-1930s had corresponded with the growing administrative demands of the organisation, and had resulted in 'a combination of centralisation and de-centralisation with no clear lines of demarcation'. For example, both ordnance and commercial departments were responsible for their own manufacturing and selling activities, while the technical, buying and accounting functions had been partially decentralised. Second, there was a problem with 'the span of control'. At Hadfields there were as many as 21 subordinate managers who reported to one senior executive, which was virtually impossible to co-ordinate.[171]

---

[165]   Box 130, Minutes of Local Directors, July 1938, Commentary of P. B. Brown.

[166]   Box 130, Minutes of Local Directors, August 1938.

[167]   Box 130, Minutes of Local Directors, November 1938.

[168]   Hadfields Records, Box 101, Urwick Orr and Partners, Correspondence file, P. B. Brown to Lord Dudley Gordan, 13 May 1944.

[169]   Box 101, J. B. Thomas to Urwick, Orr, 21 June 1944.

[170]   Box 101, Urwick. Orr to Hadfields, 16 August 1944.

[171]   Hadfields Records, Box 132, Urwick, Orr, and Partners Report, March 1945.

Perhaps the greatest legacy left by an aging management elite was the lack of young executives capable of taking over the leading positions in the company.[172] This could be taken as a criticism of the personal capitalist nature of the firm, in which a small, close-knit elite in power had failed to exploit the opportunities of the local board, which had been intended to act as a forum for recruiting and nurturing the next generation of directors. Even in 1945, faced with meeting the challenges of the post-war world, Brown and his co-directors prevaricated. After sitting on the Urwick, Orr preliminary report for a number of weeks, the directors, at a special board meeting, could come to no agreed position and effectively backed away from a full investigation.[173]

Conclusion

The business record of Hadfield from its foundation as a public company in 1888 to the 1940s was a mixed one. Prior to the First World War, under the leadership of Robert Hadfield, the company made considerable profits, paid high dividends to its shareholders, and was at the forefront of technological change in steelmaking. During this war, the company became one of Sheffield's leading munitions producers, making a valuable contribution to the production of shell and armour plate. The quality of its products, and an association with skilled work, were core cultural values that defined the relations between executive management and their workforce and with customers that purchased their products. Governance of the company was characterised by the personality of Robert Hadfield, who in the boardroom often exhibited an authoritarian style of management, while at the same time building a loyal elite of trusted directors, which reflected his views on collective responsibility at the head of the organisation, and the importance of internal promotions. Notable amongst the managerial elite was the rise of Brown and Clerke to executive management positions, and the latter was to be a major figure in the company during the 1930s, as Robert Hadfield's control of business affairs waned due to ill health.

As the leading shareholder in the company, Hadfield shaped the culture of the board, and governance relations with shareholders exhibited a personal style. The floating of the company's preference shares, which paid dividends but allowed no voting rights, symbolised Hadfield's insistence on maintaining personal control, and he viewed shareholders almost as loyal subjects who should be satisfied with their pecuniary rewards while trusting in the judgement of the board to deliver effective business outcomes. Hadfield viewed shareholders as investors and derided those he defined as speculators who had no long-term interests in the fortunes of the company. During the inter-war years, however, investors may have had much to complain about in the strategic direction of the company. During these troubled

[172] Ibid.
[173] Box 101, P. B. Brown to Urwick, Orr, 30 March 1945.

decades, the company's policy of diversification was unsuccessful, and in the case of the Bean cars venture turned into a fiasco. Many of these problems, which brought with them financial implications for the company, were not fully reported to shareholders, who were asked to remain patient and trust in the discretion of executive management. The governance of the company was characterised by a low level of financial disclosure, and there is evidence to suggest there was a careful management of disclosure policy at AGMs by Hadfield and his senior executives. The voice of shareholders did not provide a major challenge to personal control within the company, and the board emerged from the Bean fiasco with its reputation intact, a remarkable achievement considering that profits and dividends remained low for most of the inter-war period.

The business deficiencies of the company after 1920 owed much to the decision-making of Hadfield and his senior directors, and organisational change was slow to materialise. By the 1930s, and despite the changing fortunes of the company after 1936 due to growing government demand for armaments, evidence suggests that internal efficiency was at a low level. With an aging managerial elite, and by the late 1930s a largely inactive chairman, Hadfield's successor, Peter Brown proved inadequate to the task of instigating radical organisational change. While in 1929 there seemed every intention to devolve responsibility to a local board of directors, in reality Brown resisted a more hierarchical approach to management, and the major changes advised by a series of consultants, and supported by board members such as Roebuck, were either dismissed or quietly shelved. Brown's growing influence in the 1930s, and his eventual succession on Robert Hadfield's death in 1940, typified the continuation of a deep personal control of the governance of the company.

Chapter 4

Losing Trust: The BSA Board and Corporate Governance, 1900–1939

Introduction

This chapter examines the evolution of corporate governance and personal capitalism at one of Britain's leading engineering companies, Birmingham Small Arms (BSA). The case study is of relevance to the understanding of corporate governance in British industry for a number of reasons.[1] BSA was a long-established company, which could trace its origins back to 1861, and by the beginnings of the twentieth century it had a business reputation for the engineering quality of its diversified range of products. By the standard of British business at the time, it was a large company, securing a place amongst the largest 100 manufacturing concerns in the country throughout the period represented in this study.[2] BSA was an innovative firm, evolving from its traditional production of small arms to manufacture bicycles, motor cycles and motor cars. It made a major contribution to Britain's First World War effort by developing a number of products that were at the leading edge of technological development for their time. BSA's technical competencies established its reputation as an important engineering company, and put it on the War Office list of approved armament firms in 1914. Finally, the company is of considerable interest to the business historian because of the development of its organisational structure, especially the creation of a holding company in 1919, which attempted to co-ordinate the operation of a number of manufacturing subsidiaries, including the well-known automobile manufacturer Daimler. As Wilson observes, the personally controlled holding company was a feature of British business organisation in the inter-war years, the numbers of which proliferated in the merger waves of the 1920s and 1930s.[3]

Throughout most of the period studied, top management at BSA was subject to controversy, often within the managerial hierarchy itself, and this intensified

---

[1]   See R. Lloyd-Jones et al., 'Control, Conflict and Concession: Corporate Governance at Birmingham Small Arms, 1906–1933', *Accounting Historians Journal*, Vol. 32, No. 1 (2005), p. 153.

[2]   L. Johnman, 'The Largest Manufacturing Firms of 1935', in R. P. T. Davenport-Hines (ed.), *Business in the Age of Depression and War* (London, Frank Cass, 1990), pp. 20–39; C. Shaw, 'The Largest Manufacturing Firms of 1907', in Davenport-Hines (ed.), *Business in the Age of Depression and War*, pp. 1–19.

[3]   Wilson, *British Business History*, p. 133.

after 1919 when BSA adopted a holding-company structure. While BSA directors won accolades from shareholders for their stewardship of the company during the First World War, in the subsequent peace-time economy dissident directors and shareholders challenged both the form of governance at the company and the appropriateness of the business and financial strategy pursued by the board. An exploration of these controversies touches on a number of themes – accountability, managerial autonomy, information flows and the purpose of financial reporting, and the response of top management to the volatile business environment of the 1920s and 1930s – which are crucial to the understanding of corporate governance in this period. BSA, we argue, is a particularly rich case study because of the number of issues that affected it in the early twentieth century and the volume of archival material available to document these: hence the length and the detail of this chapter.

As an explanatory device for the study of corporate governance at BSA, use is made of Hirschman's notion of 'Exit, Voice and Loyalty', providing a basis for discussion of the relatilonship between executive management and shareholders at the company. Hirschman suggests that dissatisfied shareholders may express their unhappiness by choosing to exit the company, exercise their voice by protest to management, or demonstrate loyalty in the hope that change evolves from within the organisation.[4] Voice may take on the form of individual complaint or collective criticism of executive action. In the case of BSA, shareholder dissatisfaction was expressed with growing vehemence, at first individually by a former director, and then, under his leadership, via complaint and criticism in letters and protests at successive AGMs.

The pre-war years: secret reserves and the Daimler acquisition

In the years before the First World War, BSA had evolved to become a multi-faceted engineering firm manufacturing a broad range of products. In 1910, the company made a major strategic decision to extend its activities in the new sector of motor vehicles and by the eve of war employed nearly 10,000 workers at its two main factories in Birmingham and Coventry. During the Edwardian era, two episodes related to corporate governance drew public attention to BSA and had long-term effects on the relationship between directors, shareholders and other financial providers, both at the company and in a wider corporate context. The first was essentially concerned with an insider–outsider conflict, which erupted into a legal case in 1906 and attracted wide contemporary comment as it involved the directors' use of secret reserves, the rights of shareholders and the transparency of the board to its stakeholders.[5] The second involved a major strategic decision to diversify operations in 1910 through the merger with Daimler, which resulted

---

4   Hirschman, *Exit, Voice and Loyalty*, p. 77.
5   See Lloyd-Jones et al., 'Control, Conflict and Compromise', pp. 154–9.

in a change in the internal composition of the board, and the involvement of an outsider, Dudley Docker, in the company's affairs.

As shown in Chapter 6, the issue of secret reserves became a focus for those advocating more transparency in Britain's system of corporate governance in the inter-war years.[6] In January 1906, the BSA directors put forward a special resolution at an Extraordinary General Meeting (EGM), which replicated the actions of 'one or two other Birmingham industrial concerns',[7] to empower them to create an 'internal reserve fund' out of profits that could be allocated for any purpose they thought fit. This was tantamount to the directors establishing a secret reserve, whereby transfers into and out of the fund could be made in any year in which the company had passed a 10 per cent dividend on the ordinary share capital and paid all dividends to preference shareholders.[8] Following a second EGM in February, shareholders carried the motion to introduce the reserve fund. At this meeting, a small shareholder, Sir Alfred Newton, proposed that they record their thanks to the company chairman, the newly appointed Sir Hallewell Rogers, for his 'courteous conduct',[9] but *The Accountant* later reported that the motion to carry the reserve fund had only been passed 'after a somewhat stormy discussion'.[10] Despite Newton's platitudes at the EGM, he later applied for an injunction against the BSA board to prevent the implementation of the resolution to create a secret reserve, and his actions attracted wide publicity in the financial press. *The Accountant*, for example, commented that 'It is some years since a legal decision has been delivered of such far reaching importance to the profession'.[11] For the legal and accounting profession BSA was a test case, which would establish through the rule of law a precedent for shareholder voice and its role in determining and challenging the power and responsibility of directors as constituted in the governance criteria of the company's articles of association. As Newton argued, the directors were

---

[6]   See A. J. Arnold, '"Publishing your Private Affairs to the World': Corporate Financial Disclosures in the UK 1900–24', *Accounting, Business and Financial History*, Vol. 7, No. 2 (1997), p. 145, who observes that during the first quarter of the twentieth century the three most problematic, although overlapping, issues in corporate financial reporting concerned the appropriate means of dealing with investments in long-term or fixed assets (depreciation), the degree of prudence or conservatism advisable in an uncertain environment (secret reserves) and the amount of information provided to stakeholders.

[7]   *The Statist*, 29 September 1906, p. 537.

[8]   Solihull Library, BSA 19, The Birmingham Small Arms & Metal Company Limited, Shareholders' Minute Book covering the period 1897–1952, 24 January 1906; Modern Record Office (MRC), University of Warwick, MSS 19C/31/1, Notice of EGM, 24 January 1906.

[9]   BSA 19, Shareholders' Minute Book, 1897–1952, 21 February 1906.

[10]   *The Accountant*, 3 March 1906, p. 271.

[11]   *The Accountant*, 14 July 1906, p. 29.

exceeding their powers under company law and eroding the rights of shareholders to access information concerning 'the true position of the company'.[12]

Presiding over the *Newton v Chambers* case in June 1906, Mr Justice Buckley upheld the principle of the secret reserve, and endorsed the rights of directors to exercise prudence in reporting, despite the fact that the balance sheet may underestimate the 'true' financial 'position' of the company. It followed that directors had a responsibility to act prudently by the publication of financial accounts that were 'conservative rather than optimistic', even if the existence of internal reserves, '*ipso facto*', negated their accuracy.[13] Buckley acknowledged that 'Assets are often, by reason of prudence, estimated, and stated to be estimated, at less than their possible real value'.[14] This judgement, however, did not give unlimited power to directors, and Buckley upheld the objections of Newton over the rights of the company auditors to have information relating to the existence of the fund, which was a principle enshrined in existing company law.[15] To comply with this ruling the BSA directors permitted their auditors to know about the fund and to monitor financial transactions, but reserved the right to refrain from the disclosure of information to shareholders or to enter it as a separate item in the annual balance sheet.[16] At an EGM in July 1916, the BSA directors submitted a revised resolution acknowledging the role of auditors in the internal governance process:

> The Directors shall keep full accounts of the Internal Reserve and of the investment or application thereof, and the Auditors of the Company shall at all times have access to such accounts together with all other books, accounts and vouchers of the Company. It shall be the duty of the Auditors to report to the Shareholders whether the Internal Reserve has been invested and applied in accordance with the provisions hereinbefore contained, but except in cases when it is their duty so to do, under Section 23 of the Companies' Act, 1900, the Auditors shall not disclose in such report either the amount of the Internal Reserve or any other information concerning the same or the investment or application thereof.[17]

By complying with the legal judgement, the BSA directors elevated the auditors to be the guardians of the shareholder interest, but this did not restore trust and shareholders continued to oppose the decision to maintain the internal reserve.

[12]   Law Report 2 Chancery, 1906, p. 382.

[13]   L. R. Dicksee, *Published Balance Sheets and Window Dressing* (London, Gee & Co., 1927). Reprinted in L. R. Dicksee, *Business Methods and the War: The Fundamentals of Manufacturing Costs; Published Balance Sheets and Window Dressing* (New York, Arno Press, 1980), pp. 38, 43.

[14]   Law Reports 2 Chancery, 1906, pp. 378–9.

[15]   *The Accountant*, 4 August 1906, p. 122.

[16]   *The Times*, 23 July 1906; 25 July 1906.

[17]   MSS 19C/31/1, Notice of EGM, 16 July 1906.

At the July AGM, attended by 7 BSA directors and 73 shareholders, a motion to accept the revised resolution was initially defeated on a show of hands by 36 votes to 27. Facing a shareholder revolt, Rogers 'demanded a poll' of all shareholders. The result was overwhelming support for the directors, the combined votes of shareholders personally present and those voting by proxy carrying the motion to adopt the revised resolution by 27,993 votes in favour to just 95 votes against.[18] An EGM on 31 July confirmed the decision; of the 148 shareholders, including directors, present, the resolution passed on a show of hands by 79 votes for to 42 against, and by a poll of 33,000 for to 9,000 against.[19]

The pattern of voting indicated that small-minority shareholders could exercise a considerable voice by their presence at company meetings, and they again demonstrated their tenacity at the October AGM when Newton returned to the issue of secret reserves. During the chairman's speech, Rogers steered well clear of the issue of internal reserves, but Newton persisted in an attempt to resurrect the discussion. Despite the fact that Rogers received support from shareholders who declared Newton out of order, the dissenting shareholders then tabled an amendment that the meeting should not accept the company report and accounts until subjected to an enquiry into the amount invested and application of the internal reserve. Apparently, 'amid some uproar', Rogers ruled that this was out of order, as due notice of the amendment had not been given, and the reports and accounts were finally adopted.[20] There is no record of any further resistance by Newton and the directors of BSA eventually got their way, without falling foul of the Companies Act, 1900. The internal reserve was duly established; it remained in place during 1907 and 1908, but in 1909 it was incorporated into the general reserve. When the internal reserve was finally announced by Rogers in 1909, it amounted to just £30,000, compared to a general reserve of £100,000. Despite the small amount of the reserve, it raised serious questions of governance in British business.

Newton v Chambers was a minor victory for shareholders, in that it defined in law the role of auditors in monitoring financial reporting and as guardians against fraudulent activity. Nevertheless, it also represented a powerful restatement of the rights of directors to retain control over financial disclosure, which enhanced their powers to govern the company and only to disclose information that they saw as in the best interests of the organisation. Central to the thinking of company directors on matters of governance, as it had been in Buckley's judgement, was the importance of prudence in relation to financial disclosure. Certainly, commentators at the time equated prudence with the setting up and use of secret reserves, and recognised that banking companies, insurance companies and large holding companies considered this sound business practice.[21] *The Accountant*, for example, considered that the

[18]   BSA 19, Shareholders' Minute Book, 1897–1952, 16 July 1906.

[19]   BSA 19, Shareholders' Minute Book, 1897–1952, 31 July 1906.

[20]   *The Accountant*, 13 October 1906, p. 401.

[21]   E. E. Spicer and E. C. Pegler, *Practical Auditing* (London, H. Foulks Lynch & Co., 1914), p. 339; H. B. Samuel, *Shareholders' Money: An Analysis of Certain Defects*

balance sheet could never 'be an absolutely accurate statement of the position of affairs and it must be over-favourable or over-cautious'. Prudence demanded conservative accounting, and there was 'in connection with every sound company a secret reserve'.[22] Thus, in defending their position the BSA directors made a distinction between two different types of shareholders: the 'speculator', who purchased shares solely in order to extract a large dividend and then sold the shares in a now depleted company, and the 'prudent', who was prepared to invest for the long-run and place their trust in the director's judgement. Prudence dictated that the BSA directors were empowered by shareholders to govern in the long-term interests of the company, and they held the right to exercise discretion over the extent of public disclosure. If shareholders required additional information then they were obliged to seek advice from the company directors.[23]

Businessmen created an image of an ethical universe, a self-regulating business community, in which trust, reputation and secrecy were paramount to their understanding of the governance of the organisation and their relationship to shareholders as guardians of a company's future. At BSA, Rodgers defined his company's board of directors as men of business acumen, who had detailed knowledge of the operations of the company, and who had a reputation for honest dealing. Regardless of the concern of individual shareholders for greater disclosure, Rogers remained adamant that the board knew best, and that shareholders could trust executive management to deploy internal reserves in their best interests. The use of secret reserves at BSA was acceptable business practice, and consistent with that practised 'by several of the leading commercial companies'.[24] In Birmingham, these included reputable firms such as Guest, Keen & Nettleford (GKN), Metropolitan Amalgamated Railway Carriage & Wagon Co. (MARCWC), W. & T. Avery, Kynoch & Co., Docker Bros., and Bellis and Morcom.[25] Additional credence for this practice was supplied by the BSA auditors, Carters & Co., who publicly acknowledged that it had audited the accounts of several other companies which used secret reserves 'in every case … to the advantage of the companies and their shareholders'. Advantage accrued through maintaining public secrecy, as 'great injury may be done to the business [as] difficulties may be caused between rival traders or between capital and labour'.[26]

A high trust culture symbolised this interpretation of corporate governance, but for shareholders such as Newton there was a high degree of suspicion concerning the actions of executive management. Newton challenged the directors' interpretation, not, he claimed, because he was a 'speculator' only desiring high dividends, but

in Company Legislation with Proposals for their Reform (London, Pitman & Sons, 1933), p. 276.

[22]   *The Accountant*, 4 August 1906, p. 124.

[23]   Law Report, 2 Chancery, 1906, p. 387.

[24]   *The Times*, 22 February 1906.

[25]   *The Accountant*, 3 March 1906, p. 271.

[26]   *The Accountant*, 14 July 1906.

rather that he was a 'prudent' shareholder who had lost his trust in the board over the secretive nature of accounting practices.[27] Despite the fact that Newton only held 40 shares, he brought the case to court, and was prepared to launch a challenge to the board in the public arena of the AGM. Newton's tenacity, a classic illustration of idiosyncratic behaviour, may have been influenced by support from Arthur Chamberlain, a member of one of the West Midlands' most powerful industrial families, and who had personal connections to the BSA board through his uncle, Harold Chamberlain, the chairman at BSA between 1900 and 1904. In addition, Arthur's cousin, Neville Chamberlain, was later to be a director of the company at various times between 1913 and 1922. Arthur opposed the decision of the board to establish a secret reserve, and *The Times* reported his opposition following the defeat of the dissident shareholders during July 1906. He believed that his uncle's replacement as chairman in 1904 had set off a chain of events that had led to the introduction of the secret reserve. In particular he pointed out that, as shown in Table 4.1, between 1897 and 1902 BSA had paid dividends of 20 per cent, but in 1903 this was reduced to 12.5 per cent. Although a 15 per cent dividend was paid in 1905 and 1906, Arthur believed that the departure of his uncle had coincided with the introduction of the secret reserve, which resulted in a lower dividend to shareholders.[28]

Table 4.1   BSA profits and dividends 1897–1909

	BSA Profit (£000)	Dividend rate (%)
1897	88	20
1898	60	20
1899	56	20
1900	58	20
1901	88	20
1902	95	20
1903	65	15
1904	51	12.5
1905	81	15
1906	74	15
1907	80	15
1908	99	15
1909	84	10

Source: *The Statist*, 1 October 1910, p. 773.

[27]   Law Report, 2 Chancery, 1906, p. 387.

[28]   *The Times*, 2 August 1906; R. Lloyd-Jones et al., 'Control, Conflict and Concession', p. 158.

The inference was that the board had introduced a secret reserve to hide its own failings. Consequently, in a good year, the directors could hide a given proportion of profits, which they could subsequently pay out in a bad year, and thus the secret reserve was a device that deprived shareholders of the appropriate information to monitor the board's performance.[29] That a secret reserve existed at BSA was not an issue of concern in itself for shareholders, but rather it was the fact that discretion lay in the hands of directors to determine the allocation of these funds.[30] 'The gravest objection to which the creation of these reserves is open', as Spicer and Pegler observed in 1914, 'is that they may be utilised in an improper manner for the personal advantage of the Directors or their friends'.[31] Impropriety, however, was not the charge made by shareholders at BSA, but rather what they objected to was the power that reserves gave to directors to set the strategic direction of the firm, outside the scrutiny of its stakeholders. *The Accountant* commented that there was a potential to create an insider coalition, 'a business within a business'.[32]

The emergence of an insider coalition of top executives at BSA occurred between 1906 and 1910 when the company pursued an ambitious acquisition policy, which concluded with the take-over of Daimler. By 1910, the company was dominated by a triumvirate of leading directors consisting of two Daimler men, Percy Martin and Edward Manville, who became managing director and deputy chairman respectively at BSA, and Hallewell Rogers, who retained the chairmanship. This group of powerful directors was to dominate company life until the early 1930s, and set the tone for strategic decision-making. Central to understanding their rise to power was the influence of Dudley Docker in the affairs of the company. Docker was an advocate of industrial rationalisation through merger, and 'Birmingham's industrial titan', who had risen to national prominence through effecting an amalgamation between five railway carriage and wagon companies, three in Birmingham and two in Lancashire, to form the MARCWC in 1902.[33] Described by Davenport-Hines as 'a showpiece of modern, rationalised combination', the MARCWC was the 'largest and most powerful rolling-stock manufacturers in Britain', eventually integrating production, distribution and marketing.[34] The MARCWC also collaborated with Dick, Kerr & Co., a Scottish electrical firm that under Docker's initiative became a central player amongst a

---

[29]   For Samuel, *Shareholders' Money*, pp. 280–81, who was mainly concerned about the impact of secret reserves on stock market share prices, the major problem was the ability of directors to draw on them in times of bad trade to show a profit and pay dividends to shareholders when, in fact, the business had actually made a loss. Such a practice he considered an intolerable abuse. See also Dicksee, *Published Balance Sheets*, p. 40.

[30]   *The Accountant*, 4 August 1906, p. 123.

[31]   Spicer and Pegler, *Practical Auditing*, p. 342.

[32]   *The Accountant*, 4 August 1906, p. 123.

[33]   R. P. T. Davenport-Hines, *Dudley Docker. The Life and Times of a Trade Warrior* (Cambridge, Cambridge University Press, 1984), pp. 24–6.

[34]   Ibid., pp. 28, 31; Wilson, *British Business History*, p. 109.

group of firms who responded to the foreign challenge in the field of electrical engineering.[35] Such was Docker's reputation for 'business infallibility' that he joined the boards of several companies prior to the war, where he played a leading role in 'arranging mergers'.[36] One of these companies was BSA, which Docker joined in early 1906, coinciding with the appointment as chairman of Rogers and with the shareholder challenge by Newton. According to a business associate of Rogers, Sir Patrick Hannon, Docker was directly responsible for elevating Rogers to chairman of BSA.[37] Docker's relationship to BSA is interesting from a business-network perspective, which relates to interaction between business people to promote their economic interests, but may also involve 'associations' of a social and/or political nature.[38] Both Rogers and Docker interconnected with the circuits of local Birmingham business,[39] and at a political level Rogers was active in the right-wing pressure group the British Commonwealth Union (BCU), an organisation of which Docker happened to be President.[40] Docker's influence on boardroom selection at BSA was illustrated further by the appointment of Lincoln Chandler, his colleague on the board of the MARCWC, as a BSA director in 1907.[41]

Docker's arrival at BSA also coincided with the decision to create a secret reserve, a practice pursued by the MARCWC. On its formation in 1902, the articles of association empowered the directors of the MARCWC to build up secret reserves not published in the balance sheet; by 1910 these amounted to £450,000. Apparently, the MARCWC used reserves for dividend smoothing, especially in the depressed year of 1909, but also fulfilled the ambition of Docker for funding potential future acquisitions.[42] It is reasonable to suggest that secret reserves could aid an acquisition; the financial means of the potential buyer were not evident to the selling company, which had implications for price negotiations, and furthermore enabled the purchaser to move fast when a suitable target appeared if the reserve consisted of liquid assets. Under Rogers and Docker, the BSA reserve may well have been a financial device to pursue a policy of diversification, the acquisition of companies to expand the range of activities undertaken. The creation of the reserve in 1906 coincided with a review of the company's core business activity,

---

[35]   Wilson, *British Business History*, p. 110.

[36]   Davenport-Hines, *Dudley Docker*, pp. 32, 35, 47.

[37]   Ibid., p. 48; R. P. T. Davenport-Hines, 'Rogers, Sir Hallewell', in D. J. Jeremy (ed.), *Dictionary of Business Biography* (London, Butterworths, 1985), pp. 923–7. Hannon was later in 1925 to become a BSA director and was a Tory MP.

[38]   See M. Casson, 'An Economic Approach to Regional Business Networks', in J. F. Wilson and A. Popp (eds), *Industrial Clusters and Regional Business Networks in England, 1750–1970* (Ashgate, Aldershot, 2003), pp. 28–9, 39–40.

[39]   Davenport-Hines, 'Rogers', p. 924.

[40]   Ibid.; A. Marrison, *British Business and Protection, 1903–1932* (Oxford, Oxford University Press, 1996), pp. 346, 353.

[41]   Davenport-Hines, *Dudley Docker*, p. 48.

[42]   Ibid., pp. 32–3.

with BSA facing serious uncertainty over its gun business and orders from its main customer the War Office.[43] The precarious nature of the gun trade was evident to BSA directors by the autumn of 1906, and under Rogers and Docker the company attempted to branch out into bicycles and motor vehicles, which became paramount with the failure of the War Office to requisition large orders in the 'precarious armaments business' between 1907 and 1911.[44] In late 1906 BSA embarked on negotiations with the cycle and motor cycle makers the Eadie Manufacturing Co., which was accordingly acquired. The acquisition represented an opportunity to develop bicycle and motor cycle production, and the capabilities of the board in this area were extended by the appointment to the BSA board of Albert Eadie, the managing director, Robert W. Smith, the works manager, and George Cartland, the chairman of Eadie (Table 4.2). Eadie became the managing director of the BSA Cycle and Motor Cycle Department.[45]

Table 4.2   Pre- and post-merger boards at BSA

1906–10	Post-1910 merger with Daimler
Sir H. Rogers (chair 1906)	Sir H. Rogers (chair)
F. D. Docker (Deputy chair 1909)	F. D. Docker
A. Eadie	A. Eadie
Lincoln Chandler	Lincoln Chandler
W. L. Powell	Percy Martin (managing director)
E. M. Goodman	A. H. E. Wood
W. E. Hipkin	Edward Manville (deputy chair)
H. Wallis	
G. H. Cartland	
R. W. Smith	

Source: Lloyd-Jones et al., 'Control, Conflict and Compromise', p. 156.

BSA's involvement in the motor trade took on a more ambitious direction following the Eadie acquisition with the conversion of the Sparkbrook factory in Birmingham. Sparkbrook, formerly the Royal Small Arms Factory, was purchased by BSA from the government in 1906 for the prototype production of motor cars. By 1908 the company had developed three models but these proved not to

---

[43]   Ibid., p. 49.

[44]   Ibid.; Davenport-Hines, 'Rogers', p. 924.

[45]   *Stock Exchange Official Intelligence Book*, 1907; M. J. Cannons, 'Eadie, Albert', in Jeremy (ed.), *Dictionary of Business Biography*, pp. 222–4.

be a commercial success.[46] According to Davenport-Hines, such was Docker's dissatisfaction with the performance of the motor business at BSA in 1908 that he informed Sir Edward Holden, the chairman of the Midlands Bank, that he would be prepared to accept the responsibility of attaining the chairmanship of the company.[47] This represented a clear indication both of his commitment to the policy of diversification and his potential influence in the boardroom. Although Docker did not succeed Rogers as chairman, he did nevertheless become deputy chairman in 1909, and from this position was instrumental in focusing attention on policies to remedy deficiencies in the BSA motor car business. In 1910 an internal Motor Committee produced a damning report on the deficiency of operations at BSA. These included inaccurate stocktaking and non-standardisation of component parts, meaning that cost control was impossible, low-quality production relating to defects in design engineering, and inadequate after-sales service. On the quality of management, the report condemned senior staff, who had failed to organise production effectively and to develop marketable design standards.[48] Given this context, Docker was influential in brokering the merger with the Daimler Motor Co. of Coventry.[49]

Daimler's past record in the motor industry was a chequered one. In 1904, such were the financial problems of the company that Daimler restructured its capital base, enabling it to raise additional public capital through the issue of debentures and preference shares, a policy consistent with the early history of motor manufacturers, who called on public subscriptions to support ailing firms. Between 1904 and 1910, Daimler raised £81,000 in preference shares, £100,000 in debentures, and £100,000 in ordinary shares, demonstrating the high level of public confidence in this relatively new industry.[50] The restructuring of 1904 placed Daimler on a sound financial footing, and in 1905 it expanded its production facilities and modified its plant, largely under the direction of the managing director Percy Martin, who had experience of production engineering in both Europe and the USA, and was a large shareholder in Daimler.[51] In 1906 *The Statist* reported that Daimler had 'built up a very fine reputation for its cars', and 'a remarkable rate of profits had again occurred'. Gross profits for the year ending September 1906 were £212,416, and the concern was an efficient business enterprise pursuing a prudent financial strategy of building reserves from profits to meet future long-term investment.[52] Business success was not inevitable; between 1906 and 1909

---

[46]   *The Times*, 2 October 1906; J. St Nixon, *Daimler 1896–1946* (London: G. T. Foulis and Co., n.d.), p. 132.

[47]   Davenport-Hines, *Dudley Docker*, p. 50.

[48]   MRC, MSS 19A/1/2/16–17, 22 June 1910.

[49]   Davenport-Hines, *Dudley Docker*, p. 50.

[50]   D. Thoms and T. Donnelly, *The Motor Car Industry in Coventry since the 1890s* (London, Croom Helm, 1985), p. 54.

[51]   Ibid., pp. 44, 62–3.

[52]   *The Statist*, 3 November 1906.

the company faced intense price competition, and typical of many firms in the fledgling motor car industry had to navigate the sharp trade fluctuations in the British market. By 1908 Daimler was pressed to balance income with expenditure, recording in that year a loss of £50,000, and with unsold inventories of £300,000 and debts of £92,000 the company faced a mounting liquidity problem.[53] To tide the company over, Daimler negotiated an overdraft of £65,000 with the Midlands Bank,[54] through the auspices of Sir Edward Holden, who was 'an outstandingly helpful, sympathetic and constructive banker to many other industrial clients'.[55] Holden, as we have seen, was a close associate of Docker, as were key members of the Daimler board: Percy Martin, Edward Manville, the chairman, and their co-director George Flett. Like Rogers at BSA, the Daimler directors had business and political links to Docker. Manville has been described as 'being in a close orbit to Docker',[56] both were directors of the MARCWC, and during the war they were to become 'political adherents' when Docker was President of the Federation of British Industry and Manville headed the Association of British Chambers of Commerce.[57] Docker's association with Flett, who sat on the board of the MARCWC and was a leading executive at another Docker interest, Dick Kerr & Co., may well have aided further his knowledge of Daimler's business affairs.[58]

By 1910 Daimler represented an ideal business opportunity for Docker and the BSA board, and this dovetailed with their policy of diversification. The failure to develop the motor business at BSA led Docker to the conclusion that if BSA could not develop internally the managerial capabilities for its motor division then these would have to be acquired from outside.[59] In addition, Daimler now represented a potentially profitable business asset. During 1910 Daimler had an extraordinarily successful year, its profits reaching £100,000, prompting *The Financial Times* to report in September 1910 that the BSA–Daimler 'combination' represented 'one of the most important ever effected in the motor industry'. In particular, it offered a potential to inject fresh share capital in the Daimler business, as well as a profitable asset for existing shareholders. As *The Financial Times* informed the public, during 1906–07, Daimler had paid a dividend of 12.5 per cent on ordinary shares plus a bonus of 10 per cent, and the financial backing of BSA now held the prospects for the development of a highly profitable venture.[60] Daimler shareholders did not miss out; the terms of the amalgamation were on 'very modern lines'. Daimler retained its trading identity, the existing company was liquidated and a new company was launched with all shares held by BSA.

[53] Thoms and Donnelly, *The Motor Car Industry in Coventry*, pp. 50, 52, 57.
[54] Ibid., pp. 56–8.
[55] Davenport-Hines, *Dudley Docker*, p. 33.
[56] Marrison, *British Business and Protection,* pp. 369–70.
[57] Davenport-Hines, *Dudley Docker*, p. 51.
[58] Ibid., p. 51; Wilson, *British Business History*, p. 110.
[59] Davenport-Hines, *Dudley Docker*, p. 50.
[60] *The Financial Times*, 2, 27 September 1910; Nixon, *Daimler*, pp. 128–30.

The Daimler preference shareholders received a 25s payment in cash for each £1 share, and ordinary shareholders a conversion rate of 4 Daimler ordinary £1 shares for 5 fully paid BSA £1 shares, which were ranked *pari passu* with the latter company's ordinary script. Further adding to shareholder confidence was the BSA guarantee for all Daimler liabilities, and the restructuring of the board around the key executives of both companies.[61]

The restructured board was undoubtedly a signal to shareholders of continuity of policy and sound financial judgement by respected business leaders who were in tune with both companies. In the history of corporate governance and strategic direction at BSA, 1910 marked an important turning point. The post-merger board had all the hallmarks of a Daimler-led managerial coalition, with the incoming directors gaining strategic control over decision-making. The key to the acquisition was a trade-off between the financial circumstances of the deal and a major change in the governance of the new amalgamation that brought a fundamental restructuring of the BSA main board. Daimler was required to pay BSA a dividend of £100,000 a year, while the incumbent BSA directors were culled and the main board reduced from 11 to 7, with 4 from BSA and 3 from Daimler. Although Docker resigned from the BSA board, his acolytes Percy Martin and Edward Manville became managing director and deputy chairman respectively (see Table 4.2), and they, together with Rogers, constituted the dominant coalition that determined strategy at the company and shaped decisions relating to governance. The terms of the deal also consolidated ownership and control at BSA and it retained the form of a personal capitalist organisation. Martin and A. H. E. Wood, the latter another Daimler man, were two of the largest shareholders at Daimler, and became substantial shareholders in BSA.[62] Although the shareholdings of the new board members were not substantial enough to guarantee outright ownership, they could, when it suited them, assert that they were strongly identified with the interests of the company's shareholders at large. As Quail argues 'the theoretical justification for the larger powers of ... directors remains their role as a group of proprietors standing for the proprietors as a whole'.[63]

Acquiring Daimler in 1910 was to set the tone of governance of the company until the early 1930s, but Daimler also came to represent by the inter-war years an increasing financial burden on the company. As Davenport-Hines observes, in the long-run the acquisition did not ensure a combine distinguished throughout by even and consistent management, whether in finance, marketing or product development.[64] The performance of Daimler, as we shall see, raised serious questions about the governance of BSA in the inter-war era, and tested shareholder loyalty and trust in executive management. Adding to the governance issues were

[61] Nixon, *Daimler*, pp. 129–30; *The Statist*, 1 October 1910.

[62] *The Statist*, 1 October 1910.

[63] J. Quail, 'The Proprietorial Theory of the Firm and its Consequences', *Journal of Industrial History*, Vol. 3, No.1 (2000), p. 3.

[64] Davenport-Hines, *Dudley Docker*, p. 50.

the increased diversification of the company during the First World War, and the decision in 1919 to create a holding company structure.

BSA and the role of the directors: war and reconstruction, 1914–20

The war years were an important period for BSA for a number of reasons. The company both profited from the urgent and ever increasing demand from the War Office, Admiralty and Ministry of Munitions for war materials and developed its long-run strategy for post-war growth. It achieved a strong financial position, including excellent returns to investors, and the directors strengthened their position, thanks to good relations with shareholders, and vigorous networking with government and within industrial and political pressure groups. At the end of the war, BSA also underwent a reorganisation of its structure and of its Board, which had important consequences during the troubled inter-war period. These changes are discussed in the following section of this chapter.

At the outset of the war, BSA was added by the War Office to its approved list of armament firms, and in his speech to shareholders at the AGM in October 1914 Sir Hallewell Rogers explained that the company had 'placed the entire factory at the disposal of the government', the company's plants working 'day and night' to meet contracts. Directors had also sanctioned 'at the wish of the War Office … large extensions which would enable us to increase output considerably'.[65] By the summer of 1915, the Ministry of Munitions had placed BSA on the list of 'controlled establishments' under the Munitions of War Act, which entailed a number of restrictions on armament firms relating to the regulation of employment and the control of profits.[66] Excess profit duty was to become a major issue between business and government during the conflict.[67] As Rogers informed shareholders in October 1915, the company's profits had increased and this was 'only to be expected', given the firm's prime concern with the supply of arms, but he assured shareholders that they could take a relaxed view over state controls. In terms of profit control, the chairman believed, they could be expected to be treated by the authorities with 'fairness and consideration', given due recognition of the services that BSA had 'rendered in the past and is continuing to render'. Certainly, the directors would have allayed any fears that shareholders may have expressed

---

[65]   Birmingham Archive, MS/321/A/1, BSA Directors' Reports, Speech of Chairman, AGM, 5 October 1914.

[66]   MS/321/A/1, BSA Directors' Reports, Speech of Chairman, AGM, 6 October 1915. For the mobilisation of the industrial economy see H. Strachan, *The First World War*, Vol. 1, *To Arms* (Oxford, Oxford University Press, 2001), Ch. 11.

[67]   For the control on profits see B. W. E. Alford, 'Lost Opportunities: British Businessmen during the First World War', in N. McKendrick and R. B. Outhwaite (eds), *Business Life and Public Policy. Essays in Honour of D .C. Coleman* (Cambridge, Cambridge University Press, 1986), pp. 213–14.

over profit controls, when they announced a net profit of £408,000, a 40 per cent dividend on ordinary shares, plus a one-shilling bonus per share for all ordinary shareholders.[68]

High rewards to stakeholders were not justified simply in terms of the escalating demand for the various munitions of war, but rather by the efficient manner in which the BSA management conducted the business. Shareholders were informed in 1915 that despite the increased cost of materials and labour, the company having conceded a 12.5 per cent wage increase to all adult workers in 1915, 'the unit price of their supplies to the government are not more than ruled for some time prior to the commencement of the war'.[69] BSA supplied a wide range of war products including rifles, machine-guns (particularly the Lewis machine-gun, which became the standard for the British Expeditionary Force), projectiles, military bicycles, and a range of small tools and special machine tools, the last two a direct response to the demands by the Ministry for increased equipment for the munitions factories. Furthermore, via Daimler, BSA supplied aeronautical engines, and towards the end of the war the complete aircraft, as well as engines for the latest weapon of war, the tank.[70] According to Rogers, by 1916 the company had gained the approval of 'high officials at the Admiralty, War Office and the Ministry of Munitions', particularly for its ability to keep its promises concerning increased output and its commitment to capital investment in plant and machinery.[71] In his last war-time address, Rogers read to shareholders a letter from the Ministry praising the efficiency of BSA's management and commenting favourably on the company's capability in keeping down its cost of production below that of many other suppliers. His concluding remarks were positive; the company had supplied the authorities with articles 'at a time when they are wanted, and not at a much later date as is unfortunately the case in many directions'.[72] At the same time, he could celebrate with shareholders a rising profit performance, a healthy payout in dividends to the company's shareholders, and an escalation in retained reserves for future investment (Table 4.3).

---

[68] MS/321/A/1, BSA Directors' Reports, Speech of Chairman, AGM, 6 October 1915.

[69] Ibid.

[70] Nixon, *Daimler*; G. H. Frost, *Munitions of War: A Record of the BSA and Daimler Co. during the First World War* (Birmingham and Coventry, BSA and Daimler, n.d.); J. Singleton, 'The Tank Producers: British Mechanical Engineering in the Great War', *Journal of Industrial History*, Vol. 1, No. 1 (1998), p. 94; R. Lloyd-Jones and M. J. Lewis, *Alfred Herbert Ltd. and the British Machine Tool Industry* (Aldershot, Ashgate, 2006), p. 61.

[71] MS/321/A/1, BSA Directors' Reports, Speech of Chairman, AGM, 5 October 1916.

[72] MS/321/A/1, BSA Directors' Reports, Speech of Chairman, AGM, 9 October 1918.

Table 4.3   BSA profits, dividends and profit to reserve, 1914–19

	Net profit (£000)	Dividend (%)	Profit to reserve account (£000)
1914	190	15	50
1915	408	20	133
1916	382	20	150
1917	428	20	150
1918	435	20	155
1919	373	10	100

Source: Lloyd-Jones et al., 'Corporate Governance in a Major British Holding Company', p. 84.

Rogers's self-congratulatory tone, however, requires a consideration of the overall contribution of the firm to the war effort. While it is true that BSA did make an important contribution to the supply of rifles and Lewis machine-guns, the efforts of Daimler in terms of tank-engines were less than exemplary. As Singleton has pointed out, the engine used in the original Mark 1 1916 tank, a 105 h.p. Daimler model, was insufficiently powerful to cope with the muddy conditions of the Somme and Daimler 'failed to deliver' an improved version.[73] A different type of engine was developed for British tanks, its manufacture taken up by other firms, and Rogers's claim that Daimler 'has a very large share in the production of materials for new and ingenious engineers of war'[74] must, as far as tank engines are concerned, be taken with a degree of scepticism. Nevertheless, by the end of the war BSA had gained a reputation as an efficient supplier of a range of war products, and the directors had delivered in this area of strategy. Consequently, in the latter years of the war, the management executive turned its attention to the company's post-war priorities, and the long-term future of the concern.

Relations between capital and labour epitomised the growing concern amongst businessmen and shareholders over the shaping of the post-war consensus. The 'First World War marked a watershed in economic and business development as well as in political and social life', and during the conflict 'the pattern of production over a wide range of industries was to be transformed as business strove to meet wartime requirements'.[75] State intervention during the war had given rise to ideas of co-operation between business, labour and government, in the interests of

---

[73] Singleton, 'The Tank Producers', p. 94.

[74] MS/321/A/1, BSA Directors' Reports, Speech of Chairman, AGM, 5 October 1916.

[75] Hannah, *The Rise of the Corporate Economy*, p. 29.

enhancing Britain's industrial performance.[76] A group of leading industrialists, the most 'vociferous' of whom was Dudley Docker, took on the mantle of the productioneers, advocates of rationalisation and a new co-operative spirit. Such ideas transcended the realm of the firm itself, and required a platform to present a social message to the public.[77] In 1917, at the BSA AGM, Rogers informed shareholders that 'the natural concern of business firms was the development of trade after the war', which was at the 'forefront of their future policy', and in this context 'the cooperation of labour and capital' was central to the long-term 'welfare' of the company. To pursue this strategy, the company joined the newly established National Alliance of Employers and Employed (NAEE), a vehicle formed for the specific purpose of enabling business interests to promote closer co-operation between capital and labour.[78] Signalling BSA's support for this initiative the deputy chairman Edward Manville joined the executive committee of the NAEE and his membership was given added weight by the fact he was also a senior vice president of the Association of Chambers of Commerce of the UK. According to Manville 'It is [a] very first object of the board of this company, to promote the best possible relations between employers and employed', and consequently they had joined the NAEE 'at its very inception'.[79] Manville and the board seemed keen to promote BSA's reputation as a progressive employer, but there was in this an element of self-service. As Middlemas has pointed out, during 1916–17 the NAEE became part of 'a joint Liberal–Conservative propaganda campaign' with the aim of promoting 'anti-socialist trade union groups'.[80] Rogers, for example, asserted the need to consider the welfare of workers but added that such 'action would mean [the workers] could avoid being misled by the few' and that the NAEE would act as a 'bulwark against the spread of a revolutionary spirit'.[81] Nevertheless, it would be unreasonable to dismiss Rogers and Manville as simply indulging in the rhetoric of industrial politics. In 1918, Rogers gave shareholders details of the action taken by the board to improve the welfare of the BSA workforce, which included the provision of an 'up-to-date surgery with a fully trained nursing staff',

[76]   Wilson, *British Business History*, p. 168. See also Davenport-Hines, *Dudley Docker*, pp. 84–7.

[77]   For a discussion of 'social reporting' as a function of the AGM see J. Maltby, 'Hadfields Ltd: its Annual General Meetings, 1900–1939 and their Relevance to Corporate Social Reporting', *British Accounting Review*, Vol. 36, No. 4 (2004), pp. 415–39.

[78]   According to K. Middlemas, *Politics in Industrial Society. The Experience of the British System since 1911* (London, Andre Deutsch, 1979), pp. 112, 117n, 128–9, 139), the NAEE gained support from the Engineering Employers Federation but support declined from 1919.

[79]   MS/321/A/1, BSA Directors' Reports, Speech of Chairman, AGM, 12 October 1917.

[80]   Middlemas, *Politics in Industrial Society*, p. 117.

[81]   MS/321/A/1, BSA Directors' Reports, Speech of Chairman, 12 October 1917, 9 October 1919.

the opening of a large canteen, a works gymnasium, and a training and education programme for boys that had been 'developed on modern lines'. 'Confident' in the fact that he had secured the goodwill of the shareholders in matters of labour relations, he assured them 'that all should be done that is commercially possible for the improvement of the conditions of their employees'. Correspondingly, Rogers announced the establishment of a Special Committee of the Board and Management of both BSA and Daimler to concern itself with matters of workers' welfare.[82] In addition, the BSA board appointed Lieutenant-Colonel A. Warden as 'Welfare Supervisor for all the works' in July 1918, charged with producing a report on strategy to be submitted to the company's labour committee.[83]

Despite these overtures of industrial welfare, labour relations at BSA were fraught in the immediate post-war years as inflationary pressures led to wage rises, and the ending of the brief post-war boom in mid-1920 to falling output and orders.[84] In the same way, BSA's cordial wartime relations with its shareholders deteriorated sharply afterwards. At the 1915 AGM shareholders congratulated the Board on the company's performance, and proposed and unanimously carried the motion to double directors' fees for the financial year.[85] The following year ordinary shareholders received a dividend of 20 per cent, and at the AGM they proposed and sanctioned 'a similar sum' for directors' fees to that granted in 1915. Given the crisis of the war, Rogers considered this a 'splendid' gesture by shareholders, but considered that it was the board's national duty to decline the magnanimous gesture. As recompense, a shareholder tabled a motion for payment of directors' fees free of tax, which Rogers duly accepted.[86] By the 1917 AGM, the Board could bask in the compliment that they 'had served the shareholders in the very best possible way' by waiving the increase in directors' fees. At that meeting, a letter from Dudley Docker, who had been unable to attend, was read, in which he proposed that directors should again receive a doubling of fees. Introduced to shareholders as someone who 'knows the inner workings of this company', Docker's letter acknowledged that at the time of the Daimler merger directors' fees had been set at a 'very inadequate' level, and on his appeal for 'a more adequate remuneration' shareholders voted the increase, which was accepted by Rogers on behalf of the Board.[87] Directors were compensated for the added time and effort in the management of a company central to the war effort, and their reputation was constantly enhanced.

---

[82]   MS/321/A/1, BSA Directors' Reports, Speech of Chairman, AGM, 9 October 1918.

[83]   MS/137/Acc/91/114, Minute Books of BSA Directors No. 5, 1917–20, 13 September 1918.

[84]   Lloyd-Jones and Lewis, *Raleigh*, p. 109.

[85]   MS/321/A/1, BSA Directors' Reports, Speech of Chairman, AGM, 6 October 1915.

[86]   MS/321/A/1, BSA Directors' Reports, Speech of Chairman, AGM, 5 October 1916.

[87]   MS/321/A/1, BSA Directors' Reports, Speech of Chairman, AGM, 12 October 1917.

During the war shareholders could well afford to take a generous line on the issue of directors' fees, secure in the knowledge that they received 'a very handsome dividend free from tax'.[88] Nevertheless, Rogers, perhaps with a wider constituency in mind, was careful to point out that the Board had continued to pursue a prudent financial policy. He reflected on this policy at the 1918 AGM:

> If, in the past, instead of taking the prudent course of making provision out of profits for contingencies, your board had recommended the payment of dividends to the full extent possible each year, we certainly should not have been able to cope with the demands of the past four years without coming to you for more capital.[89]

A further positive result of the war for BSA was its impact on the external reputation of the board, a point that Rogers constantly projected to shareholders. In addition to being an executive committee member of the NAEE and a vice president of the Association of Chambers of Commerce of the UK, in 1916 Manville joined the executive council of the newly founded Federation of British Industry.[90] BSA directors were closely involved in the business politics of the period, and in the general election of 1918 Manville and Hallewell Rogers were elected to Parliament as Tory MPs, secretly supported by Docker's British Commonwealth Union.[91] Directors also contributed to the national planning for war production. Percy Martin enhanced his national profile when he became Director for Internal Combustion Engines at the Ministry of Munitions in 1917. Daimler's chief engineer, A. E. Berriman, who later was to become a BSA director, joined the Ministry in 1918 as Deputy Director (Technical) of Aeronautics.[92]

BSA built up substantial reserves during the war (Table 4.3).[93] The company was in safe hands, made a substantial contribution to the war effort, and had pursued a prudent policy for directors' remuneration and shareholder reward. Reviewing their performance at the time of the Armistice the BSA board could reflect on having had a 'good war'; they were held in high esteem by their shareholders, who were confident in their stewardship of a much enlarged company, and were ready to meet the challenges of the post-war years.[94] The company's stakeholders could look optimistically to the future, safe in the knowledge that BSA was in a strong financial position, as evidenced by the £1 million bonus they received in

---

[88]   MS/321/A/1, BSA Directors' Reports, Speech of Chairman, AGM, 5 October 1916.
[89]   MS/321/A/1, BSA Directors' Reports, Speech of Chairman, AGM, 9 October 1918.
[90]   MS/321/A/1, BSA Directors' Reports, Speech of Chairman, AGM, 5 October 1916.
[91]   Davenport-Hines, *Dudley Docker*, p. 72. The BSA Board had in fact agreed to apply for membership of the BCU in July 1918 and had sent a cheque for £2,000 as a first payment. MS/137/Acc/91/114, Minute Books of BSA Directors No. 5, 1917–20, 26 July 1918.
[92]   MS/321/A/1, BSA Directors' Reports, Speech of Chairman, AGM, 9 October 1918.
[93]   Ibid.
[94]   Ibid.

1918.[95] Post-war strategic thinking at BSA firstly involved the impact of the war on productive capacity, and the ability of the company to re-shape its direction to meet uncertain post-war conditions. A direct consequence of the war was the enormous increase in productive capacity. The Board sanctioned two capital reconstructions, one in 1915, the other in 1918. On the eve of the Armistice, BSA employed over 13,000 workers and Daimler in the range of 4,000 to 4,500 workers.[96] Explaining this to shareholders, at the 1918 AGM, Rogers emphasised the need to plan for the utilisation of the company's additional capacity 'after the war', which 'is constantly engaging the attention of your Board'. Whilst anticipating that BSA would be able 'to speedily turn on to a peace time programme which would ensure the continued prosperity of the company', Rogers did not specify in detail what this entailed. He did, however, float the suggestion of a possible combined venture with Docker's MARCWC, a vague reference to a scheme whereby the two companies would cooperate in a 'key industry' whose products were largely imported.[97] Such a co-operative venture, involving a proposed scheme aimed at import substitution, came to nothing. The BSA board made no further reference to it, and it is probable that Docker was too concerned with the consolidation of his extended business interests in 1918–19, following the merger of MARCWC with the American-owned British Westinghouse and the electrical division of Vickers in 1917, 'an impressive consolidation of firms within the electrical industry'.[98]

During 1919, the BSA strategy focused on rising demand and the need to increase output rapidly. This entailed an expansionary investment policy for its core business activities, the development of mass production, and the streamlining of product lines to reap economies of scale. In addition, the company committed to its pre-war policy of acquisition 'as opportunity offered of businesses carrying on kindred or complementary trades'. Acquisitions were designed to facilitate further vertical integration between the diverse product groups. Thus, in the summer of 1919, BSA acquired William Jessop & Sons and Saville & Co., two Sheffield steel producers, the former with steelmaking plant in the USA. These companies were important producers for export markets and offered the capability to produce steel and forgings for BSA engineering products. At the same time, BSA acquired Burton, Griffiths & Co., a firm of London machine-tool merchants with extensive sale networks in the USA to facilitate the marketing of BSA machine tools, an engineering activity which had been introduced and expanded during the war.[99]

---

[95]   *The Financial World*, 22 July 1933; *The Economist*, 5 October 1918.

[96]   Birmingham Archive, MS/137/Acc/91/114, Minute Books of BSA Directors No. 5, 1917–20, 18 October 1918.

[97]   MS/321/A/1, BSA Directors' Reports, Speech of Chairman, AGM, 9 October 1918.

[98]   Wilson, *British Business History*, pp. 144–5; Davenport-Hines, *Dudley Docker*, pp. 156–8.

[99]   Coventry Archive, PA 594/1/1/2/4, BSA Ordinary General Meeting, October 1921.

Economies of scale and scope[100] determined the BSA strategy to meet what they anticipated to be expanding post-war markets. Expansion initiated board-level discussions on the appropriate organisational form for the development of the post-war business in October 1918, but the board did not communicate a decision to shareholders until the AGM of October 1919, when they announced the formation of a holding-company structure.[101]

In 1919 BSA represented a diversified engineering organisation, and to effect increased administration and co-ordination it was constructed as a holding company in that year. Its executive board was considerably enlarged (Table 4.4), the existing production departments – Cycles, Rifles and Tools, and Daimler Motors – were converted into subsidiary companies, together with the new acquisitions in steel and machine tools. Rogers rationalised the conversion to shareholders in October 1919: 'in view of the increasing importance of these departments, each one now constitutes a large business, it is better for the efficient management of each, that they be constituted into more or less separate concerns, having separate detailed management'. Each subsidiary was organised as a separate entity, with appointed boards of directors, but to ensure centralised administration the boards included one or more directors from the main parent company board, together with leading managers from each subsidiary. To enable an overview of business performance, the subsidiaries were to 'report to the parent Company Board periodically and ... on matters of importance and policy be subject to the decision of the main board'. The financial assets 'of all the companies will be retained under the control of the main [parent] board', who leased fixed and variable assets to the subsidiaries, which were represented in their balance sheets by corresponding shares held by the parent company.[102] Within a year of the end of the war, the executive had radically transformed the company, and shareholder confidence and trust was high. Nevertheless, during the 1920s and early 1930s, trust in the triumvirate of top directors gradually evaporated, and led to a crisis of governance at BSA.

---

[100] Economies of scale relate to the introduction of high-volume production, while economies of scope result from the use of the same materials and processes to make and distribute a variety of different products. These are seen as essential to cost-effective organisations. See Chandler, *Scale and Scope*, p. 17; D. Teece, 'Economies of Scope and the Scope of the Enterprise', *Journal of Economic Behaviour and Organisation*, Vol. 1, No. 3 (1980), pp. 223–47.

[101] MS/137/Acc/91/114, Minute Books of BSA Directors No. 5, 1917–20, 18 October 1918, 24 October 1919; PA 594/1/1/2/3, BSA Meeting File, Ordinary, AGM, October 1919.

[102] PA 594/1/1/2/3, Ordinary General Meeting, October 1919.

Table 4.4   BSA board of directors 1919

Şir Hallewell Rogers – chairman	Albert J. Hobson – chairman of Jessops
Edward Manville – deputy chairman	Brigadier General Sir Henry Holden
Percy Martin – managing director	Walter H. Thomas – director of Savilles
A. Neville Chamberlain	A. H. Wood
Albert Eadie	Thomas S. Walker
Edward M. Griffiths – chairman of Burton, Griffiths	

Losing trust: from individual to collective voice, 1920–31

At BSA's AGM in 1921, Rogers outlined the problems facing the company and its subsidiary operations. Acknowledging that all its business ventures had felt the full impact of falling demand, Rogers appealed for understanding that the company's performance was determined by external market factors outside their control. In the case of Jessops, for example, the company had virtually ceased production, affected by falling orders in Britain and the USA. Both steel and machine-tool production were seriously affected by the world-wide recession and their heavy reliance upon export markets. Problems in the motor car, motor cycle and bicycle markets also came under consideration. Rogers informed shareholders that both Daimler and BSA Cycles remained 'extremely vigorous and vital enterprises', but their performance reflected depressed market conditions. At the same time, Daimler faced particular market constraints given the decision to adopt a mass production strategy based on the standard Daimler 45 and the Daimler 30 modules, both of large engine capacity and at the higher price range. Consequently, BSA abandoned a mass production strategy, and alternatively made arrangements with dealers to sell exclusively a wide range of Daimler cars under batch production methods. Rogers summed up the policy u-turn: 'If in 1919 we plumped for mass production, it was because we thought conditions justified it. But we have not forgot our cunning, and what our present experiences show is that we can abandon one system and go back to the other.' He further reassured shareholders that while the war had provided a lesson in mass production, it had also given 'an education in flexibility and adaptiveness few other firms in the world can ever have enjoyed'. Shareholders could thus rest assured that BSA had the flexibility to adapt to changing markets, while at the same time, strict economy in manufacture would reduce costs and realise the full potential of unsold stocks.[103]

---

[103]   PA 594/1/1/2/4, BSA Ordinary General Meeting, October 1921.

Shareholders may well have been reassured, but in 1921 'some' were clearly 'disappointed'. In April 1921, at a general meeting of ordinary shareholders, there was disquiet concerning the announcement of a 'conservative' dividend policy, the company paying only 5 per cent, despite a 'satisfactory' profit of £567,000 (Table 4.5), while at the same time writing down stocks of all subsidiary companies 'to the lowest possible point'.[104] A conservative outlook of holding 'cash in light of no future expectations of increased profits' may well be considered as a prudent policy, given that by 1922 BSA recorded substantial losses (Table 4.5). However, at the general meetings in 1921 Rogers referred to numerous requests from shareholders for further information on the financial and business performance of the subsidiaries, to which he supplied the usual answer that it would not be in the best interests of the company to disclose information which 'is sometimes of very great value to competitors'.[105] At meetings, the detail of this information was never recorded, but top of the agenda for shareholders was the wisdom of BSA's acquisition policy, and the ill-fated decision in February 1920 to diversify into aircraft manufacturing by the acquisition of the Aircraft Manufacturing Co. (AMC) and the aviation engine makers Peter Hooker & Co.

Table 4.5   BSA profits, dividends and profit to reserve, 1919–39

	Net profit (£000)	Dividend (%)	Profit to reserve account (£000)
1919 (to 31 July)	373	10	100
1920–21 (18 months to 31 Jan)	567	5	0
1921–22	-469	0	0
1922–23	-167	0	0
1923–24	125	0	0
1924–25	179	5	0
1925–26	185	6	0
1926–27	112	0	0
1927–28	72	0	0
1928–29	90	6	0
1930	148	0	0
1931	-204	0	0
1932	-798	0	0

continued

[104]   PA 594/1/1/2/4, BSA Ordinary General Meeting, April 1921.

[105]   Ibid.; PA 594/1/1/2/4, BSA Ordinary General Meeting, October 1921.

Table 4.5   *concluded*

1933	245	0	136
1934	128	0	15
1935	112	0	110
1936	171	0	133
1937	398	0	140
1938	431	11	8
1939	411	6	67

Source: Lloyd-Jones et al., 'Corporate Governance in a Major British Holding Company', p. 84.

Both these ventures were at best overambitious and at worst foolhardy and incompetent. The board minutes provide no satisfactory explanation why diversification into the aircraft business by BSA was sanctioned, but it is probable that Manville and Martin wanted to build on Daimler's growing activity in aircraft (engine and airframes) production and services into the post-war era. However, within a few months of their acquisition in February 1920 both the AMC and Hooker were in receivership.

J. Holt Thomas established the AMC prior to the war, and it produced from a factory along the Edgware Road in London. Before 1914, the company 'seemed to be among the very few concerns' that was 'well established and competently managed in the making of aeroplanes'. During the war 'it increased its output enormously', and diversified in 'many new directions' through an ambitious acquisition programme to become 'not merely a great industrial concern, but the financial centre of a network of outside companies numbering altogether about a dozen', including the specialist aviation engine makers Peter Hooker. The fact that the company appointed De Havilland as its chief designer did much to enhance its business reputation, and the AMC secured close relations with government agencies, with two of its directors acting on the government Air Board.[106]

BSA opened negotiations for the share holding of Holt Thomas in AMC and Peter Hooker in 1918, and at that time it certainly seemed to be a prospective profit-making business. BSA eventually acquired the ordinary shares in the two companies for £586,000, payable in 293,000 BSA shares at £2 each, a deal that Martin thought was in the very best interests of his company and its shareholders.[107] On the face of it, the BSA directors had taken the right option in acquiring a company with an 'impressive air of solidarity and wealth'. *The Economist*, however, was more circumspect. Just nine months after the purchase, 'Mr Thomas and his fellow [ordinary] shareholders understood the value of what they had sold

---

[106] 'Castles in the Air', *The Economist*, 6 November 1920.

[107] MSS 19A/1/2/42, letter from Percy Martin to BSA, January 1920; 19A/1/1/1/13 BSA board Meeting 19 March 1920.

far better than the BSA had understood the value of what they had bought'.[108] Indeed, in October 1920 the BSA board received the unwelcome news that they would have to provide their bankers with guarantees of up to £700,000 to cover the accounts and liabilities of the AMC.[109] To keep the AMC afloat, Manville met a representation of the company's note holders, and proposed a scheme that would allow Daimler to lease the Hendon works of the AMC for up to five years with an option to purchase at the end of the lease. This proved to be a disappointment, and Manville reluctantly informed the board that BSA was 'immediately' retiring 'from the position which we had proposed to occupy'. Consequently, both the AMC and Hooker entered into receivership, and in April 1921 Percy Martin reported that the £586,000 investment in the two companies had been written off.[110]

Public scrutiny of the AMC affair came from *The Economist*; the journal asserted that there were 'certain questions' that BSA shareholders would be 'clearly entitled to make'. They would 'want to know from their directors why in the spring [of 1920] they made a bargain which by the summer had proved to be so bad'.[111] At board meetings, the directors referred to the AMC and Hooker affair on four occasions in 1920, three times in 1921, six times in 1922 and twice in 1923.[112] On no occasion was there any detailed discussion of how the directors had led BSA into such a predicament, and they waited until the 1921 AGM before an explanation was given to shareholders. The meeting attracted a 'large attendance of shareholders', and Rogers put the best possible gloss on the misguided affair. The deal had been premised upon 'investigations' made in 1918, and

> Had we been able as originally intended, to acquire the control of these concerns with vacant possession, or had the contracts into which both concerns had entered, prior to our entry, been as remunerative as they were represented to us … then, in either event, the investment would have been amply justified and most remunerative.[113]

Roger's defence was therefore premised upon shareholders accepting that the BSA directors had been misled by AMC over the financial viability of the two companies, but his defence leaves open the question of why the purchase proceeded without guarantees of vacant possession of the properties, and why there was no careful vetting of the contracts. What exposed the BSA board to direct culpability was Roger's admission to shareholders that Hooker was 'unfortunately, hopelessly involved in burdensome contracts, which moreover could not be executed except

---

[108] *The Economist*, 6 November 1920.

[109] MSS 19C/11 BSA Directors' Minutes, Special Meeting of the Board, 8 October 1920.

[110] MSS 19C/11, Board Meeting 17 December 1920; Board Meeting 1 April 1920.

[111] *The Economist*, 6 November 1920.

[112] MSS 19C/11, various dates of board meetings.

[113] *The Statist*, 16 April 1921.

by the investment of very large further capital'. Rogers admitted that, in order to fulfil the contracts, BSA would have had to find 'probably half a million' but he offered no explanation why these considerable financial discrepancies appeared only after the acquisition. Nevertheless, he did make clear was that there was no alternative to liquidation. The only positive that Rogers could offer to shareholders was that although the AMC and Hooker bank overdrafts had to be recorded on the BSA balance sheet 'we are responsibly advised ... that it is improbable that any charge will fall upon us in this regard'.[114] Despite such reassurance, BSA assumed the bank liabilities on two redundant companies, and it was not until 1923 that the sale of their assets finally closed the sorry episode. At the 1924 AGM Rogers on behalf of the board acknowledged the financial costs of the aircraft venture to the company, and placing it in a wider context accepted that the expansion and diversification policy overall had been based on a false optimism:

> The misfortunes of the company have been due largely to its expansionist programme, which led it to increase its fixed assets during the boom by nearly £1,000,000 and its interests in subsidiaries by over £3,000,000. These firms have, with few exceptions, proved to be unfortunate investments, and two of them are in the process of liquidation. It was thought at one time that the Company would have to meet part of its contingent liability of £950,000 in respect of bank loans which had been granted to them. The contingent liability has however, been since reduced to £154,400, and, in the opinion of the directors, need cause no anxiety.[115]

Shareholders, who had not long ago demonstrated trust in the governance of the company, now found only belated reassurances by the board concerning the AMC–Hooker affair. While the BSA directors may well have assumed that this was sufficient, there is evidence that the AMC–Hooker affair damaged their reputation. Shareholders now questioned the effective stewardship of the company, and the trust they had placed in the governing elite. They submitted an amendment to the 1921 directors' report, in which they demanded that the final approval of the report should be adjourned, pending an inquiry 'by a committee of shareholders into the activities of the directors in respect of AMC and Peter Hooker'. The amendment was subsequently lost, only 12 voting in favour.[116] While this represented a considerable vote of confidence in favour of the board, shareholder voice now made its first appearance since the spat over secret reserves in 1906. Although the AMC–Hooker affair can hardly be described as leading to a shareholder revolt, it nevertheless demonstrated that some shareholders would not remain passive as they called into question the conduct and performance of top executives. It also masked deeper

---

[114] Ibid.

[115] *The Statist*, 3 May 1924.

[116] *The Economist*, 16 April 1921.

issues about the overall management of the holding company, which were taken up by dissident directors who challenged the competency of top executives.

A holding company is organised through a parent company, which assumes 'controlling interests in or authority over legally separate and mainline subsidiaries [operating companies] which are given responsibility for production or operations'.[117] Thus, holding companies raise important issues about the performance of management and the transparency of disclosure of financial information relating to its various subsidiaries. The degree of administrative centralisation exercised by the parent company may well affect efficient business performance, and transparent accountability takes on more importance for stakeholders who require detailed information relating to the performance of the operating companies. What takes on added significance here is the role of the directors of the parent company, in the case of BSA its top executive, who are trusted with the effective administration of the subsidiaries, and the level and quality of disclosure on operating performance. In 1921, when the AMC–Hooker affair was prominent in the minds of shareholders, a prominent member of the parent board and a director of BSA Cycles, T. S. Walker, raised pertinent issues relating to control by the parent company of the subsidiaries, and the transparency of the accountability of the leading executives.

Walker had joined the board of BSA in 1919, and until succeeded by J. N. Chamberlain in January 1921 had been chairman of BSA Cycles.[118] In December 1921 Walker resigned his directorship of BSA on matters of principle, and writing to Rogers he impressed on him that that he was unable to sustain loyalty to Percy Martin, the managing director, as he had been uneasy 'for some time as to the policy we are pursuing'. His main objections may be categorised under three heads: excessive expenditure on expansion, the selection of managerial staff, and over-centralisation. Walker was convinced that following the formation of the holding company, the whole concern was becoming unmanageable:

> Too much of the detailed management of the subsidiary companies is in the hands of the Parent Company's Staff. As a result of this Mr [W. L.] Bayley is not only Mr Martin's Chief Engineer but he is responsible also for the control and management of a number of other companies in the group. This system I believe is wrong and must result in inefficient management of the subsidiary companies in a concern of the magnitude of the BSA. It is not a question of Mr Bayley not being the right man, but that I do not believe it possible to find anyone who could undertake satisfactorily such multifarious duties. A company such as BSA Cycles under the present centralised system has very little chance of competing satisfactorily with a compact, specialised business, managed by one

---

[117] R. Fitzgerald, 'The Competitive and Institutional Advantage of Holding Companies: British Business in the Inter-war Years', *Journal of Industrial History*, Vol. 3, No. 2 (2000), pp. 2–3.

[118] PA594/2/1/59, E. M. Griffiths to J. N. Chamberlain, 11 February 1922.

man of sound commercial training with a thorough knowledge of the cycle trade who gives the whole of his time and attention to the business, and who controls both manufacture and distribution of the goods produced.[119]

The critical observations made by Walker implied that the holding company was over-centralised, and that management was stretched across too many activities. In particular, Walker questioned the ability of the executive management of the BSA holding company to effectively manage and co-ordinate the activities of an enlarged and diversified business. 'I think the proper course', Walker suggested, 'is to aim at making the subsidiary companies as far as possible separate, independent units, each controlled by a managing director, both as to manufacture and distribution.' A delegation of more control to the subsidiaries, however, was fundamentally opposed by Martin. Responding to Walker, through Rogers, Martin insisted that 'by virtue of a small specialised staff surrounding me in the Parent Company we have obviated numerous and extravagant appointments in each of the subsidiary companies which would have been necessary in order to carry out Mr Walker's ideas'. Martin championed himself as a guiding hand, inducing a spirit 'of team work in each of the companies … and we have brought about a gradual and improved co-operation between the various companies to the end aimed at in our initial decision to increase the scope of the BSA after the war period.'[120] In a direct communiqué to Walker, Rogers acknowledged that 'The main difference between us comes to this, that, in your opinion we are never likely to obtain sufficient trade to justify an organisation or premises in excess of what we had before the war'. On this point, he reminded Walker that the leading directors controlled strategy, and 'We take a different view and we regret that you did not give yourself the opportunity of discussing with the board … or the Managing Director the situation and future policy of the company.'[121]

While Walker was prepared to use individual voice to question the strategic direction of the company, there was no further correspondence with the directors following his resignation. Walker chose exit, and the exercise of individual voice passed to E. M. Griffiths. Prior to his appointment to the BSA board in 1919, Griffiths had been a founding partner and chairman of Burton, Griffiths & Co., which became a subsidiary of BSA. In April 1919 he announced the advantages of acquisition to his own shareholders, which included additional capital injections from BSA, the continuation of management on 'similar lines', and by the appointment of W. L. Bayley, BSA chief engineer, as a representative of the parent company, an extra 'source of [managerial] strength'.[122] The appointment of Griffiths to the BSA board, while retaining the chairmanship of Burton, Griffiths, clearly gave him a presence in decision making in both concerns, but at the Burton,

[119] PA594/2/1/59, T. S. Walker to H. Rodgers, 15 December 1921.

[120] PA594/2/1/59, P. Martin to H. Rodgers, 29 December 1921.

[121] PA594/2/1/59, H. Rodgers to T. S. Walker, 30 December 1921.

[122] PA 926/12/1/1, Burton, Griffiths & Co., General Minute Book, 10 April 1919.

Griffiths AGM in March 1920 tensions were clearly evident. Attending the AGM were Rogers and Martin, representing the BSA board, as well as in their capacity as shareholders of Burton, Griffiths. Griffiths used this occasion to announce his dissatisfaction with the BSA parent board's allocation of additional capital for expansion. At the January 1921 AGM Griffiths again unsuccessfully approached the issue of additional capital expenditure, but now also objected to a decision made by the BSA board to appoint Rogers and Martin as directors of Burton, Griffiths.[123]

Events at these AGMs embroiled Griffiths in a power struggle for control of the subsidiary company, and during 1921 he was engaged in negotiations with BSA to sell Burton, Griffiths back to him. These negotiations foundered; no satisfactory agreement emerged on the valuation of the concern. Nevertheless, as a key member of the BSA parent board, Griffiths was now directly opposed to the strategy of its leading directors. Writing to J. N. Chamberlain in December 1921, Griffiths was 'compelled to remind' him 'that when I sold the business to the BSA Co. it was with a view of not continuing in harness and in active management, and therefore it would be more from a matter of sentiment because I do not want to see the concern wrecked'.[124] Griffiths clearly believed that his control over policy at the subsidiary was being undermined by the interference of Martin, and this was evident in the area of marketing. He had been 'over-ruled … with regard to salesmanship … with which I disagreed, as they were not for the benefit of the company generally, and which have proved disastrous in their results'.[125] Within a short period, Griffiths became disillusioned with BSA policy towards the subsidiary, and especially the role of Martin as managing director of the parent concern. As Chamberlain acknowledged, 'it is clear to me that you cannot work with our managing director and that unless some other arrangement can be arrived at either you or he must leave the board on that ground'.[126] A compromise was finally reached whereby Griffiths resigned his chairmanship of Burton, Griffiths, and signed a condition, under protest, that he would not hold directorships of rival machine tool concerns for a period of 12 months after his leaving.[127]

Martin may well have forced Griffiths to resign his position on the subsidiary, but he was still a director of the parent board, and was to prove a tenacious adversary in his condemnation of the running of the business by the BSA directors. Added weight was given to his criticisms by the fact that Griffiths was not only

---

[123] Burton, Griffiths, General Minute Book, 19 March 1920; 28 January 1921.

[124] PA 594/2/1/59, E. M. Griffiths to J. N. Chamberlain, 8 December 1921.

[125] PA 594/2/1/59, E. M. Griffiths to H. Rogers, 21 February 1922.

[126] PA 594/2/1/59, J. N. Chamberlain to E. M. Griffiths, 5 December 1921.

[127] PA 594/2/1/59, E. M. Griffiths to J. N. Chamberlain, 9 December 1921. The agreement specifically mentioned leading machine-tool companies Buck and Hickman, Alfred Herbert and Charles Churchill.

a director of BSA but also a leading BSA shareholder.[128] He reminded Rogers of this fact in February 1922, when he tendered his resignation as a BSA director. 'My resignation will be very serious in view of the very large number of shares I hold in your company', but he had 'been out of sympathy with the views of the majority of the directors [of BSA] … and its subsidiary companies for many months past'.[129]

The decision of Griffiths to resign may be interpreted simply as a reaction over what he considered to be the mismanagement of Burton, Griffiths, a company that he had founded, but as a large shareholder, and a man with insider knowledge, his criticisms reflected a growing concern with the overall strategy of the parent board. His dissatisfaction with the heavy losses of BSA between 1921 and 1923 (Table 4.5) prompted him to act, and Griffiths, in tandem with Walker, raised serious concerns about the performance of subsidiary companies within a centralised holding company. In February 1922, for example, he wrote to Chamberlain, who had succeeded Walker as the chairman of BSA Cycles, requesting an explanation for losses of £651,532 for 1921. The changes in management, Griffiths observed, had occurred 'little more than a year ago and I am wondering whether a like result would have happened under the old regime, seeing that results were previously uniformly successful'.[130] Chamberlain denied the inference, and based his defence on adverse 'post-war conditions', but did admit that BSA Cycles was conducting operations in a depressed market 'in a works three times their normal size'.[131] Griffiths was not appeased, and criticised the failure to reorganise the sales department 'by putting practical and commercial men at the head of it'. This, Griffiths argued, had been advocated by Walker before his resignation, and Griffiths concluded that Walker's 'rather despondent outlook of the future' of the Cycle Company 'will prove correct'.[132]

The critique of Griffiths clearly focused on the incompetence of the triumvirate at the head of the company, and he believed that there was a disparity between action and performance at executive level. The holding company was 'overly-bureaucratic'; there was 'too much red tape, reports, routines, hampering production and producing unsatisfactory results'. Further, despite constant references made by the board to shareholders concerning attempts to install 'economy' in operations, Griffiths argued that that this did not represent 'Economy with Efficiency'. Rather, it was a 'False Economy', BSA employing:

---

[128] In the 1920s Griffiths was the second-largest BSA shareholder, holding 44,875 ordinary shares in 1929. PA594/2/1/59, List of Holders of 5,000 and Over Ordinary Shares, 22 March 1929.

[129] PA 594/2/1/59, E. M. Griffiths to H. Rogers, 21 February 1922.

[130] PA 594/2/1/59, E. M. Griffiths to N. J. Chamberlain, 11 February 1922.

[131] PA 594/2/1/59, N. J. Chamberlain to E. M. Griffiths, 14 February 1922.

[132] PA 594/2/1/59, E. M. Griffiths to N. J. Chamberlain, 21 February 1922.

Two sets of auditors ... two lawyers ... two engineers at Daimler – a chief and a consultant ... At Jessops – three managers, but no one responsible for the whole – besides which there are other highly paid officials with non specific title or responsibility.

All this added up to a condemnation of executive management, who in the judgement of Griffiths lacked 'foresight and forethought'. 'The test of highly paid management' is their 'efficiency' in running the business, claimed Griffiths, and this 'is proved by the results obtained by it in *bad* times, and we know these results have been poor'. That this condemnation of executive management was directed at Martin was all too obvious, as Griffiths recommended to Rogers the appointment of two additional managing directors, who have 'real knowledge and experience of the particular business they have to manage, and having proper and specified responsibilities, also with equal status to the present managing director'.[133]

Griffiths' recommendation was promptly dismissed by Rogers,[134] who remained loyal to Martin, but for the longer-term performance of the company it did raise two key issues relating to the administration of the holding company. First, Griffiths, like Walker, had criticised the board for over-centralisation, effectively meddling in the affairs of the subsidiary boards in which they had no specific knowledge of their business and routines. Second, both Griffiths and Walker had raised serious concerns over the ineffective co-ordination of the subsidiaries by the parent company. It appears from their arguments that they were not advocating the dismantling of the holding company. Rather, they focused on the issue that one managing director could not effectively administer its disparate subsidiaries, when an executive in fact sat on the boards of all the subsidiaries, but had no overview of the operations of the group at large.[135]

Similar to many British holding companies of the inter-war era, BSA was little more than a loose federation of semi-autonomous companies, with limited overall co-ordination.[136] Parent companies left the operating companies largely 'responsible... for the day to day production and distribution of their products', with the 'central office ... usually little more than a meeting place for a board of directors who, as representative owners of the constituent firms, determined through negotiation both output and profits'.[137] The attempt by Martin and his co-directors to create a unitary structure did not materialise, and the inefficiencies this brought to the co-ordination of the subsidiaries were central to the attack of both Walker and Griffiths. In the 1920s such problems manifested themselves particularly in the area of co-ordinating sales and output. For example, when BSA purchased Burton, Griffiths the intention was for it to assume the sales function of the producing

[133] PA 594/2/1/59, E. M. Griffiths to H. Rogers, 21 February 1922.
[134] PA 594/2/1/59, H. Rogers to E. M. Griffiths, 24 February 1922.
[135] PA 594/2/1/59, E. M. Griffiths to H. Rogers, 21 February 1922.
[136] Camfferman and Zeff, 'The Apotheosis of Holding Company Accounting', p. 171.
[137] Chandler, *Scale and Scope*, p. 288.

subsidiary, BSA Tools, the latter concentrating 'purely' on 'manufacturing ... without any sales organisation'. The reality, however, was that in the 1920s these two subsidiaries remained 'two self-contained companies'.[138] This meant that by 1928 BSA Tools had expanded its manufacturing programme without close 'co-operation with the sales department'.[139] At Daimler, under the leadership of Martin and Manville, there was a persistent failure to integrate the productive and marketing elements of their business, which resulted in limited design innovation, inadequate costing, and an inability to meet changing fashions.[140]

Until the late 1920s, Griffiths' concerns over the management of BSA failed to generate a substantial collective shareholder voice. Although a large shareholder, Griffiths failed to challenge the established executive team, who, although willing to communicate from a distance, simply ignored his protestations. In many ways Griffiths remained a loyal company man; he did not choose exit, and took a genuine interest in the well-being of the concern. Writing in 1932, Martin recognised this, commenting that he 'has been a severe critic of the company and especially the board ... but, I must say, has always been perfectly fair and reasonable in his criticism and is only interested in the ultimate success of the company'.[141] By the late 1920s, however, the performance and management of the group had become a main focus of shareholder discontent, and an individual voice transformed into more collective action.

To understand this, there is a need to recognise that issues relating to the holding company were not divorced from the key question of accountability and disclosure. As early as 1921, Walker raised the question of adequate financial disclosure in a holding company. If each subsidiary was allowed more autonomy, he claimed, 'Each company would stand alone and there would then be no difficulty in seeing where the profit or loss was made.'[142] The fundamental issue of the transparency of financial reporting was seized upon by Griffiths. Writing to Rogers in 1922 Griffiths questioned the reduction of 'the usual' 10 per cent dividend to 5 per cent, and considered that shareholders should be given more information not only of the performance of the company overall, but of its individual subsidiaries.[143] Rogers responded in what was to become a typical manner, reminding Griffiths that the BSA directors were the guardians of the shareholder interest, and that the reduction was consistent with their judgement of a 'sound' financial policy.[144] The private intervention of Griffiths, however, and his possible influence on shareholders at

---

[138] PA 594/1/1/3/3, BSA Board Minutes, 29 February 1924, Memorandum on BSA Tools and Burton, Griffiths Ltd.

[139] PA 594/1/1/3/58, BSA Board Minutes, 30 November 1928, Report by F. W. Turrell, Managing Director BSA Tools on Organisation of Sales.

[140] Davenport-Hines, *Dudley Docker*, p. 226.

[141] PA 594/2/1/2/10, Part 1, P. Martin to Sir Alexander Roger, 4 November 1932.

[142] PA594/2/1/59, T. S. Walker to H. Rodgers, 15 December 1921.

[143] PA594/2/1/59, E. M. Griffiths to H. Rodgers, 21 February 1922.

[144] PA 594/2/1/59, H. Rogers to E. M. Griffiths, 24 February 1922.

the AGM, struck a warning note amongst the directors, leading them in advance of the 1922 AGM to craft carefully prepared answers:

> Question: Do the losses shown include the losses of all subsidiary companies? Answer [by Chair]: This is a very natural question, and I am not surprised at it being asked. I think on reflection you will agree with me that it is not in the interests of the company, and therefore the shareholders, that I should answer this question as put. I can say however, that in no instance is there a debit balance on the profit and loss account of any subsidiary company, in fact in the aggregate there is a considerable credit balance carried forward.[145]

A reluctance to disclose the detailed financial accounts of the subsidiaries was tempered with a guarantee that the balance sheet of the subsidiaries were sound, and that shareholders could trust the board to safeguard their interests. Such guarantees would seem to have sufficed. While Griffiths might protest, the vast majority of shareholders remained passive, trusting in the ability of the directors to manage their financial affairs. By the late 1920s, however, shareholders were no longer willing to stand patiently by, and a wider group of them raised issues concerning the level of financial disclosure. As BSA's profits deteriorated, shareholders now made the connection between the performance of the subsidiaries and the ability of management to effectively manage the concern, and in this context the issue of transparency became a focal point of shareholders' collective concerns. The position of the triumvirate was seriously challenged, and long-standing executives were held accountable for BSA's poor performance.

The issues of transparency that were raised by shareholders at BSA needs to be considered within the context of an extended national debate on the extent of financial reporting in the 1920s, which particularly questioned the actions of holding companies.[146] A fundamental issue was the relative contribution of the operating companies to the overall performance of the holding company, and the transparency of this to shareholders in financial accounts. A commentator on accounting, W. Back, insisted in 1924 that:

> The withdrawal of detailed accounts of working, the manipulation of stocks and reserves, and still more the formation of holding companies whose balance sheets give no real information as to their affairs have progressively withdrawn from the capitalist all real knowledge of the use of his capital.[147]

---

[145] PA594/1/1/2/6, BSA, Notes on the Accounts and Possible Questions and Answers for the 1922 AGM.

[146] See Lloyd-Jones et al., 'Corporate Governance in a Major British Holding Company, pp. 74–8; Camfferman and Zeff, 'The Apotheosis of Holding Company Accounting', pp. 171–206; Edwards, 'The Accounting Profession and Disclosure', pp. 289–303.

[147] W. Back, 'The Natural History of the Industrial Organiser', *The Accountant*, 21 June 1924.

Another commentator, Gilbert Garnsey, argued that holding companies should radically examine the level and quality of their disclosure to shareholders.[148] Important to contemporary debate in business and the accounting profession was the provision of a consolidated balance sheet. Although conservatives challenged increased disclosure, reformers called for more transparency through the publication of a consolidated balance sheet, which would amalgamate the accounts of the holding company with those of the subsidiaries to improve the reliability of information to shareholders. These debates fed into the Green Committee on Company Law and the Company Act of 1928. However, the reformers were to be disappointed; the Committee recommended only a very low level of disclosure for holding companies, and the Act simply required the parent company to publish the holding company's balance sheet/profit-and-loss account, treating the interest in subsidiaries as an investment and the dividends from them as part of profit. There was no legal requirement placed on holding companies to provide a consolidated balance sheet, and this was not enforced in Britain until the Companies Act of 1947.[149]

It was in this in the context of these national debates that Griffiths in 1927 again posed serious questions about the transparency of financial reporting, while at the same time holding accountable executive management for the performance of the company. Writing to Martin, he claimed that the holding company allowed directors to 'hide' relevant or sensitive information on the comparative performance of the operating companies.[150] Prepared to make a stand on this issue, Griffiths contacted the two auditors responsible for the BSA accounts, Carters & Co. and Touche & Co. In a letter to Carters he enclosed a cutting from *The Times* complaining that the shareholders of holding companies 'all too frequently received insufficient information', and expressed the hope that the auditors would see their 'way to give more detailed information in the coming balance sheet, to which the shareholders are justly entitled'.[151] Both auditors refused to take issue with the directors on behalf of shareholders. They considered that shareholders had no rights to force directors to disclose information which they thought inappropriate. 'Power' of disclosure rested at the discretion of directors. Nevertheless, they did acknowledge a basic logic in Griffith's arguments. Writing to Carters & Co., Touche & Co. conceded:

> As a matter of fact we have a good deal of sympathy, and we think you do too, with the point of view which Mr Griffith expresses. The grouping of assets under a few conglomerate headings is a fault in a great many balance sheets, but we agree that the BSA balance sheet offers little ground for objection under this head, beyond the very important one that the balance sheet of a holding company gives practically no information about the position of the operating

---

[148] *The Accountant*, 6 January 1923.

[149] Lloyd-Jones et al., 'Corporate Governance in a Major British Holding Company', pp. 75–7.

[150] PA594/2/1/59, E. M. Griffiths to P. Martin, 7 July 1927.

[151] PA594/2/1/59, E. M. Griffiths to Carters & Co., 10 December 1927.

companies, unless it is in the consolidated form with the assets and liabilities of the real undertakings grouped under suitable headings, and, even then, the position of the individual operating companies is not revealed.[152]

Despite their recognition of the inadequacies of financial disclosure, the auditors considered it undesirable that they should be 'inveigled into a discussion with a shareholder' about the accounts.[153] The justness of Griffiths' case was acknowledged, but his effectiveness in bringing about change was constrained by the right of the directors to use their discretion concerning the disclosure of information. Griffiths, however, could not be lightly dismissed. He was a large shareholder, a successful businessman, and an knowledgeable investor, and he represented a formidable challenge. The directors were well aware of the threat, and Rogers ensured that he remained in contact with the auditors, and insisted on being informed of all correspondence with Griffiths.[154] A director of Savilles, R. A. Rotherham, went further when he suggested to Martin in July 1928 that the BSA board would have to consider means to 'fight' him, even if this entailed offering him a place back on the board as a precursor to Griffiths buying back his interests in Burton, Griffiths.[155] Griffiths, however, was not to be so easily cajoled.

A letter to Carters from Griffiths demonstrated the dangerous nature of his accusations to the reputation of the BSA board. In it he referred to financial scandals at 'Messrs Vickers, Armstrong, Whitworth, Marconi etc', and attached a list of suggestions for information that might be included in the BSA reports.[156] The board was forced to make concessions in April 1928, providing a consolidated statement that listed the aggregated assets and liabilities of the subsidiaries. This progressive move by the directors, which reflected general trends in the 1920s towards modest increases in group disclosure,[157] did not satisfy Griffiths, who pointed out that all the reserve accounts, including profit-and-loss and depreciation, were 'lumped together'. Consolidated balance sheets did little to reveal the actual performance of the individual operating companies, and while he acknowledged that the board had shifted its ground he continued to assert that the information provided to shareholders remained 'difficult and obscure'.[158] Despite this, by the standard of the times, BSA's financial report for 1929 was ahead of regulatory requirements. Its consolidated balance sheet was praised for its clarity by *The Economist*, as 'hitherto the company's accounts have been presented in an obscure form'. In 1931 BSA revealed the 'identity' of its subsidiaries, and at the AGM the

---

[152] PA594/2/1/59, Touche & Co. to Carters & Co., 15 December 1927.

[153] PA594/2/1/59 Carters & Co. to Touche & Co., 11 January 1928.

[154] Ibid.

[155] PA 594/2/1/59, Memorandum by R. Rotherham to P. Martin, 18 July 1928.

[156] PA594/2/1/59, E. M. Griffiths to Carters & Co., 3 January 1928.

[157] See Edwards, *A History of Financial Accounting*.

[158] PA594/2/1/59, E. M. Griffiths to E. Manville, 5 April 1928.

chairman provided some clues as to 'status and conditions'.[159] Indeed, Edward Manville, chairing his first AGM in 1929, following the resignation of Rogers in 1928 through ill health, stated that his directors had met the 'wishes' of the shareholders.[160]

Changes to reporting standards were one thing, but they did little to appease shareholders. A conjuncture of forces in the late 1920s and early 1930s acted to place increasing pressure on the parent company board. These included the deteriorating financial performance of the company (Table 4.5), the mounting problems at Daimler, and Griffiths' mobilisation of wider shareholder support in which he linked the management record of the company with its disclosure policy. In periods of business uncertainty, and decline, organisational problems might lead to rapid exit by the firm's customers with little loss to themselves. But the choice between exit and voice for shareholders is more complex because decisions to exit might involve financial loss if the problems facing the business depress the share price. Shareholders might choose to remain loyal and passive and hold their stock, assuming that any action on their part would be unlikely to influence the decisions of directors. Alternatively, they might decide to exercise voice and use the governance mechanisms, such as the AGM, to hold directors to account.[161] BSA shareholders largely chose not to exit, and their motives reflected the interaction of long-standing loyalty with falling share prices, which significantly increased the cost of exit. Griffiths informed Martin in 1931 that 'British stockholders are called "patient oxen" and suffer silently, still there are many in the company whose money has been invested for them by their forefathers and who depend largely for dividends as their means of livelihood'.[162] Only on three occasions were ordinary dividends paid between 1921 and 1931 (Table 4.5). Share prices remained low throughout the 1920s, and in 1931 were just 7s 6d compared to 59s 6d at their peak in 1918.[163] Such a trend saddled ordinary shareholders with shares on which they were bound to make a loss on disposal and which did not generate a satisfactory return. One of many shareholders who communicated was R. Harold Smith, a retired teacher, who insisted that 'the first duty of any board' was to ensure regular dividends 'which … is all they have to live on'. A female shareholder 'of many years' protested her loyalty, but 'the shares cost me 57s 3d and you see what they are today, and no dividend'.[164]

---

[159] *The Economist*, 1 April 1929; 12 December 1931.

[160] PA594/1/1/2/10, BSA Meeting File, Transcript of AGM, 3 May 1929.

[161] Lloyd-Jones et al., 'Corporate Governance in a Major British Holding Company', pp. 71–2.

[162] PA594/2/1/59, E. M. Griffiths to P. Martin, 23 November 1931.

[163] Lloyd-Jones et al., 'Control, Conflict and Concession', p. 168.

[164] PA594/1/1/2/13, BSA Meeting File, R. Harold Smith to Secretary BSA, 2 December 1931; Transcript of AGM, December 1931.

Foregoing exit, shareholders rallied around Griffiths, who was also 'in the painful position of owning 47,000 shares'.[165] In early 1929, Griffiths made a bold move to organise collective shareholder action, when he proposed to Manville that the board should appoint a prominent business leader to represent large shareholders. Griffiths even suggested his own nominees, a choice between Sir Herbert Austin and Sir Alfred Herbert. At the same time Griffiths suggested that a committee should be appointed to investigate the poor profit record of the company, and when Manville politely declined, he circulated to large shareholders (holding 5,000+ shares) a letter reviewing the profits. Over the previous eight and a half years, BSA had produced an average return of 1.75 per cent on its share capital and paid no ordinary dividend in 1927 and 1928; Rolls-Royce had paid an 8 per cent dividend, the Enfield Cycle Co. 10 per cent, and Edgar Allen & Co. and Kayser Ellison, two prominent Sheffield steelmakers, 2.5 per cent and 5 per cent respectively.[166] These comparisons were representative of companies producing similar commodities to the BSA group, and they delivered to their shareholders a far better financial return.

By 1929 Griffiths may be described as an unelected representative of the main body of shareholders who began to protest as an organised group. He engaged in personal correspondence and negotiations with the parent board directors, circularised shareholders, produced alternative financial statements, asked awkward questions at AGMs, mooted the formation of a committee of large shareholders, and attempted to instigate a committee of inquiry into the management of BSA.[167] Griffiths identified himself with shareholders whom he considered as investors, rather than speculators. Investors were the 'backbone of the company', displaying loyalty to the long-term future of BSA.[168] Such actions provided encouragement to other shareholders to voice their complaints concerning the board's stewardship, and directors such as Martin and Manville came under increasing pressure. This led to a crisis, which undermined the governance of the leading directors in the early 1930s.

As BSA's finances deteriorated from the end of the 1920s, the board's stewardship came under increasing scrutiny and shareholders expressed growing scepticism over the strategy pursued by Manville and Martin. Following the lead of Griffiths a growing number of shareholders believed that crucial aspects of the holding company's performance were being obscured. This problem applied in particular to Daimler, BSA's most prestigious subsidiary, which was under Manville and Martin's direct control. The 1910 merger with Daimler left Manville and Martin as chairman and managing director respectively, positions they continued to hold in additions to their roles on the main board. Daimler performed poorly in the 1920s. Its commitment to the high-quality range of the market proved

---

[165] PA594/1/1/2/15, BSA Meeting File, Transcript of AGM, November 1932.

[166] PA594/2/1/59, E. M. Griffiths to E. Manville, 21 February 1929; Manville to Griffiths, 22, 26 February 1929; Circular by E. M. Griffiths to shareholders, March 1929.

[167] Lloyd-Jones et al., 'Control, Conflict and Concession', pp. 170–79.

[168] PA 594/1/2/15, BSA meeting file, Transcript of AGM, 15 November 1932.

unsuccessful as it experienced a number of embarrassing technical problems with its engines. For example, Manville and Martin had bought the rights to the sleeve valve engine in 1908. Despite problems with its design and manufacture, they persisted with applying it to the company's vehicles until 1933.[169] A move into omnibus production in 1920 through the formation of Associated Daimler, a joint venture with the Associated Equipment Co., proved yet another failure. By 1928, Associated Equipment had become disillusioned with the inability of Daimler to produce competitive vehicles using engines and chassis supplied by them. Deficiencies in engineering capability led to a catastrophic relative fall in Daimler's sales in the depression of the early 1930s (Table 4.6), and precipitated a financial crisis at the holding company which undermined the reputations of Manville and Martin. Their control weakened, and shareholder voice became louder and more focused at the company's AGM in 1931.

Table 4.6   BSA sales, 1930 and 1932

	1930 (£)	% total sales	1932 (£)	% total sales	% change
Daimler	390,963	35.2	164,220	18.7	-58.0
BSA Cycles	370,706	33.4	316,596	36.1	-14.6
Jessops	106,315	9.6	134,484	15.3	+26.5
Savilles	83,299	7.5	76,212	8.7	-8.5
Burton Griffiths	74,293	6.7	47,877	5.5	-35.5
BSA Tools	44,503	4.0	81,130	9.3	+82.3
BSA Guns	25,315	2.3	39,604	4.5	+56.8
Arthur Andrews	7,857	0.7	6820	0.8	-13.2
British Abrasive Wheel	6,336	0.6	10,076	1.1	+59.3
Total	1,109,587	100.0	877,019	100.0	-20.9

Source: PA594/2/1/2/14, Coventry Sales Summary.

The 1931 AGM proceeded in a hostile atmosphere. Shareholders launched scathing attacks focused on the performance of Daimler, managerial inadequacies,

---

[169] Davenport-Hines, *Dudley Docker*, p. 225; B. Thackery, *The AEC Story: Part One* (Glossop, Venture Publications, 2001), pp. 96–102; PA 594/4/4/1/6, Part 1, Memorandum by P. Martin on AEC, 16 April 1928.

the level of financial disclosure, and a zero dividend while directors continued to accept generous salaries. In the run-up to the AGM letters from shareholders to the chairman, Manville, already indicated that the meeting was not going to be easily managed: A. Sells castigated the company's performance and brought attention to the fact that 'directors drew something like £100,000', and E. van Notten Pole thought it 'the worst report ever given, and I can only hope that in the future some law may be passed to protect the investor and make the men who so misuse their money responsible for it'. Another shareholder, F. H. Thompson, considered that 'the directors allocate to themselves almost autocratic powers to purchase any sort of business without consulting the shareholders'. A caustic letter from 'a fed up BSA shareholder', with a long memory, pointed out that 'if you want to buy any more dud companies I have one or two I should like to sell including an aircraft company'.[170] At the AGM itself, Sells questioned the accuracy of financial reporting, and condemned the payment of £8,600 to directors which compared to just £5,500 at 'A magnificent concern like Tube Investments'. Further, in a throwback to 1906, a number of shareholders questioned the substantial build-up of reserves, totalling £2 million in the general BSA reserve and £2.2 million in the reserves of the subsidiaries. Despite the usual plea of prudence by the directors, shareholders remained dissatisfied when they equated the reserve with the fact that they received no dividend. As tensions rose, they targeted the ineffective marketing of Daimler cars. Morris and Austin, claimed Sells, had a highly effective marketing policy, and what BSA required was 'hard headed businessmen' such as William Morris or Herbert Austin; if these had been connected with the company 'we would have been rolling in wealth'. Sells concluded, 'unfortunately there had been no one of that sort connected with the company'. Other shareholders continued to berate Manville, who became embroiled in a heated debate with Sells, which exposed his own deficient knowledge of the accounts and the status of individual subsidiaries. Manville finally ended the trial with the statement 'It is too complicated to explain in a few words. If you want a detailed explanation I will see that you are written to'.[171]

To the dismay of his fellow directors, Manville failed to stem the tide of criticism, and attempts to pacify shareholders by plans to strengthen the management on the BSA board came under intense shareholder scrutiny. Manville, supported by Martin and Arthur Pollen, the latter a director since 1923, advocated the appointment of four of the managing directors of the subsidiary companies to the BSA board, but this was perceived by shareholders as a means to perpetuate a board based on personal ties and loyalties. In the words of Sells it equated to 'a family party'. Shareholders now questioned the personalised style of management, involving a clique of long-standing directors, who lacked the capability and

---

[170] PA594/1/1/2/13, BSA Meetings File, A. Sells to E. Manville, 9 December 1931; E. van Notten Pole to Manville, 24 November 1931; F. H. Thompson to Manville, 24 November 1931; anonymous, dated 23 November 1931.

[171] PA594/1/1/2/13, BSA Meetings File, Transcript of AGM, December 1931.

knowledge to manage the specialised and diverse activities of the company.[172] These allegations owed much to the machinations of Griffiths, who prior to the 1931 AGM had roundly rejected any suggestion of hand-picked directors, who 'were expected to "say yea to your yea and nay to your nay"'. Griffiths, back on the topic of the inefficiency of centralised management, registered his concern over 'the number of officials with titles which appear to be growing', and these appointees, drawing 'lucrative salaries', were 'not commensurate' with the profit record of BSA. Rather than extend centralised management, Griffiths proposed a more rationalised managerial board. His alternative consisted of Martin as president, able to have an 'over-looking capacity of the whole concern', a vice president, appointed from outside, who would be a business and financial man of 'push and go', and a consultative technical director, to support them. 'The old style Board of Directors is out of date; it has had its trial since the war and has been found wanting'. This had resulted, according to Griffiths, in an 'unfortunate system of appointing directors having no knowledge of the business [which] has been tolerated too long in this country ... Directors serving on multiple companies are a great source of weakness'.[173] There was to be no place for either Manville or Pollard in the Griffiths scheme. At the 1931 AGM Manville's knowledge of BSA affairs and his understanding of the overall performance of the company were tested by shareholders to the full, while at the same time they observed that his outside business interests were distracting him from effective management. That Manville was over-stretched was well known to shareholders; not only did he sit as a director on all the subsidiary boards, but he also held directorships in 25 other companies, both British and foreign, industrial and service.[174]

Arthur Pollen rightly described the 1931 AGM as a 'fiasco',[175] and it certainly did little for Manville's reputation with shareholders. The AGM witnessed a significant outpouring of shareholder discontent, but it did not necessarily mean that they could pressure the executive into making radical managerial changes. Control still rested with a dominant executive, and the board's resolution at the 1931 AGM to appoint directors, drawn from the subsidiary companies, to the parent board was carried unanimously. This owed much to the fact that members of the board were also major shareholders (Table 4.7), with a direct interest in protecting their own positions. In addition, many shareholders did not attend AGMs, but voted by proxy, displaying what Sells referred to as a high degree of apathy. Sells went further, accusing the directors of 'the skilful use of proxies', which 'rendered helpless' shareholders attending meetings.[176] Despite a more collective and focused voice, shareholders still remained impotent to force change. Manville's eventual demise owed as much to external forces, and the role of Dudley Docker and the

---

[172] Ibid.

[173] PA594/2/1/59, E. M. Griffiths to P. Martin, 23 September 1931.

[174] PA594/2/1/1/2, Directors' Declaration of Interest under Companies Act, 1929.

[175] PA594/2/1/2/23, A. H. J. Pollen to P. Martin, 8 December 1931.

[176] PA594/1/1/2/13, BSA Meeting File, A. Sells to Secretary, BSA, 9 December 1931.

Midland Bank, which responded to growing shareholder protest, as it did to the 'fiasco' of the AGM.

Table 4.7   BSA board: holdings of BSA shares 1932

A. H. Pollen	10,000
E. Manville	7,000
P. Martin	87,000
A. H. E. Wood	70,000
Hannon	2,000
Chapman	1,000
Capt. E.G. Wood	3,000

Source: PA594/1/1/2/15, BSA Meeting File, 15 November 1915.

Reconstruction, the Midland Bank, and corporate governance, 1931–35

The key factor that brought the Midland Bank into governance at BSA from 1931 was the issue of liquidity. In 1928, BSA had instigated a capital restructuring, supported by the bank, by issuing debenture stock. Falling sales and revenue by 1930 constrained revenue generation and the company was hampered by high debenture interest payments.[177] A liquidity crisis at BSA greatly concerned senior bank officials, especially given the faltering business in motor cars. General manager of the Coventry branch of the Midland Bank, H. A. Astbury, registered his concerns in March 1931:

> The demand for their cars has fallen off and production has practically stopped. There is no doubt price has something to do with this as well as performance ... I have also heard it stated the management is not what it should be and complaints are rife as to excessive charges for repairs. Frankly I am not at all comfortable with the present position. If further accommodation [of the overdraft] is required I think the question of security should be raised.[178]

At the time of the 1931 AGM, Astbury's concerns had materialised into direct action, the bank ruling that any future extension of the BSA overdraft should

---

[177] PA594/1/1/2/12, BSA Meeting File, Transcript of AGM, Chairman's Speech, October 1930.

[178] Hong Kong and Shanghai Banking Corporation (HSBC) Archives, 358/13, Coventry Reference Book, 1923–37, 7 March 1931.

be conditional on bank representation in 'management'.[179] Initially, Martin and Manville attempted to circumvent this through 'channels by which we could influence the choice'. Consequently, they proposed to the bank T. G. Rose, a management consultant who had previously worked with Pollen when he was chairman at International Linotype Ltd. Pollen described Rose as a man 'who would know how to keep faith with the bank without being a thorn in the side of management'.[180] In the event, they were overruled and Sir Mark Webster Jenkinson, former auditor for the Ministry of Munitions, filled the supervisory role, giving the bank a direct involvement in governance.

Instrumental in Jenkinson's appointment was Dudley Docker, who had initially brokered the Daimler acquisition of 1910, and who had personally supported the careers of Martin and Manville at BSA. Docker was a member of the Midland board, and through his position as chairman of the Birmingham Advisory Committee of the bank had sanctioned the overdraft requirements of BSA. The appointment of Jenkinson went beyond a supervisory role, as the bank instructed him to investigate the policy of management and the effectiveness of the holding-company structure.[181] In a letter to Griffiths, Pollen denied that the bank had exerted pressure, claiming that Jenkinson was 'our selection and appointment', but he did add that Jenkinson was given an important position as an advisor to Martin, enabling the latter to reduce his 'responsibilities and duties'.[182] What was clear was that the appointment represented the intent of the bank to have its say in the running of the company. A meeting between Astbury and Martin, with Jenkinson in attendance, in May 1932, demonstrated the influence that the bank could now exert. Priority was given to the performance of the Daimler business, and the acquisition by BSA in 1931 of the Lanchester Motor Co. Martin's policy for the ailing Daimler business was to expand the manufacturing programme at Lanchester, which produced smaller, lower-priced cars. The finance for this required an extension of the bank overdraft to Daimler of £130,000, but Astbury only conceded on the condition that Jenkinson was satisfied with progress. Jenkinson's remit from the bank thus extended into monitoring business performance, and in July 1932 he compiled a report on operations, to be followed by a review in September. Both Martin and Astbury were fully aware that the overall financial stability of BSA rested with a resurgence of the Daimler business, of which Lanchester was a key factor, but bank concerns over indebtedness took priority.[183] The bank now assumed a direct strategic role, proposing as part of a capital restructuring plan for BSA a rationalisation of the holding company structure through the creation of clearly defined product divisions (Table 4.8).

[179] PA594/2/1/2/23, A. H. Pollen to P. Martin, 28 December 1931.

[180] PA594/2/1/2/23, A. J. H. Pollen to P. Martin, 29 December 1931.

[181] R. P. T. Davenport-Hines, 'Pollen, Arthur Joseph Hungerford', in Jeremy (ed.), *Dictionary of Business Biography*, p. 755.

[182] PA594/2/1/59, A. J. H. Pollen to P. Martin, 15 April 1932.

[183] 358/13 Coventry Reference Book, 5 May 1932.

Table 4.8   Proposed BSA divisional structure, 1932

Divisions	Subsidiaries
BSA Co.	BSA Cycles / BSA Guns
Daimler Co.	Lanchester Motors
BSA Tools	Arthur Andrews[a] / Burton, Griffiths
Jessops & Sons	Savilles

Source: PA594/9/1/3/2, Proposed Capital Reconstruction, 1932.
Note: a. Acquired in 1930.

The BSA board, while prepared to accept changes in financial arrangements, were less than enthusiastic when it came to changing the organisational structure of the holding company, and they argued that any practical advantages accruing from the proposed reconstruction would be 'outweighed by the expenses and dislocation involved'.[184] Facing resistance to organisational change, the bank became a party to attempts to reconfigure the executive board, with Manville as the chief scapegoat. In July 1932, R. A. Rotherham, a director of Savilles, called on Astbury to seek reassurance that the bank would continue to finance operations. During the discussion, the topic arose of Jenkinson's report on the viability of Daimler, and Astbury informed Rotherham that this had been viewed unfavourably by Docker. Subsequent to this meeting Docker had discussed with Martin and Manville their future in the company, and persuaded Martin to resign as managing director of BSA and Daimler, assuming a new role as general manager. More significant was the fact that Manville agreed to submit a letter of resignation, to be replaced by Pollen as chairman.[185] This did not end the affair, however, and Docker's intervention had not run its course. Although Pollen succeeded as chairman, Docker supported the retention of Martin as a director, who had now accepted the need to carry out the bank's reforms. Docker's support of Manville was purely pragmatic, and he reminded Astbury of the fact that Manville held a considerable number of directorships outside of BSA, which had business with the bank, and 'if he were he not offered the option of continuing as a director, he might think it due to the bank's actions'. For all intents and purposes, and despite the succession of Pollard as chairman, the old guard of Manville and Martin remained in place. Presumably aware of shareholder reaction, Docker pressed Astbury on the need to put into operation a representative governance structure with the inclusion of two shareholder directors.[186]

By the summer of 1932, the bank and Docker had taken an initiative in the reorganisation of executive management, partly as a response to growing

[184] PA594/9/1/3/2, Correspondence on Proposed Restructuring, 26 July 1932.
[185] 30/100, Diary of H. A. Astbury, 1 July 1932.
[186] 30/100, 4 July 1932.

shareholder voice, but also from the bank's perspective as a safeguard against financial liabilities. As Astbury informed Docker in July, the success of the Daimler business remained problematic, and the extension of overdraft facilities should be handled with 'considerable care'.[187] Trust by the bank in management had been dealt a serious blow. Following a meeting with Pollen, Astbury noted that Pollen had omitted to tell him that the BSA Company owed the Daimler Company £75,000, which it had on loan, and could be repaid to limit the unsecured accommodation to the Daimler Company.[188] By 1932, the bank had become central to the governance of BSA, but its role in changing management was unknown to most ordinary shareholders, as was its impact on appeasing shareholder concerns. Despite initiatives associated with shifts in top personnel, 1932 brought little respite from shareholder criticism, and at that year's AGM Pollen faced fierce shareholder attacks. Leading the assault was Griffiths. After praising the fact that the balance sheet 'was more clear than most holding companies', he nevertheless considered that it lacked detail on the trading losses of individual subsidiaries, notably Daimler. Receiving only yes/no answers from Pollen, Griffiths then turned his attention to the issue of no dividend payment, and the culpability of the executive. He observed that 'The composition of the board has changed very considerably from last year', and that Martin, 'the managing director of the whole of the companies, has resigned, and now seeks re-election as a director. Why?' Answering his own question he pointed out that both Martin and Manville, 'who also seeks re-election, are to my mind largely responsible for the position in which the company finds itself today'. On the issue of Pollen's appointment as chairman, Griffiths was equally scathing, observing that that 'this is rather a change of name than a change of policy'. For Griffiths, the changes in management were no more than a ploy to secure the continuation of a management regime that had failed. These long-standing executives represented a clique of businessmen, networked through a series of cross-directorships, both within the holding company and externally. Shareholders correspondingly held the executive to account on the matter of cross-directorships at the 1932 AGM.[189]

Renowned for his 'impulsive and dictatorial methods',[190] Pollen avoided the question of cross-directorships, and declared further discussions 'closed', safe in the knowledge that they had enough proxy votes to pass a resolution to re-elect the directors. What followed was symptomatic of the difficulties facing shareholders in their attempts to exert influence on the board, and also demonstrated the undemocratic nature of governance at BSA:

> Chair: Does any shareholder demand a poll?
> Several Voices: Yes.

[187] Ibid.

[188] HSBC, 30/100, 11 July 1932.

[189] PA 594/1/1/2/15, Transcript of AGM, December 1932.

[190] Davenport-Hines, 'Pollen', p. 755.

Chair: Right get up and demand it.

Griffiths: May I say that you need not fall into the trap gentlemen. They evidently have sufficient proxies to carry it.

Chair: Are you proposing a poll?

Griffiths: No.

Chair: Then you are not in order. No poll is demanded and the discussion is closed and the resolution is carried.[191]

The 1932 AGM, nevertheless, spelled the end for Manville. Following the AGM, he resigned as chairman, having upset several fellow board members including the reinstated Martin.[192] BSA now appointed their third chairman of 1932 when Sir Alexander Roger, described as 'a strong supporter of the bank', accepted the post.[193] Roger had the support both of Dudley Docker and the chairman of the Midland Bank, Reginald McKenna, and he held the chair for the remainder of the 1930s.[194] During the managerial shake-up, Docker finally removed Martin from the board in December 1933, allegedly after a year in which Martin had 'opposed and insulted' Alexander Roger at every opportunity.[195] The change in executives did represent an important evolutionary development in the style of governance at BSA and demonstrated that shareholders carried influence as they became more organised and collective criticism replaced individual complaint. Their voice at AGMs also became more focused around clear themes of discontent, and they became more demanding in terms of the greater accountability of directors for their stewardship of the company. Voice did matter at BSA. In 1934 and 1935 directors sanctioned the publication of more detailed accounts,[196] but the financial problems of the company continued, and Daimler remained a burden to recovery. A shareholder in 1933 asked the new chairman: 'why do our competitors in the car industry pay dividends and in some cases enormous dividends?' At the 1934 AGM another complained that 'we are told the same thing every year but we get nothing'.[197] Similar dissatisfaction resonated at the AGM of 1935, as did the issue of explanation of the financial composition of the accounts. At the latter meeting, O. E. B. Smith, a large shareholder, observed that

---

[191]   PA 594/1/1/2/15, Transcript of AGM, December 1932.

[192]   Davenport-Hines, 'Pollen', p. 755.

[193]   HSBC, 30/100, 19 March 1934.

[194]   R. P. T. Davenport-Hines, 'Roger, Sir Alexander Forbes Proctor', in Jeremy (ed.), *Dictionary of Business Biography*, p. 968; *Sunday Express*, 23 July 1933.

[195]   Davenport-Hines, 'Pollen', p. 756.

[196]   PA594/1/1/2/17, and PA594/1/1/2/18, BSA Meeting Files, Transcript of AGMs, December 1934 and December 1935.

[197]   PA 594/1/1/2/16, Transcript of AGM, December 1933; PA594/1/1/2/17, Transcript of AGM, December 1934.

our auditors are watching our interests ... but after all auditors are guided and controlled by the [1928 Companies] Act which is ... out of date in many respects, particularly in regard to holding companies, which do not empower the disclosure of the stocks and debts of individual companies.[198]

If BSA is typical, then, above all else, governance in British manufacturing by the 1930s was hardly democratic and open. The changes in executive management in 1932, although prompted by shareholders, had more to do with the political machinations of Docker, and the financial security of the bank. Docker had hinted at greater shareholder participation, but this was hardly forthcoming. As Smith put it, 'I again make the suggestion that there should be an independent, impartial investigation by experts in order to arrest the retrogression of this old established company, and the appointment of shareholder representatives to the board.'[199]

What shareholders got was Alexander Roger, a bank appointee, and the influence of the bank in governance was remarked upon by Astbury in 1937, who considered that 'all along the bank had helped this company considerably by suggesting new directors who were enhancing the reputation of the company'.[200] Shareholder trust, however, was not easily restored, and Roger, who like his predecessors, held a number of external directorships, was accused of having no knowledge of the business conducted by BSA. Summarising the views of shareholders on the appointment of Roger in 1932, Griffiths observed that 'he [Roger] is a director of twenty companies largely interested in cables and telephones ... what knowledge of the BSA Company's goods does that bring?'[201] One of the first actions of Roger was to commission a major report on the structure of the holding company, similar to that conducted by Jenkinson before him.[202] No change was instigated, and BSA remained a loose confederation of subsidiaries. Nevertheless, from 1935 profits rose sharply, and enabled a restoration of dividend payments in 1938. At last, the shareholders got their share.

Conclusion

BSA's history at the beginning of the twentieth century is of particular relevance to an understanding of the UK development of corporate governance, and in particular the implications of personal capitalism for British industry. BSA is important because it exemplified some important features of industrial history during this period. It showed the pattern of rapid growth in response to the production demands

[198]   PA594/1/1/2/18, Transcript of AGM, December 1935.

[199]   Ibid.

[200]   HSBC, 30/100, 20 January 1937.

[201]   PA594/1/1/2/15, Transcript of AGM, December 1932.

[202]   MSS 19A/1/2/56, Report to Sir Alexander Roger' by D. H. Allan, 3 February 1933.

of the First World War, followed in quick succession by peace-time optimism and then slump, which is seen in the stories of Hadfield and Raleigh. Like these latter two companies, BSA made unsuccessful post-war attempts at diversification – in Hadfields' case the motor manufacturer Bean, in Raleigh's the development of cars and a three-wheeler, in BSA's most notably the airline manufacturers AMC and Hooker. Financial disclosure was a continuing preoccupation for BSA's shareholders, from the 1906 *Newton v Chambers* case to the complaints surrounding uninformative accounts in the 1920s and 1930s. Similarly, reporting was an issue for Raleigh until the late 1940s, and it was only the passing of the 1947 Companies Act that obliged it to produce informative group accounts.

Perhaps the most revealing aspect of governance at BSA is the light it casts on the relationship between its directors and its shareholders. BSA's directors made considerable efforts to join influential networks, in politics and in industrial associations, as well as their numerous cross-directorships, and enjoyed considerable status outside the company. This was no different from Harold Bowden at Raleigh, or Robert Hadfield, but unlike these business leaders the directors of BSA experienced tense and frequently acrimonious exchanges with their shareholders. The correspondence surrounding the AGMs and the meetings themselves highlight the shareholders' dependence on dividend income and their acute disappointment at the company's persistent failure to compete with, for instance, other motor manufacturers in the inter-war period.

Cheffins, in his discussion of shareholder behaviour in the inter-war period, concludes that shareholders 'generally … adopted a passive stance', but he does have to concede that it was at least theoretically possible for dissident shareholders to mount a challenge that had to be taken seriously.[203] Inter-war events concerning BSA illustrate the point. The 'fiasco' AGM of 1931 and the rapid changes in chairman the following year represent a challenge to the view of personal capitalism as a bulwark for directors against shareholders whose opinions they could safely ignore. The BSA case study suggests that the relationship between directors and shareholders of other inter-war companies deserves to be studied in the same detail.

---

[203] Cheffins, *Corporate Ownership and Control*, p. 295.

Chapter 5

Alfred Herbert Ltd: The Individualistic Element in Corporate Governance and the Legacy of Personal Control

Introduction

Personal capitalism, and an individualistic style of leadership, permeated the history of Britain's largest machine-tool maker, Alfred Herbert Ltd of Coventry. Indeed, of all the companies discussed in this book, in no other did the role of its founder endure the test of time for so long. Founded by Alfred Herbert in 1887, the company remained a private concern until its public conversion in 1944, guided by its self-styled 'chairman and governing director'. Thereafter, until his death aged 90 in 1957, Alfred Herbert continued to remain the dominant figure, and was supported by selected directors who had been groomed to succeed him. To understand the governance of the company, a number of key themes are explored in the chapter. First, the chapter examines the characteristics of the British machine-tool industry, a sector of key importance to the nation's overall performance in manufacturing industry and in which personal capitalist forms of organisation predominated, at least until the 1960s. A second theme explores the evolution of corporate governance at Herbert, and the formation of a private limited company, which established a close-knit board of departmental directors. From its establishment to 1918 it achieved considerable business success, built upon the quality of its engineering products. The third theme concentrates on the inter-war years, and shows how the company weathered the depression without significant recourse to external finance, while at the same time maintaining a reputation for the high quality of its engineering. Under the leadership of Alfred Herbert, the company evolved an individualistic style of governance, which had wider implications for the machine-tool industry in general. The final theme of the chapter focusses on the legacy of personal capitalism after the company's conversion to public status. Alfred Herbert and his established managerial team of loyal long-term directors remained firmly in command, displaying an attitude to shareholders that may at best be described as ambivalent. But on Herbert's death in 1957 the company faced the legacy of its long personalised control as succession became a major issue in a period of rapid change.

The context: individualism in the British machine-tool industry

The British machine-tool industry, although small in scale compared to other industrial sectors, was of strategic importance to British manufacturing. Aldcroft describes machine tools as a 'barometric' industry, 'the basis on which all manufacturing industry ultimately depends'.[1] The industry exerted an influence far greater than its actual size, identified, for example, as a key sector during both world wars in the twentieth century, and central to the debates concerning the industrial problems of Britain during the inter-war years and to controversies over the modernisation of British industry in the late 1950s and the 1960s.[2] Consequently, its business history engages at various points with broad themes associated with the performance of the twentieth-century British manufacturing industry, for example the debates over declinism, the technical capabilities of British manufacturing, the reliance on American sources of machine tool technology, and from the 1960s the problems of management in reacting to organisational changes in the industry.[3]

A key characteristic of the industry was its highly fragmented structure, which reflected the population profile of the majority of firms in Britain's general engineering industries. Rationalisation and concentration did not accelerate until the 1960s, and from 1945 to the late 1950s the number of firms in the industry remained more or less constant at approximately 350. Large numbers of small, often family-controlled firms characterised the industry, and in 1959 out of the 350 firms in the industry 200 had an average annual turnover of up to £40,000.[4] The industry did possess one large firm, which quickly gained a national and international reputation; this was Alfred Herbert Ltd, which supplied a wide range of standard machine tools to the general engineering trades, both those of its own make and those of other domestic and foreign manufacturers, the latter through its factoring department. By the eve of the First World War, Herbert produced twice the output of its nearest European rival,[5] and in the 1950s it described itself as the 'largest machine tool organisation in the world', a claim based upon its extensive sales networks as a factor of machines.[6]

---

[1]   D. H. Aldcroft, 'The Performance of the British Machine-Tool Industry in the Inter-war Years', *Business History Review*, Vol. 40, No. 3 (1966), p. 282.

[2]   See Lloyd-Jones and Lewis, *Alfred Herbert Ltd.*

[3]   See Ibid., p. 1.

[4]   E. W. Evans, 'Some Problems in the Growth of the Machine Tool Industry', *Yorkshire Bulletin of Economic and Social Research*, Vol. 18 (1966), pp. 46–7; H. W. Breeley and G. W. Troup, 'The Machine Tool Industry', in D. Burn (ed.), *The Structure of British Industry: A Symposium*, Vol. 1 (Cambridge, Cambridge University Press, 1958), p. 363.

[5]   A. J. Arnold, 'Innovation, Deskilling and Profitability in the British Machine Tool Industry, 1887–1927', *Journal of Industrial History*, Vol. 1, No. 2 (1999), p. 53. This study provides a meticulous investigation of the Herbert accounts, which are extensively cited in this chapter.

[6]   *Machine Tool Review* (published by Alfred Herbert Ltd), Vol. 43 (1955), p. 113.

Within the industry, a distinctive feature of firms was a strong attachment to individualism and personal capitalist forms of ownership and control, and there was little scope until the 1960s for merger, or indeed for collaboration. Machine firms developed their products on individual lines, and the industry generally lacked institutional arrangements. For example, firms remained highly secretive in relation to the dissemination of technical knowledge to their competitors. In 1918, when the Department of Scientific and Industrial Research (DSIR) invited the Machine Tools Trade Association (MTTA) to form a research association for machine tools, it rejected the offer, preferring instead to respect the prerogative of 'individualistic' firms to conduct their own business affairs.[7] During the 1920s, when rationalisation through amalgamation was seen by many business leaders as a panacea to depression, the firms in the machine-tool industry resisted change. With the exception of Associated British Machine Tool Makers Ltd, a sales organisation formed in 1917, there was no centralised marketing in the industry to co-ordinate the activities of large numbers of small producers, and larger firms operated individually, organising marketing through their own domestic branch offices or overseas sales companies.[8] An engineer, W. George, believed in 1929 that collaborative action was unfeasible because of the problems of reconciling 'the conflicting thoughts that exist in groups of employers [and] the many personal jealousies and fears in individuals who are essentially in competition with each other'.[9] In 1929, the leading trade journal *The American Machinist* considered that 'Although rationalisation is put forward as a partial solution to trading problems, many machine firms 'adhere to the individualistic feature which has characterised British production up to the present'.[10] Prominent Scottish machine-tool maker W. J. Lang had no doubt that 'individualism' was a central attribute of the industry, bringing with it a technical knowledge of engineering practices, when he informed the MTTA in 1930 that it is 'as important today as ever it was despite combination and amalgamation among firms' in British industry.[11] Individualistic behaviour, as we shall see, permeated the boardroom of Alfred Herbert Ltd, Britain's largest and leading machine maker. The evolution of this individualistic style of governance at Herbert, and of the ideal of private enterprise for the governance of business, is explored below.

---

[7]   Private Records of the MTTA, Machine Tool and Engineering Employers Association, Minute Book, 3 October, 13 November 1918.

[8]   *The American Machinist*, 8 January 1925, p. 2E.

[9]   *The American Machinist*, 20 April 1929, pp. 124–5E.

[10]   *The American Machinist*, 24 May 1930, p. 219E.

[11]   MTTA, Annual Report, 1930.

Sir Alfred Herbert: governance in a private company, 1887–1919

The company was founded as a partnership between Alfred Edward Herbert, who was just 21, and William Hubbard, in 1887, employing 12 workers. Alfred became the sole owner in 1894 of a limited company, with a nominal capital of £25,000. In 1894, Herbert was the only shareholder in the company, but as the company expanded in the 1890s the capital base was widened to include family members and managers as shareholders.[12] Between Alfred's accession and 1897 the company grew rapidly, building machines and supplying components to the rapidly expanding bicycle industry in Coventry.[13] When the bicycle boom collapsed in 1897, the company diversified into building machines for the emerging Coventry motor car industry, and gained a reputation as a high-quality producer of capstan and turret lathes, which were influenced by American designs.[14] By 1914, Herbert was one of 17 firms in Coventry that specialised in supplying machinery to the bicycle, motor vehicle and small arms trade.[15] Total employment rose from 12 in 1887 to 500 by the end of the bicycle boom in 1897, 930 in 1903, and 2,000 by 1914. On the eve of the First World War Herbert had become the largest machine-tool maker in Europe, and by this date accounted for an estimated 42 per cent of all British machine-tool output.[16]

Expansion reflected the rising demand for both the company's own machine tools and those of foreign and other British makers, which were sold and marketed through Herbert's factoring operations, and the extension of its sales networks. As Table 5.1 shows, Herbert sales expanded considerably from 1888 to 1914, subject to the cyclical pattern which was a characteristic of capital goods makers who were reliant upon the fluctuations in demand in the engineering trades.[17] Prior to 1914, the company experienced generally rising profitability (Table 5.2). Its net profits rose rapidly between 1896 and 1907, and despite a fall during the recession of 1908 and 1909 they accelerated again during the boom that preceded the war. Net profit percentage averaged 21 per cent between 1896 and 1907, and 15.4 per cent between 1908 and 1914. Herbert's success was based upon its ability to sell a range of machine tools at highly remunerative prices, and shareholders duly received the rewards from the high net profit. Between 1896 and 1907 the rate of return on capital employed averaged 23 per cent, and between 1910 and 1914 14 per cent. Relative to average returns on industrial investment at this time,

---

[12] Lloyd-Jones and Lewis, *Alfred Herbert Ltd*, p. 29.

[13] *Machine Tool Review*, Vol. 18 (1930), p. 58.

[14] Records of Alfred Herbert Ltd, PA 1270/4/1, Oscar Harmer for the Alfred Herbert Testimonial, 22 July 1917.

[15] R. Floud, *The British Machine Tool Industry, 1850–1914* (Cambridge, Cambridge University Press, 1976), p. 38.

[16] Ibid., pp. 57, 61; Lloyd-Jones and Lewis, *Alfred Herbert Ltd*, p. 28.

[17] See Arnold, 'Innovation', pp. 56–7, 61–3.

it represented a very high level of profitability.[18] From this perspective, and in relation to the fact that the British machine-tool industry faced intense competition, especially from American makers, during this period, Herbert was an example of a highly innovative company which responded to competition by developing novel machine tools, and through its factoring activities, which represented at various times a high proportion of total sales, could supply a wide range of machines to meet the needs of its customers.[19]

Table 5.1   Alfred Herbert sales: own and factored machine tools (£000), 1888–1914

	Factored	Own	Total	% factored
1888	0.0	2.5	2.5	0.0
1889	3.6	4.4	8.0	45.0
1890	12.9	7.7	20.6	62.6
1891	19.4	9.6	29.0	66.9
1892	14.1	8.7	22.8	61.8
1893	5.4	9.7	15.1	35.8
1894	3.3	14.0	17.3	19.1
1895	3.5	18.0	21.5	16.3
1896	7.5	41.3	48.8	15.4
1897	4.0	62.6	66.6	6.0
1898	1.0	86.2	87.2	1.1
1899	0.0	99.2	99.2	0.0
1900	27	91	118	22.9
1901	26	91	117	22.2
1902	29	113	142	20.6
1903	23	131	154	15.0
1904	21	142	163	12.9
1905	35	183	217	16.1
1906	52	198	250	20.8
1907	92	232	324	28.4
1908	47	142	189	24.9

continued

[18] Ibid.
[19] Lloyd-Jones and Lewis, *Alfred Herbert Ltd*, p. 33.

Table 5.1   *concluded*

1909	68	165	233	29.2
1910	82	250	332	24.7
1911	148	281	429	34.5
1912	224	295	519	43.2
1913	220	306	526	41.8
1914	270	325	595	45.4

Source: Arnold, 'Innovation', pp. 60–61.

Table 5.2   Profitability at Alfred Herbert Ltd, 1888–1914

	Net profits (£000)	Net profit: total sales (%)	Return on capital employed[a] (%)
1888	-0.1	-4.0	-2.8
1889	1.0	12.5	21.7
1890	2.4	11.7	63.2
1891	5.7	19.7	61.3
1892	2.9	12.7	24.4
1893	2.0	13.2	14.8
1894	2.8	16.2	15.7
1895	2.9	13.5	13.6
1896	14.3	29.3	41.7
1897	13.8	20.7	31.0
1898	13.6	15.6	22.1
1899	21.3	21.5	24.3
1900	31	26.2	25.5
1901	20	17.4	14.7
1902	22	15.6	14.4
1903	34	22.4	19.3
1904	31	19.3	15.9
1905	41	18.7	19.3
1906	56	22.3	22.4
1907	76	23.4	25.1
1908	20	10.6	6.5

continued

Table 5.2   *concluded*

1909	21	9.0	6.5
1910	55	16.6	15.1
1911	79	18.4	18.7
1912	99	19.1	19.9
1913	90	17.1	15.9
1914	100	16.8	15.6

Source: Arnold, 'Innovation', pp. 60–61.
Note: a. Return on capital employed, or what Arnold refers to as 'net profits: shareholders' interest' = total value of shares and reserves. Arnold, 'Innovation', p. 61.

Three key factors explain the success of the company to 1914. First, it developed a reputation for the high quality of its machines and their adaptation to British engineering requirements. The engineering of machines followed closely that of American practices, but Herbert did not simply imitate American technology. For example, when the firm displayed its machines at the Paris Exposition of 1900, it was observed that they were 'constructed on American lines, and are yet not American machines nor blind copies of them, but included features thought by the builders to better adapt them to the British market'.[20] Like other British machine firms prior to the war, Herbert developed key improvement innovations which increased the speed and durability of the products, as well as adapting high-speed steel to their machines for cutting metals.[21]

Second, Herbert machine-tool design was influenced by a knowledge of American machines, which was gained through their development of a highly successful factoring business, especially for the sale of American machine tools. Factoring consolidated the Herbert reputation for using American practices and laid the foundation for 'an effective selling organisation', both at home and abroad. The company sold imported American machine tools and their own capstan and turret lathes, 'which made use of American practices'. Factored machines represented a profitable part of the company's business; they were usually purchased on credit, and did not necessitate a heavy investment in fixed plant. Factoring also enabled Herbert to supply a wide range of products to the engineering trades, which met its commitments to meet customer demand, and the ideal of the company to provide not just a product but a comprehensive engineering service.[22] Its involvement with factoring helped build the 'reputation' of the company, a fact noted by John Milburn, a leading departmental director, in 1918, who considered that they had a

---

[20]   *American Machinist*, 4 August 1900, p. 682E.

[21]   See Lloyd-Jones and Lewis, *Alfred Herbert Ltd*, pp. 21–8, 33–4.

[22]   Arnold, 'Innovation', pp. 55, 63–4; Lloyd-Jones and Lewis, *Alfred Herbert Ltd*, p. 33.

responsibility to supply machines 'for the full equipment of workshops, from both Herbert and factored machines'.[23]

Finally, the engineering quality of the company, its market reputation and its rapid rise to prominence in the industry owed much to the technical qualities of Alfred Herbert and his senior managerial team. Under Alfred's leadership from 1894, the company acquired a group of talented managers with the accumulated knowledge to advance the business on progressive lines. Alfred Herbert, like many of the pioneers of the British machine-tool industry, was a trained engineer, having served apprenticeships in engineering firms prior to the formation of his business in 1887.[24] In the early days of the company, as Alfred later reflected, he was 'general manager, traveller, and odd job man'.[25] Until 1897, management was conducted largely by Herbert with the support of Arthur Marston, a close friend who took on the responsibility of works manager. As the company expanded and the management became stretched, Herbert recruited prominent engineers to managerial positions, and particularly selected men who had experience of American workshop practices in the making of machine tools. In 1897, Oscar Harmer, an American engineer who had worked for the American Capwell Machine Co. before joining the engineers Babcock and Wilcox in Glasgow, was appointed by Herbert as production manager. Harmer was also a close friend of Charles Churchill, another American, who had developed a successful business in London importing American machine tools, and these networks were important for the development of Herbert's factored business. Two key managerial appointments followed Harmer's arrival. Percy Vernon, an engineer who had worked for a number of American makers, was persuaded by Harmer to become general manager, and John Milburn from Rhode Island, who had worked with Harmer at Babcock and Wilcox, became works manager. Together with Harmer, their knowledge of American methods enabled Herbert to perfect new designs to diversify when the bicycle boom collapsed in 1897, and to rapidly build for itself a high market reputation.[26]

The extension of the management of the company was accomplished under the governance of Alfred Herbert, who remained overwhelmingly the majority shareholder in what became very much a family concern. Alfred's initial venture into the machine-tool industry, through his partnership with Hubbard in 1887, had been partly financed by Alfred's brother, William Henry Herbert, the owner of the Premiere Cycle Co. of Coventry, who invested £20,000 of his own capital into the concern. As the business expanded after 1894, family members invested

---

[23]   Records of Alfred Herbert Ltd, PA 926/1/4/1–3, Minute Books of the Departmental Board of Directors, 1911–1941, 23 September 1918.

[24]   Lloyd-Jones, *Alfred Herbert Ltd*, p. 29.

[25]   Records of Alfred Herbert Ltd, PA 1270/9/1, *Alfred Herbert News*, December 1926.

[26]   PA 1270/4/1, Oscar Harmer for the Alfred Herbert Testimonial, 22 July 1917.

in new share issues, and became important stakeholders in the company.[27] The capital of the company was periodically increased by the issue of new shares; in 1898 nominal capital was increased from £20,000 to £25,000, and 950 preference £5 shares, paying 5 per cent, were issued, with a total value of £4,750. These were allotted to existing shareholders only, on a pro rata basis, which perpetuated Alfred's control of the company and the familial nature of shareholding. As shown in Table 5.3, the new allocation of 1898 went primarily to Alfred Herbert and family members, with a small holding taken by managers.

Table 5.3   Distribution of 5 per cent preference shares in Alfred Herbert Ltd, 1898

	No.	Value (£)
Alfred E. Herbert (founder)	677	3,385
William Henry Herbert (brother of Alfred)	212	1,060
Fannie Millicent Herbert (wife of Alfred)	15	75
E. A. Herbert (son of Alfred, died during the First World War)	5	25
William Herbert (son of William Henry)	24	120
Sarah Ann Herbert (Daughter of William Henry)	3	15
A. E. Marston (works manager)	12	60
F. Floyd (Father-in-law of Alfred)	2	10
Un-issued shares	50	250
Total	1,000	5,000

Source: PA 586/11 General Minute Book, 14 April 1898.

In 1899 the nominal capital was raised from £25,000 to £35,000, by the issue of 2,000 new preference shares of £5 each. At the 1900 AGM nominal capital was increased further to £85,000, by the creation of 10,000 new preference bonus shares of £5 each, which were distributed pro rata amongst existing shareholders only,[28] and at the 1905 AGM to £200,000.[29] Following the end of the war in 1920, nominal capital was increased to £1 million, 'by the creation of 160,000 bonus ordinary shares of £5 each. The allocation of 1920 was largely funded from the company's 'reserve fund and undistributed profits', which had expanded considerably during the war, and thus £724,000 was 'accordingly capitalised and

[27]   Lloyd-Jones and Lewis, *Alfred Herbert Ltd*, p. 29.

[28]   Records of Alfred Herbert Ltd, PA 586/11, General Minute Book, 14 April 1898; 15 June 1900.

[29]   PA 586/11, General Minute Book, 15 May 1905.

applied in payment up in full at par of 144,990 ordinary shares in the company of £5 each', and to be distributed to existing ordinary shareholders in the ratio of nine new shares for every one existing share.[30] Of the £1 million of nominal capital established in 1920, £752,590 had been taken up as paid-up capital by 1926, all distributed amongst existing shareholders.[31] The information in Table 5.4 compares the shareholding of issued capital in 1900 and 1926, and shows that Alfred retained the overwhelming majority of the shares, that family stakeholders remained important, and that the shareholder base was marginally widened by the inclusion of company managers, and their family, as stakeholders. The company remained a private one.

Table 5.4   Issued capital: share ownership in Alfred Herbert Ltd, 1900 and 1926 (£)

	1900[a]		1926[b]	
	Ordinary	**Preference**	**Ordinary**	**Preference**
Alfred Edward Herbert (F)	34,880	21,290	398,325	51,630
William Henry Herbert (F)	11,110	5,000	67,015	30,590
William Herbert (F)	1,235	745		
W. J. Hutchens (M)	1,000			
Oscar Harmer (M)	1,000		19,500	7,735
P. V. Vernon (M)	1,000		15,600	6,435
A. E. Marston (M)	865	575		2,080
Fannie Millicent Herbert (F)	740	1,745		200
Mrs F. H. Marston (MF)	640	325	16,725	7,715
Thomas Woof (M)	500			
J. Pickin (M)	300		5,515	
E. A. Herbert (F)	285	170		
F. Floyd (F)	125	65		
Sarah Ann Herbert (F)	120	85		
Mrs F. K. H. Blythe (F)			2,735	1,695
J. Millman (M)			4,800	1,890
Mrs Hollick (F)			825	380

continued

---

[30] PA 586/11, General Minute Book, 17 March 1920.
[31] PA 586/11, General Minute Book, 12 January 1926.

Table 5.4   *concluded*

Mrs G. F. Harmer (MF)			825	475
G. O. Herbert (F)			65,475	29,580
J. Johnson (M)			375	125
J. T. Haddock (M)			560	190
D. M. Gimson (M)			1,125	375
Gimson and Marder (accountants)			1,650	5,850
A. H. Lloyd (M)			1,875	625
A. W. Perkins (M)			320	605
S. H. March (M)			785	260
G. Kelway (M)			95	30
Total	53,800	30,000	604,125	148,465

Source: PA 926/1/5/4/23, Capital Account, 31 October 1900; PA 586/11, General Minute Book, 12 June 1926.

Notes: (F) denotes family connection, (M) denotes management connection, and (MF) denotes a family connection to a manager; a. £83,800 of total shares were issued in 1900 out of the nominal capital of £85,000; b. £752,590 shares were issued by 1926 out of the nominal capital of £1 million.

The private company and its governance

A key characteristic of British industrial capitalism before the First World War was the reluctance of firms to finance expansion through recourse to the capital markets, demonstrating the weak link between industrial and financial capital in Britain, and the determination of personal entrepreneurs to retain ownership.[32] Prior to the First World War, private limited liability was a major characteristic of the evolution of British industrial enterprise. Thus, in 1907 it is estimated that only about 10 per cent of industrial ventures were financed by public issue of shares.[33] Following the 1908 Companies Act, which defined in law the private company, firms tended to adopt private, rather than public limited status. By 1913, approximately 80 per cent of all companies in Britain came under the legal definition of 'private limited', which enabled them 'to gain the advantage of limited liability on shares at the same time as allowing them to retain control by rejecting the issue of those

---

[32]   See Cottrell, *Industrial Finance*, p. 182; Collins, *Banks and Industrial Finance in Britain*, p. 34.

[33]   Cottrell, *Industrial Finance*, p. 190.

shares to pre-selected groups; to themselves, members of their family, personal acquaintances, and so on'.[34]

To maintain the ownership by the family Alfred changed the company's articles of association in 1908 to make it a private company in accordance with the recent Companies Act. The articles prohibited the transfer of shares, restricted the number of shareholders to a maximum of 50, and stated that 'No invitation to the public has been or shall be made or issued to subscribers for any shares or debentures of the Company'.[35] The ideal of the private company was reflected in Alfred's style of governance, and in 1911 further changes to the articles of association reflected his overwhelming control over the direct management of the concern, when he was appointed 'sole governing director', with the right to act as chairman at board or company meetings and to hold office until his death or resignation, or until he ceased to hold 1,000 ordinary shares. In addition, Alfred wielded considerable power over the appointment of managers to the firm, and in 1911 the creation of a departmental board of directors reflected his overarching control. He was empowered to determine whether he governed the company 'with or without departmental directors ... and either with or without any ordinary directors'.[36] The distinction made between departmental and ordinary directors was a complex one. The former were managers of departments, with no share qualification, while the latter were departmental directors who owned a minimum of 100 ordinary shares in the company and were entitled to vote at AGMs.[37] Thus, leading departmental directors such as Oscar Harmer (technical director), Joseph Picken (director factored department), P. V. Vernon (general manager and design director), J. Millman (works manager), D. M. Gimson (finance director) and A. H. Lloyd (sales director) also qualified as ordinary directors, as shown in Table 5.4, by their holding of more than 100 ordinary shares.

What distinguished all directors were that they were employees of the company, subject to the right of Alfred Herbert to appoint and dismiss them as he saw fit, and to determine their financial rewards in the form of salaries and bonuses.[38] As holders of equity, directors were also stakeholders in the company, which gave them a personal interest in the long-term fortunes of the enterprise. But as departmental directors they were also contracted to the company itself, and 'The relations between the Company and the Departmental Directors shall be those of employer and employed in all respects'.[39]

---

[34]   Collins, *Banks and Industrial Finance*, p. 34.

[35]   PA 586/11, General Minute Book, 31 March, 11 April 1908.

[36]   PA 586/11, General Minute Book, 24 August 1911.

[37]   Records of Alfred Herbert Ltd, PA 1270/1/1–3, Memorandums and Articles of Association of Alfred Herbert Ltd, 1894–1954.

[38]   Ibid.

[39]   PA 926/1/4/1–3, Minute Books of the Departmental Board of Directors, Legal Documents Appointing Departmental Directors, 13 September 1911.

The creation of a departmental board in 1911, however, did represent a change in the governance of the company; it enabled Herbert to devolve responsibility for the day-to-day running of the company, albeit to selected hand-picked directors under his governing directorship. The meetings of the departmental directors, which occurred on a fortnightly basis, were reflective of a group of managers that maintained a tight monitoring of the company's business affairs, and set the strategic direction of the firm in terms of machine-tool design, the range of machines developed, the costing of production, and the sale of machines, both of their own make and those sold through its factoring department.[40] It was, to all intents and purposes, a board of engineers, which consisted of managers with specific knowledge of the industry and the markets in which the company operated. The board itself had direct responsibility for the management of the 'business of the company', which included financial accounting, the provision of an audited balance sheet, and the determination of dividends on the ordinary shares. Accountability and disclosure thus rested with the departmental board, whose responsibility was to record in the private ledgers 'true accounts' of the financial affairs of the company, and after acceptance by the auditors present a balance sheet to the AGM,[41] a document that came under the careful scrutiny of Alfred Herbert himself.

Herbert was well versed in the details of the accounts, and demanded high standards from both the auditors and the departmental directors in accounting procedures. In 1903, Herbert wrote to Wilshere & Sons, the company auditors, concerning a discrepancy between his own valuation of stocks and that of the auditors: 'I am getting rather anxious to know when your people are coming over to endeavour to put right the mistakes in our last year's figures.' Herbert was indeed his own accountant, and as he reminded the auditors 'the difference should have been discovered by them'.[42] The governing director was the key figure in internal accounting, working in tandem with the auditors 'before any final entries are made in the private ledgers'.[43] Departmental directors also came under his watch. For example, in September 1918 he wrote to the departmental board concerning the 'disturbing' effects of the government's excess profit duties, and reminded them of the need for the careful monitoring of departmental expenditure. It was the duty of all board members, in their 'own sphere', to produce accurate figures, investigate items of expenditure, and keep Herbert regularly informed.[44]

Governance at Herbert's was very much a private affair. At the AGM a detailed balance sheet was presented to the private shareholders, with little or no detailed explanation from the governing director. Herbert's role at the AGM was to provide

---

[40]   See PA 926/1/4/1–3, Minute Books of the Departmental Board of Directors.

[41]   PA 1270/1/1–3, Memorandums and Articles of Association of Alfred Herbert Ltd, 1894–1954.

[42]   PA 926/1/5/16/15, Alfred Herbert to Wilshere & Sons, 27 February 1903.

[43]   PA 926/1/5/17/7, Alfred Herbert to Wilshere & Sons, 24 December 1903.

[44]   PA 926/1/4/1–3, Minute Books of the Departmental Board of Directors, 23 September 1918.

a short speech, often outlining the company's business progress during the year, announce the distribution of profits by dividend, and then proceed to pass the resolution accepting the audited accounts.[45] The AGM was a family gathering, together with departmental directors who held the ordinary share qualification, and the business was routine and conducted behind closed doors. The public disclosure of financial information remained the prerogative of the company, and there is no evidence of the reporting of the Herbert AGM in either the local press or the financial press, at least before its conversion to a public company in 1944. This typified the private nature of firms within the British machine-tool industry, and, as *The American Machinist* observed in 1922, 'few' makers 'issue reports on the year's working that find their way into the press', and seldom did they use the advertisement columns in the local press to announce the returns made at AGMs. As the journal concluded, in the public domain 'the finance of the industry is rather obscure, and … the true standing of firms is difficult to estimate'.[46]

Even during the war, when private business came under increasing scrutiny over profiteering, the company's accounts seem to have remained obscure as far as the public press were concerned. Nevertheless, the company expanded its business reputation during the war, playing a major role in supplying its own general purpose machine tools to Britain's war industries, as well as single-purpose machines of American origin through its factoring connections.[47] The governing director gained a national reputation as a mover and shaker at Lloyd George's Ministry of Munitions, where he became controller of the Machine Tool Department of the Ministry, and was instrumental in gradually introducing dilution into Britain's machine-tool shops. He also became president of the Machine Tool and Engineering Trade Association, which was renamed the MTTA in 1918, and in 1916 was knighted for his services to the war effort.[48] Not only did he serve the country well, but the profits of the company accelerated during the first two years of the war, and although they fell between 1917 and 1918 high dividends accrued to its founder and private shareholders, as well as increasing salaries and bonuses.

Table 5.5 shows the profit figures for 1915 to 1939. Between 1915 and 1918 the shareholders received an average dividend on ordinary shares of a staggering 52.5 per cent. At the same time, Herbert and his departmental directors received generous salaries, the departmental directors also being awarded substantial bonuses by way of commissions paid on sales of machinery, as shown from the returns available for 1914–15 and 1917–18 (Table 5.6). The high profits and dividends of the war years receded in the depressed climate of the 1920s, and following the short post-war boom the British machine tool industry faced an intense and prolonged economic depression, with declining export markets, low and uncertain domestic demand,

---

[45]   See PA 586/11, General Minute Book.

[46]   *The American Machinist*, 2 December 1922, p. 91E.

[47]   See Lloyd-Jones and Lewis, *Alfred Herbert Ltd*, pp. 49, 63–5, 67–70.

[48]   Ibid., p. 52. Percy Vernon also held a key ministerial job as assistant controller at the Machine Tool Department. PA 1270/9/1, *Alfred Herbert News*, October 1927.

falling prices, lowered profit expectations, and rising foreign competition. The next section of the chapter examines the response of the company during the inter-war years and the evolution of its individualistic style of governance.

Table 5.5   Profits and returns to shareholders at Alfred Herbert Ltd, 1915–39

	Net profits (£000)	Net profit: total sales (%)	Return on capital employed (%)[a]	Ordinary share dividend (%)[d]
1915	149	11.3	20.0	50
1916	222	9.4	24.2	50
1917	114	3.9	11.5	50
1918	143	4.6	13.2	60
1919	230	10.6	18.2	6
1920	-48.0	-1.8	-4.1	3
1921	-33	-3.4	-3.0	3
1922	-21	-2.7	-2.0	3
1923	140	18.2	12.0	5
1924	146	14.5	11.6	5
1925	263	21.5	17.8	5
1926	179	14.0	11.3	5
1927	151	10.3	9.0	7
1928				
1929[b]	319	17.6		15
1930[c]	295	13.8		7.5
1931	-38	-4.0		0
1932	28	2.9		0
1933	153	18.4		17.5
1934	217	16.5		35
1935	243	14.1		40
1936	385.0			40
1937	667.6			65
1938	633.2			65
1939	175.3			55

Source: Arnold, 'Innovation', pp. 60–61; 926/1/5/42–49, Alfred Herbert, Annual Accounts and Schedules, 1928–35; 586/11; Alfred Herbert General Minute Book, 1894–1950.

Notes: a. Capital employed = total value of shares and reserves. Arnold, 'Innovation', p. 61. Arnold calculates these figures to 1927 only. b. For 17 months ending March 1929. c. For 19 months ending October 1930. d. Preference dividends were fixed at 5 per cent for 1915–25, and 6 per cent for 1926–35.

Table 5.6   Salaries paid to Alfred Herbert and leading departmental directors, 1914–15 and 1917–18 (£)

	1914–15			1917–18		
	Salary	**Commission**	**Total**	**Salary**	**Commission**	**Total**
A. Herbert	3,000	0	3,000	5,000	0	5,000
O. Harmer	850	1,735	2,585	850	2,048	2,898
P. Vernon	850	841	1,691	850	1,454	2,304
J. Pickin	850	694	1,544	1,000	1,500	2,500
J. Milburn	350	2,192	2,542	350	3,097	3,447

Source: PA 926/5/30/24, Analysis of Salaries and Private Sales, 1914–15; PA 926/5/33/35, Analysis of salaries and Private Sales, 1917–18.
Note: Commission was paid on sales attributable to each departmental director.

The inter-war years: Alfred Herbert and the individualistic element in governance

The world economic crisis of the 1930s impacted heavily on the machine tool industry, and by 1933 its output was some 48 per cent lower than the peak year of 1929. After 1935, the industry did recover rapidly, given a boost by the rising government demand for re-armament.[49] Herbert felt the full effects of the depression. In 1921 sales of Herbert machines in the home market fell by 72 per cent, and even in 1927 were 16 per cent below those of 1920.[50] Sales slumped further between 1929 and 1933, before recovery set in from 1934.[51] Profits fell, and dividends were curtailed, but only in 1931 and 1932 did shareholders receive no payment on their ordinary shares. Indeed, in the expansion phase after 1934 profits again accelerated and dividends reached the highs of the First World War years (Table 5.5). In the 1920s, the ratio of net profits to shareholders funds declined from an average of 17.4 per cent between 1915 and 1918 to 6.6 per cent between 1920 and 1927, representing 'a poor return for the risks involved'.[52] But the company weathered the storm, and maintained its dividend to its private members, and in the long-run the stakeholders reaped the rewards of their enforced loyalty to a private limited venture, where there was no public market for the exit of shareholders.

---

[49]   See Aldcroft, 'The Performance of the British Machine-Tool Industry', pp. 281–5; Lloyd-Jones and Lewis, *Alfred Herbert Ltd*, pp. 71–3, 125.

[50]   Arnold, 'Innovation', pp. 60–61.

[51]   Lloyd-Jones and Lewis, *Alfred Herbert Ltd*, p. 86.

[52]   Arnold, 'Innovation', pp. 59–62.

The British machine tool industry was characterised by a commitment to internal financing as a means to fund the enterprise, and as *The American Machinist* observed in 1922, firms in the industry had 'not to any great extent in the past appealed for ... capital to the ordinary public'.[53] Herbert was no exception to this principle, and from its foundation the company pursued a prudent strategy of business finance. Despite the high rewards to shareholders and directors down to 1920, the expansion of the company relied upon the reinvestment of profits, a fundamental characteristic of the private enterprise, which was continued in the downturn after 1920. Between 1887 and 1927, as Arnold shows, 'in most years' the funds received from the company's business operations were more than sufficient to provide for 'taxes, interest payments, dividends', and investments in fixed capital for plant expansion. The flow of funds from business operations produced '92 per cent of total inflows, with new shares providing less than one per cent and the remainder coming in the form of trade finance from creditors'. The business success of the company, especially in the years to 1920, ensured that the owners had no need to resort on a large scale to outside finance. They did so on only three occasions, in 1890, 1898 and 1920, raising short-term loan finance in the form of bank overdrafts. Given the company's accumulated reserves, and for most of the period sufficient funds from business operations, these were quickly repaid, and over the period 1888 to 1927 the company raised only £283,400 in loan finance. Over the same period, it invested £1,400,000 in expanding its fixed assets, but this did not depend either upon outside capital or the use of family investment. The company's share capital, as we have seen, did expand over the period, 'but the major increases in 1900, 1905 and 1920 were all provided as bonus issues out of accumulated retained profits'. The expansion did not rely upon the private funds of family shareholders, and the high dividends they received were paid out of accumulated profits.[54] During the 1920s the company pursued a policy of thrift and retrenchment.

Thrift and retrenchment

Internal funding was not just the preserve of the private limited company, but permeated the industrial sector in Britain, reflecting the personalised nature of industrial capitalism. As John Wilson observes, internal funds 'continued to act as the major contributor to capital formation, and business savings still accounted for approximately eighty per cent of total industrial investment in the inter-war era'.[55] An indication of an individual ethos was provided by Alfred Herbert in 1930, in a speech to the AGM of Barclays Bank. His remarks were targeted at the recent findings of the Macmillan Committee on industrial finance and the alleged

[53]   *American Machinist*, 2 December 1922, p. 91E.
[54]   Arnold, 'Innovation', pp. 58–9.
[55]   Wilson, *British Business History*, p. 183.

gap in bank funding of the industrial sector. Herbert acknowledged that additional investment from the banks would be 'a good thing', but in his experience 'he had never found any difficulty in getting the necessary capital for the development and expansion of a sound enterprise'. A 'sound enterprise' was equated with the accumulation of internal reserves for capital expansion:

> The most valuable kind of capital that could be held in any business was the capital that business had been able to save for itself by care, economy, and a conservative policy in dealing with its accounts ... £1 of capital which they themselves had saved was worth as much to them as £2 of capital which they could borrow from outside.[56]

Such a statement reflected not only Herbert's ideal of the need to retain personal control over the affairs of the company, but also a deep mistrust of financial institutions, which at times could border on contempt. At the AGM of the MTTA in 1932, Herbert informed the audience that

> it was fairly obvious that the financiers did not appear to have made a very good job of world finance ... and the financiers were at the stage where the Chinese were when they attempted to make needles by the process of filing down crowbars (Laughter) ... the ultimate function of the financier was to be the servant and not the master of industry.[57]

Thrift was the order of the day, and this was a deeply held personal belief, consistent with his protestant values, and a message constantly projected to his own workers through the company's in-house magazine, *The Alfred Herbert News*. Thus, in 1929, Herbert encouraged workers towards 'thrift and saving', a virtue which was in line with the policy of 'their company' to accumulate funds for future investment.[58] In his definition of capital, Herbert referred to it as 'accumulated savings', which a capitalist 'may invest and re-invest in his own business'.[59]

Throughout the 1920s the company had a consistently conservative policy of capital expenditure, and of maintaining adequate cash. Herbert remained determined not to over-extend the business financially, and kept a careful watch over output and design policy and the capital commitment of the company. A sign of his caution was his warning of over-expansion to his departmental directors in October 1918, when there was considerable debate in the board over the company's

---

[56]   Cited in *American Machinist*, 25 January 1930, p. 287E.

[57]   MTTA, Annual Report, 1932. A similar view was given to the employees of the company in 1931, when Alfred observed that 'Commerce is apparently far more affected by finance ... than it ought to be [it] should be the servant of industry and in no sense the master'. PA 1270/9/1, *Alfred Herbert News*, January 1931.

[58]   PA 1270/9/1, *Alfred Herbert News*, January 1929.

[59]   PA 1270/9/1, *Alfred Herbert News*, November 1928.

post-war output policy. In response to the arguments of John Milman that the company should rapidly expand its manufacturing programme to meet a surge of expected post-war demand, Herbert insisted on caution, outlined the future unpredictability of post-war markets, and concluded that 'the best position the company could be in at the end of the war would be to have as few commitments as possible and the maximum amount of money in the bank to be ready to jump off in any direction'.[60] As Table 5.7 shows, during the post-war boom the company pursued a cautious capital investment policy, the investment in fixed assets falling during 1917 and 1918, as the company re-organised its plant for peace-time production, and it was only in 1919 that expenditure increased as the company faced problems of under-capacity, often relying upon sub-contracting to meet orders.[61]

Table 5.7   Selected financial data on Alfred Herbert Ltd, 1916–27 (£000)

	Total inflows[a]	Total outflows[b]	Investment on fixed assets	Increase/decrease in cash[c]
1916	1,421	1,377	456	44
1917	850	704	-162	146
1918	254	502	-53	-248
1919	346	413	148	-67
1920	29	114	78	-85
1921	-409	-437	41	28
1922	-28	-127	-48	99
1923	-137	-17	103	-120
1924	380	324	143	56
1925	-11	-84	41	73
1926	124	90	66	34
1927	278	200	118	78

Source: Arnold, 'Innovation', pp. 57–8.

*Note*s: a. Value of new shares, funds from business operations, loans and overdrafts, payments from creditors. b. Investments on fixed assets, taxation, interest and dividend payments, increase in stock, debtors. c. Inflows minus outflows.

The downturn of activity in 1920 brought an immediate warning from Herbert that 'Care should be used when placing contracts so that we should not accumulate

---

[60]   PA 926/1/4/1–3, Minute Books of the Departmental Board of Directors, 28 October 1918.

[61]   For a discussion of this see Lloyd-Jones and Lewis, *Alfred Herbert Ltd*, pp. 73–85.

stock and so lock up capital'. Retrenchment now became the order of the day; in June the board revised down its manufacturing programme to reduce output by 20 per cent, and by November they were forced to lay off workers.[62]

Retrenchment entailed a strict monitoring and control over internal costing at the level of the board, and the reduction of overhead charges as output and sales fell, through a vigorous policy of cutting administrative staff or what departmental directors termed 'non-productive workers'.[63] On the production side, the company pursued a policy of concentrating output on a limited range of machines for which there was a firm demand, while it also offered for sale machines of its own make and those it factored at substantial price discounts.[64] At the same time, the firm was at the centre of attempts to control wage costs in the industry. For example, Sir Alfred was a key figure in the MTTA who advocated the need for industrial co-operation, but at the same time was prepared to take a belligerent stance on the increase in wages, which he considered caused 'a serious injury to the prospect of the trade, and … has begun and will continue to produce unemployment on an increasing scale'. It would 'be far better to force a strike rather than to consent to any further increase whatever'.[65] During the early 1920s the company, through its association with the Engineering Employers Association, pursued a vigorous defence against the demands of labour for increased wages, and kept a 'black book' of striking employees.[66]

As governing director, Herbert played a lead role in the deliberations of the board over production policy, and rigorously sanctioned expenditure decisions. In 1923 investment in fixed assets did increase (Table 5.7), as the company geared itself to meet a potential revival in trade by launching a programme of new machines on the market, a decision that owed much to John Milburn, who argued consistently that the company should prepare for an upturn in demand.[67] While accepting Milburn's arguments in principle, Herbert nevertheless preferred

---

[62] PA 926/1/4/1–3, Minute Books of the Departmental Board of Directors, 8 June, 23 November 1920.

[63] See PA 926/1/4/1–3, Minute Books of the Departmental Board of Directors, 8 June, 13, 28 July, 15 September, 6 October, 9, 23 November 1920; 8 February 1921; 9 January 1923.

[64] See PA 926/1/4/1–3, Minute Books of the Departmental Board of Directors, 11 January, 17 October, 28 November 1922; 9 May, 21 August 1923; 2 September 1925.

[65] MTTA, Director's Minute Book, 10 June 1920.

[66] See J. M. Davies, 'A Twentieth Century Paternalist: Alfred Herbert and the Skilled Coventry Workmen', in B. Lancaster and T. Mason (eds), *Life and Labour in a Twentieth Century City: The Experience of Coventry* (Coventry, Cryfield Press, n.d.), pp. 108–109; Arnold, Innovation', pp. 56, 70 n. 55; A. J. McIvor, 'Employers Organisations and Strike Breaking in Britain, 1880–1914', *International Review of Social History*, Vol. 29 (1984), pp. 20–23; Lloyd-Jones and Lewis, *Alfred Herbert Ltd*, 93–5.

[67] PA 926/1/4/1–3, Minute Books of the Departmental Board of Directors, 21 August 1923.

a wait-and-see approach. As he informed the board in 1924, following a report by Milburn on an expected revival of demand from the motor car industry, they should exercise 'caution as regards the volume of work we are putting into the shop', and make a careful review of future capital expenditure in the context of an uncertain market environment.[68] The departmental board, nevertheless, was a forum for discussion and debate, and in its governance Herbert was prepared to listen and consider advice. Consequently, by August 1924, he had conceded the need to increase capacity, following the advice of Harmer and Milburn, who had presented evidence of rising demand in the car trades, and the problems of 'excess orders over deliveries'.[69] Herbert's cautious approach mirrored that of the machine-tool industry generally in the revival of trade between 1924 and 1928, with the consequence that they delayed future investment 'plans', an outcome of the uncertain market environment.[70]

Under-investment, of course, left a longer-term legacy for the industry, which was unable to meet a rising demand for orders in 1927 and 1928. By the latter date Sir Alfred was bemoaning the fact that their works were congested, and the company was unable to meet delivery times for orders from the car industry, and were curtailing taking on orders for machines 'of a special nature'.[71] On the other hand, the company was able to accumulate a positive cash balance between 1924 and 1927 (Table 5.7). With the exception of 1920, it was able to avoid recourse to bank finance, a key rule of Herbert's governance of the company. The bank loan of 1920, totalling £239,000, was repaid in full during the following two years, a loss of income which, with declining income from business operations, largely accounts for the negative inflow figures between 1921 and 1923. No other loans were required throughout the 1920s,[72] and financially the company weathered the storm. In 1926 Herbert sanctioned the expansion of the company's Edgwick works and the investment in new plant incorporating flow production methods, which opened in late 1927, and was extended further in 1928.[73] Between 1927 and 1930, the company did invest considerably in re-equipping their works, and Table 5.8 shows the investment in new machinery. From April 1930, however, sales fell, leading to the usual price discounting,[74] and the company was forced to cut expenditure on new machinery (Table 5.8), reduce its machine lines to customers,

---

[68] PA 926/1/4/1–3, Minute Books of the Departmental Board of Directors, 22 July 1924.

[69] PA 926/1/4/1–3, Minute Books of the Departmental Board of Directors, 26 August 1924.

[70] See *The American Machinist*, 8 November 1924, pp. 123–4.

[71] PA 926/1/4/1–3, Minute Books of the Departmental Board of Directors, 15 August 1928.

[72] Arnold, 'Innovation', pp. 57–8.

[73] Lloyd-Jones and Lewis, *Alfred Herbert Ltd*, pp. 120–21.

[74] See PA 926/1/4/1–3, Minute Books of the Departmental Board of Directors, 15 April, 17 June, 9 July 1930.

Table 5.8   Expenditure on new machinery, Alfred Herbert Ltd, 1924–35 (£000)

1924	47.0
1925	34.0
1926	33.9
1927	79.4
1928–29[a]	118.5
1930	19.2
1931	15.1
1932	11.2
1933	16.8
1934	60.6
1935	51.2

Source: PA 926/1/5/33–42, Alfred Herbert Ltd, Financial Accounts.
Note: a. For 18 months.

both own and factored makes, and restrict developments in new machine design while concentrating on updating its existing stock.[75] Nevertheless, the company maintained its reputation during the depression of the early 1930s, and avoided recourse to external financing. The latter was largely achieved by the call-up of £173,000 of stock in 1931, consisting of £122,000 in ordinary and £51,000 in preference shares,[76] but there was also an adherence to 'strict economy due to the financial position [and] difficult business conditions'.[77] With a revival of trade after 1932, the company, however, was in a position to build up its reserves (Table 5.9), a policy consistent with Alfred Herbert's insistence on funding future investment from internal profits. At the 1935 AGM, for example, he announced the transfer of £71,000 to reserves, which he perceived as vital to the future investment plans of the company, and at the same time he cautioned shareholders that the ordinary dividend of 35 per cent was 'exceptional and should not be taken as a standard'.[78]

During the early 1930s, Herbert cushioned the downturn in demand by an increasing concentration on the building of standard machine-tool lines, which were supplemented by factored machines, often of American and continental make, as well as an increased emphasis on providing an engineering service to

---

[75]   PA 926/1/4/1–3, Minute Books of the Departmental Board of Directors, 9 July, 14 October 1930.

[76]   PA 926/1/5/33–42, Alfred Herbert Ltd, Financial Accounts.

[77]   PA 586/11, General Minute Book, 11 December 1931.

[78]   PA 586/11, General Minute Book, 20 June 1935.

Table 5.9   Alfred Herbert Ltd: Reserve Account, 1927–37 (£000)

	Total reserve
1927	102.7
1928–29[a]	102.7
1930	102.7
1931	102.7
1932	117.4
1933	160.4
1934	217.9
1935	288.9
1936	427.4
1937	703.9

Source: PA 926/1/5/33–42, Alfred Herbert Ltd, Financial Accounts.
Note: a. For 18 months.

users. In particular, the company focused on supplying a demand for labour-saving equipment for high output, and during 1930 and 1931 offered customers high performance automatic chucking lathes, and new drilling machines for quantity production.[79] Its standard lines were representative of the management's uncertainty over future market trends, the departmental board rigorously debating the type of machine produced so that they could guarantee sales.[80] Herbert focussed on what was possible, given the prevailing market environment, while at the same time it relied upon its factoring business to supply a wider range of machines to engineering, especially American designs built for special machining purposes. Thus, Herbert concentrated factored sales on 'gap machines', mainly special-purpose machines not manufactured by British makers, but which were in higher demand by the motor trades due to their cost-saving attributes.[81] At the heart of the Herbert organisation lay a reputation for quality engineering.

[79]   PA 926/1/4/1–3, Minute Books of the Departmental Board of Directors, 15 April 1930; *The American Machinist*, 11 October 1930, p. 109E; 10 January 1931, p. 282E.

[80]   See PA 926/1/4/1–3, Minute Books of the Departmental Board of Directors, 14 October, 9 December 1930; 14 April, 10 November 1931; 14 December 1932.

[81]   PA 926/1/4/1–3, Minute Books of the Departmental Board of Directors, 10 November 1931; 12 July 1932.

Quality engineering

The Herbert organisation consisted of a group of talented engineers who had detailed experience and knowledge of the making of machine tools and the demands of the customer. An example of this was the philosophy of the company in relation to marketing, which was based upon the principle of meeting customer needs and providing an integrated engineering service. As early as 1926, within the board there were detailed discussions concerning the technical capabilities of sales staff to provide a service to users, and in 1927 Herbert endorsed a report by Vernon which highlighted the need for the company to re-vamp its marketing business with the aim of promoting amongst users the adaptation of labour-saving machinery. Consequently, the Herbert sales staff provided information on tool layouts and production times.[82] Furthermore, increased attention was given to co-ordinating the factoring department with the manufacturing side of the business, with the objective of meeting the needs of customers for the supply of 'the complete equipment of the machine shop'.[83] As Sir Alfred Herbert observed in late 1929, the company had the capability to withstand competition due to the fact 'that we deal in such a large variety of machine tools', and that its factored sales frequently promoted demand for larger orders of its own make 'because we are able to quote for plants complete in every detail'.[84]

By 1930, the company's domestic sales branches were supplying detailed information to customers on the comparative efficiency of firms, and overseas associate sales companies were reproducing comprehensive engineering drawings for information to potential customers.[85] The company's new demonstration department opened at Coventry in 1930, and became a base for the interaction with engineering users, as well as a school for training sales staff.[86] In conjunction with its marketing policy, the company prioritised the manufacture of small batches of turret lathes and milling machines, all of which were tested for efficiency and durability in the company's experimental workshops, and then demonstrated to users by technically knowledgeable sales staff.[87] Machines were also re-configured, to provide increased efficiency in cutting operations through the application of

---

[82]   PA 926/1/4/1–3, Minute Books of the Departmental Board of Directors, 7 December 1926; 4 January, 1 February 1927.

[83]   PA 926/1/4/1–3, Minute Books of the Departmental Board of Directors, 10 September, 11 June, 12 November 1929.

[84]   PA 1270/9/1, *Alfred Herbert News*, December 1929.

[85]   PA 926/1/4/1–3, Minute Books of the Departmental Board of Directors, 17 June, 9 July 1930.

[86]   PA 926/1/4/1–3, Minute Books of the Departmental Board of Directors, 11 September 1930.

[87]   PA 926/1/4/1–3, Minute Books of the Departmental Board of Directors, 9 July, 14 October 1930.

tungsten carbide, and special-purpose machines were supplied through agency agreements via the factoring department.[88]

A tradition of quality engineering lay at the heart of the culture of the Herbert organisation, and was a key factor in managerial promotion from top to bottom. In the first issue of the *Alfred Herbert News*, a publication designed to integrate staff 'more fully into our confidence' and 'encourage those who read it to take a greater interest in the affairs of the Company', Sir Alfred Herbert outlined his philosophy of the private limited company, and the reputation of the organisation for innovative engineering. In the governance of the company, workers were seen by Herbert as stakeholders, bound together by the reputation of the company for high-class engineering. The firm, Herbert claimed, 'is considerably more to me than a mere machine for earning profits'. His private ownership was equated with tradition, which discounted the firm as a mere vehicle for materialistic gain, and gave to the organisation a deep intrinsic value:

> All businesses that are to be of any use in the world must make profits, because it is out of last year's profits that this year's improvements are made and it is out of the profits that we get our dividends and our means of living, but ... it must be more than a mere means of livelihood. There is a certain pride in the work of one's hands or of one's brains if it is good work ... and every time we turn out a machine which does well and satisfies the user I get more pleasure from this fact than from the profit we have made on it, though I do not by any means despise that.

Such a philosophy, Herbert concluded, 'had won [for the company] a reputation in every corner of the world where machine tools are used, for sound designs, good workmanship and honest dealing'.[89] Reputation was central to business success; it could not be measured as could a tangible asset, 'Yet amongst [the] items [on a balance sheet] it constitutes the life and spirit of a business'.[90]

Reputation was built upon the talents and experience of home-grown engineers, and Herbert pursued a 'policy ... to try and fill new jobs wherever possible by promotion within the ranks of the company'.[91] That this was seen as a recipe for business success was eloquently portrayed by Alfred Herbert in 1940:

> A burnt cat dreads the fire and Experience ... makes fools wise. Experience is the main factor in all mechanical design and in all sound organisations. It forms a solid base on which to build such new and untried elements as inventiveness ... The new design, when it has in turn been tried in the furnace of experience,

---

[88]   *The American Machinist*, 9 May 1931, pp. 199–200E; 12 December 1931, p. 205E.

[89]   PA 1270/9/1, *Alfred Herbert News*, December 1926.

[90]   PA 1270/9/1, *Alfred Herbert News*, September–October 1933.

[91]   PA 1270/9/1, *Alfred Herbert News*, December 1926.

forms a fresh basis from which to start still further advances into the blue, and thus to build with soundness and success.[92]

Herbert celebrated the fact that those holding 'leading positions' in the company had 'largely risen from small beginnings', and had gained experience in an engineering environment. Consistent with this was the creation of a register of young staff in 1927 who demonstrated the attributes for promotion, which included a 'keen and energetic' spirit, and a particular knowledge of the various aspects of the business. Herbert clearly understood the importance of replenishing managerial talent, and recognised that 'Individuals grow old with the passing years and become less energetic, less enterprising, and less adventurous ... the only way to keep a business from growing old is that its staff should be constantly recruited by the addition of young blood'. In particular he pointed to the importance of this for managerial succession from the top to the bottom of the company.[93]

At the departmental board level – as we have seen in the case of leading directors such as Harmer, Milman and Vernon – selection was based upon their engineering knowledge and the capabilities they could bring to the firm. Over time Herbert was prepared to replace directors on retirement or death by recruitment from within the organisation. Joseph Pickin, for example, joined the firm in 1895 as a draughtsman, became head salesman of the company's showrooms in Birmingham in 1897 and Manchester in 1898, before his appointment as a departmental director in 1904 to manage the factored small-tools department. Pickin gained a reputation for promoting the sales of automatic lathes, and was influential in the development of connections with the American Norton Grinding Co., an important factor in the accumulation of technical knowledge in the making of grinding machines. Later recruits, such as A. H. Lloyd and C. W. Clark, also served their apprenticeship in the firm. The former had joined the company in 1906, as a draughtsman, and in 1926 replaced Milman on his retirement as the director of design.[94] Clark joined the firm in 1908, served as a colonel during the war and in the early 1920s had worked for a number of engineering firms. He rejoined his 'good friends in the Herbert organisation' in 1925, following a search by Alfred for a talented engineer to head the company's sales department for its coal pulverising equipment. After lengthy negotiations, he was offered an annual salary of £1,200, plus travelling and living expenses, on the insistence of Herbert that he was a valuable future asset to the company.[95] Clark became a departmental director in 1933, together

---

[92]   CA, PA 1270/9/11, Shots at the Truth by Sir Alfred Herbert, 'Experience', reprinted from the *Machine Tool Review*, January–February 1940.

[93]   PA 1270/9/1, *Alfred Herbert News*, September 1927.

[94]   PA 926/1/4/1–3, Minute Books of the Departmental Board of Directors, 7 December 1926.

[95]   PA 1270/3/1/1, J. Pickin to C. W. Clark, 23 September 1925; C. W. Clark to J. Pickin, 6 October 1925.

with C. W. Blair,[96] both of whom were to become future acolytes of Herbert's. In 1957, on Herbert's death Clark became chairman and Blair deputy chairman of the concern.[97] Internal promotion was reflective of the 'Herbert spirit'[98] and the individualism of the company.

The Herbert spirit and individualism

The 'Herbert spirit' was a symbol of the governance of the company, in which all employees were seen as stakeholders. Promotion at lower levels of the company, such as sales staff and foremen, were also conditioned by their loyalty and commitment to the firm. Amongst the many staff biographies in the *Alfred Herbert News* was that of 'our friend' W. Williams, who had joined the firm in 1899. Trained under the guidance of experienced foremen in the milling machine department, Williams rose to a charge-hand in 1904, and an assistant foreman in 1922.[99] The company gained a reputation as a progressive employer, providing opportunities for internal promotion and installing policies of industrial welfare which provided a range of social amenities to its workforce, as well as a pension scheme and bonus payment system.[100]

While welfare was a reflection of the paternalistic nature of Herbert himself, it nevertheless also was a means of promoting increased efficiency and reconciling differences between capital and labour, and as we have seen the company took a firm stance on industrial action by the unions. Following the general strike of 1926, Herbert insisted at the AGM of the MTTA that they needed to pursue a 'firm stance' against the action of organised labour, while at the same time he urged his own workers to accept the need for a 'spirit of co-operation, and unity of interest in the success of the company'.[101] Herbert frequently espoused the values of increased industrial efficiency, both in his own firm and in British engineering industry generally. As he informed his workers in 1929, modern production methods were central to business success, and the rising productivity of labour was central to this. Calling for a 'personal' commitment by all members of the company, he argued that the management had provided monetary incentives to increase labour productivity, but that this in itself was insufficient, and urged workers to consider the benefits of welfare provision, and work diligently to the

---

[96]   PA 926/1/4/1–3, Minute Books of the Departmental Board of Directors, 14 June, 22 November 1933.

[97]   Lloyd-Jones and Lewis, *Alfred Herbert Ltd*, p. 253.

[98]   For a detailed study of the 'Herbert Spirit' see J. M. Davies, 'Social Relations in an Engineering Factory: Alfred Herbert Ltd, 1887–1922', MA thesis, University of Warwick (1983).

[99]   PA 1270/9/1, *Alfred Herbert News*, January 1929.

[100]   See Davies, 'A Twentieth Century Paternalist'.

[101]   MTTA, Annual Report 1927; PA 1270/9/1, *Alfred Herbert News*, December 1926.

greater interest of the company.[102] Departmental managers echoed the 'Herbert spirit' in their own rhetoric, typified by the speeches of C. W. Clark at the annual meeting of foremen in the late 1940s, where he reflected on the evolution of a unified business culture. In 1947, for example, when Alfred Herbert, 'the first or original foreman or leader in this great organisation', took the chair, he extolled the values of a 'common enterprise', which meant 'greater prosperity for all'.[103] Later, in 1948, at a political forum, Clark advocated the importance of monetary incentives to industrial productivity, adding that in the history of the company there had been 'other important incentives such as the hope of promotion through merit, good working conditions, welfare, and education schemes'.[104] Amongst all this rhetoric, Alfred Herbert was portrayed as an individual leader, the iconic personality who in the company's history had showed 'the keenest interest' in the business.[105]

The 'Herbert spirit' exemplified the belief in a co-operative enterprise, but the business itself was to retain an individual style. The individual ethos was projected to a wider business audience when in 1928 Herbert considered the problems facing the machine-tool industry:

> My own business experience indicates that whenever I am in trouble I can invariably trace the trouble to some fault of my own ... machine tool builders should realise this fact and should look for the remedies for their difficulties, not in complaints against the buyers of their products, but in the elimination of their own weaknesses.[106]

Alfred Herbert recognised that 'the ideals of the tool maker [were] to lead – to make others follow – to make a reputation ... This may mean more money or perhaps not, but in any case leading is better than following, if more difficult'.[107] Leadership for Herbert meant the leadership of his own firm, and his individual style had repercussions for the low level of co-operation in the machine-tool industry.

As the largest firm in the industry, Herbert's provided only a minimal leadership to the industry in terms of the co-ordination of common policies, or in a movement towards rationalisation. For example, as President of the MTTA Herbert was party to attempts to co-ordinate prices by the industry during the 1920s, but these inevitably floundered, and Herbert observed that in times of

---

[102]   PA 1270/9/1, *Alfred Herbert News*, December 1929.

[103]   CA, PA 1270/7/1, Speech by C. W. Clark to Meeting of Alfred Herbert Foremen, 30 October 1947.

[104]   PA 1270/7/1, Speech by C. W. Clark to Meeting of Leamington Spa Young Conservatives, 13 April 1948.

[105]   PA 1270/7/1, Speech by C. W. Clark to Meeting of Alfred Herbert Foremen, 12 November 1949.

[106]   *American Machinist*, 6 December 1928, p. 242E.

[107]   *Machine Tool Review*, Vol. 14, 1926, p. 1.

'adversity it was likely that individualism would prevail'.[108] The policy pursued by the company was itself individualistic, as it used price discounts to maintain sales, and in 1925 Alfred remained aloof to attempts by members of the MTTA to establish precedents for a common policy of tender for the industry, which he saw as an infringement 'on the actions of private enterprise'.[109] At the 1930 AGM of Barclays Bank, Herbert made the impromptu remark that British industry was 'engaged in a war of industry', in which competitive individualism would be the order of the capitalist system.[110] This was most probably a reference to German competition, but it brought forth a series of articles in the *American Machinist* which condemned the comment as a recipe for 'unbridled competition' of 'a warlike kind', that would destroy any hopes of a co-operative spirit on pricing.[111] But a co-operative spirit was not Herbert's motto, and in the phase of re-armament after 1935 he rejected attempts by the government to introduce a common pricing policy under the auspices of the MTTA, and remarked that 'nearly all machine-tool makers were strong individualists, who preferred the private company with its many advantages of direct control and immediate response to stimuli'.[112]

Individual behaviour also stymied attempts to forge a common research policy for the industry. The approach by the DSIR to the MTTA in 1918 to form a research association for the industry led to Herbert commenting as president that research was the prerogative of 'individualistic' firms.[113] Summing up his own view Herbert observed that 'jealousy and secrecy do of necessity exist and … most companies would prefer to solve their own problems themselves rather than to submit same to an Institution'.[114] Alfred's resistance to industrial collaboration was exemplified in 1936, when he rejected overtures by the Board of Trade to use the MTTA to regulate the 'voluntary' planning by individual firms of priority machines for the defence programme. As Herbert insisted, his firm was quite prepared to meet the demands of the defence programme and had the internal capability to plan production programmes accordingly.[115] Above all the company rejected all talk of amalgamation and rationalisation, an issue which absorbed many columns in *The American Machinist*, which compared the inefficiency of the British industry, the duplication of its products, to the larger combined firms in America and Germany.[116] As an example of good practice for Britain to follow,

---

[108] MTTA, Directors' Minute Book, 14 April 1920.

[109] MTTA, Annual Report for 1925, p. 4.

[110] Cited in *American Machinist*, 25 January 1930, p. 287E.

[111] *American Machinist*, 8 February 1930, p. 10E.

[112] MTTA, Annual Report for 1935.

[113] MTTA, Minute Book, 3 October, 13 November 1918.

[114] PA 926/1/4/1–3, Minute Books of the Departmental Board of Directors, 28 October 1918.

[115] MTTA, Annual Report for 1935.

[116] See, for example, *American Machinist*, 20 April 1929, pp. 124–5E; 24 May 1930, p. 219E.

the *American Machinist* referred to the Association of German Machine Tool Factories, an institution which provided a forum for the exchange of ideas on engineering practice and machine design, and also co-ordinated the sales policy of its member firms.[117]

Alfred Herbert was well aware of the trends in America and Germany, and an insight into his ideas on amalgamation, and the governance of his own company, was provided by two articles in the *Alfred Herbert News* on 'Elementary Economics'. The first considered the issue of 'rationalisation and efficiency' and the second the merits of public over private limited liability. In defining rationalisation Herbert demonstrated the pedigree of the engineer entrepreneur. Rationalisation meant 'the combination of a number of competing firms into one large business', which Herbert considered that in theory offered two key advantages. First, combination would reduce competition, with merged firms acting as 'associates'. Second, it would increase administrative efficiency, by one board of directors replacing a number of boards, and by reductions in marketing costs through the concentration of sales in a larger organisation.[118] Herbert, however, while aware of the theoretical approach to amalgamation, remained unconvinced when it came to his observations of its practical implementation:

> We have many examples of combinations of this kind which have been made in recent years. Some of them have been abundantly successful but curiously enough many of them have been disappointing in their results, and it would seem that the success or failure of these large corporations does not so much depend on the economies I have just referred to as on the skill and ability of those who direct and manage their operations.[119]

Herbert concluded that 'amalgamation is only an advantage where the circumstances are such that the businesses dovetail into each other satisfactorily'.[120]

In relation to his own company, he referred to the fact that there had 'been opportunities for entering into combinations ... but I have always turned them down believing that it is better to row our own little boat without having to wrestle with the complications and difficulties which amalgamations involve'. Central to his vision of the Herbert organisation was the talent of his own hand-picked engineering team, and he referred to the fact of inefficiency in large organisations because they lost a sense of identity and 'individual effort' in the management of the firm. In a classic exposé of personal capitalism, Herbert summed up his image of his own company as a 'large business' which had built its success upon the leadership of a team of qualified engineers who had the 'keenness of enterprise' to ensure efficiency in design, production, selling and finance. As the

[117] *American Machinist*, 29 August 1931, p. 30E.
[118] PA 1270/9/1, *Alfred Herbert News*, December 1929.
[119] Ibid.
[120] Ibid.

firm expanded, he argued, the firm could recruit internally 'more and more men to the top positions'.[121] That Herbert was not a lone voice was demonstrated by the words of W. J. Lang at the annual meeting of the MTTA in 1930, who considered that 'rationalisation in engineering could not succeed, unless individualism played its full part'.[122]

A rejection of amalgamation reflected another concern, and that was with the speculative nature of mergers in British industry. As Herbert observed, 'Combinations ... are sometimes handicapped by the way in which their finance are dealt with', and he condemned the tendency towards the over-valuation of capital assets as a means to inflate share prices for the purchase of merged firms. The consequence was that 'these combinations have been handicapped from the start by having to pay interest on debentures and share capital, which ... is far too great for their earning capacity'.[123] Herbert clearly had a deep suspicion of the public company and its speculative nature, and this was taken further in a comparison with the private enterprise. While he acknowledged that limited liability formed the backbone of modern capitalism – providing the medium for the raising of capital through the allotment of preference shares, ordinary shares and debentures, which spread risk – he remained sceptical of their implication for speculation and debt. Debentures, for example, he considered a most pernicious means of raising capital, which brought with them 'a burden of long-term debt'. In general, Herbert asserted, public companies had 'opened the door to a good deal of undesirable finance', which he defined in terms of short-term speculation by financial institutions and individual investors who lacked specific knowledge of the business and its profitability.[124]

> If you look through the Stock Exchange quotations of the shares of limited companies you will notice that while the shares of sound and stable companies are quoted at par, and in many cases much above par, yet on the other hand you will find many companies whose shares are quoted at a fraction only of their nominal value. To speculate in the shares of limited companies without knowing beforehand exactly the position of the companies in question offers possibility of losing money quite as rapidly as gambling at Monte Casino or backing horses.[125]

In comparison, private companies, with their limited shareholding base, and with stipulations on the transfer of shares, created a solid foundation for the long-term governance of organisations, in which the directors acted as 'genuine

---

[121] Ibid.
[122] Cited in *American Machinist*, 24 May 1930, p. 219E.
[123] PA 1270/9/1, *Alfred Herbert News*, December 1929.
[124] PA 1270/9/1, *Alfred Herbert News*, March 1929.
[125] Ibid.

servants' of the shareholders and workers, all, he believed, stakeholders in the company.[126]

At the 1935 AGM he spoke passionately of his 'sincere appreciation of the friendly spirit which prevailed and of the kind way in which matters were brought before him and ... his constant and deep personal interest in the firm'.[127] In 1935 Herbert was 69 years of age, and since the 1920s he had increasingly left to day-to-day running of the company to his departmental board, living the life of a gentleman landowner in Dunley Manor in Hampshire, while keeping a close scrutiny of financial matters. At the 1936 AGM he personally thanked D. M. Gimson, and J. W. Ellson, the financial director and assistant financial director respectively, for producing the accounts which enabled him 'to keep closely in touch with the business'.[128] On the eve of the Second World War, the company was in a solid financial position, operating at full capacity and 'all were working together as friends'. Herbert 'knew of no other business where there was greater freedom from friction or the same friendly co-operation'.[129] During re-armament, the company had pursued a dual strategy, of expanding capacity to meet the increasing demand of the defence programme, while at the same time supplying commercial engineering, a policy which reflected Alfred's constant urging for 'caution', given what he considered to be the temporary and 'abnormal' conditions prevailing.[130] Herbert had presided over a difficult business period, carefully steering the company while building up a loyal group of departmental directors that reflected his own vision of a board of engineers. Directors had been replenished, and the board of 1940 (Table 5.10), had all been internally recruited from within the organisation.

The firm certainly behaved in an individualistic way in relation to the wider industry, but in many ways it was a success story in the history of British industrial capitalism in the late nineteenth and first half of the twentieth centuries, a testimony to the entrepreneurial drive of personal capitalists.[131] Nevertheless, personal capitalism was to leave a legacy. While Herbert may well have envisaged a continual infusion of new blood into the organisation, by the time of his death in 1957 it was an ageing management board which took over the reins of control, and thereafter the ability of management to meet change became of serious concern.

---

[126] Ibid.

[127] PA 586/11, General Minute Book, 20 June 1935.

[128] PA 586/11, General Minute Book, 10 June 1936.

[129] PA 586/11, General Minute Book, 15 June 1939.

[130] See PA 596/11, General Minute Book, 10 June 1936; 9 June 1937.

[131] See Lloyd-Jones and Lewis, *Alfred Herbert Ltd.*

Table 5.10   Herbert Board of Directors 1940

Sir Alfred Herbert	D. M. Gimson
J. C. Blair	A. H. Lloyd
C. W. Clark	G. S. Townsend
W. Core	Joseph Pickin
J. W. Ellson	E. R. Schofield

Source: Stock Exchange Year Book, 1940.

The legacy of personal capitalism

Alfred Herbert Ltd made a vital contribution to the British war effort after 1939, supplying some 65,000 machine tools during the conflict, including factored machines imported from America. The company was also at the forefront of moves to introduce labour dilution, a system for preserving skilled workers, with Alfred himself playing a major role at an industry-wide level.[132] As a controlled establishment during the war, the 'business was hedged round by restrictions and controls',[133] but in October 1944 Sir Alfred informed the AGM that they should 'plan for the future', and a year later the company was exporting 75 per cent of its output to meet the needs of the post-war export drive. Sir Alfred Herbert believed that 'if all members of the company continue to apply themselves energetically he did not feel unduly pessimistic regarding the future'.[134] The year 1944 also marked a major decision in Herbert's business history, when it was converted to a public company. The new public company acquired the business of the private company, and was formed with an authorised capital of £1 million, with £882,635 issued capital. All issued share capital was sub-divided into £1 instead of £5 shares, and 606,875 ordinary and 275,760 6 per cent preference shares were allotted.[135] No formal application, however, was made for an official stock-market quotation until 1946, a delay which was explained by Alfred Herbert in terms of the need to account for excess profit tax, and provide an accurate statement of the finances of the company to the 'press'.[136]

At the same time, the executive control of the company was secured by Alfred Herbert, who at the age of 77 was appointed 'sole chairman and managing director' of the public company.[137] Following the Companies Act of 1947, which

---

[132] Lloyd-Jones and Lewis, *Alfred Herbert Ltd*, pp. 153, 156–9.

[133] PA 586/11, General Minute Book, 9 October 1942.

[134] PA 926/1/1/1, Alfred Herbert Ltd, Minute Book of the Board of Directors, 1944–60, 26 March 1946.

[135] Stock Exchange Year Book, 1945.

[136] PA 586/11, General Minute Book, 15 May 1946.

[137] PA 926/1/1/1, Minute Book of the Board of Directors, 29 March 1944.

set the normal retirement age of directors at 70, shareholders passed a special resolution to enable executives, including Herbert, to continue beyond this age.[138] Financial control was consolidated under a Finance Committee in 1944, which consisted of Sir Alfred as chair, and his close financial directors D. M. Gimson and J. W. Ellson.[139] Despite the rhetoric of Alfred Herbert at the 1943 AGM that his board of directors 'was particularly free of any form of cliques',[140] the committee represented a board within a board and assumed key executive responsibilities, which included the allotment of shares, and the appointment of staff, other than of departmental directors which still remained the sole prerogative of Alfred Herbert. Crucially, the committee held the power to authorise the financial business of the company, which enabled Herbert and his close associates to control the key area of capital expenditure and the building-up of internal reserves. The Finance Committee created a two-tier executive, which set the overall strategy of the company, although it was responsible for reporting to the main departmental board 'for approval and confirmation of all decisions of importance'.[141]

By the mid-1950s, the company had expanded considerably, and operated three factories, two in Coventry and one in Lutterworth, near Leicester, as well as acquiring Sigma Instruments of Letchworth, a small maker of special-purpose testing machinery for the automobile industry. The company now employed 5,700 workers, operated 2,000 machine tools, and with the expansion of its factoring business it could claim to have 'achieved a reputation as the largest machine tool organisation in the world'.[142] Until the late 1950s, the company also remained profitable, its trading profits expanding rapidly in the aftermath of the Korean War (Table 5.11). It continued to develop its reputation as a progressive producer of general-purpose machine tools, as well as developing basic technologies in numerical control in machine-tool design, while at the same time it was Britain's largest agent for the import of American special machine types.[143] To finance expansion, the company retained its tradition of internal financing, and despite the public status of the company Herbert retained the major shareholding, still holding 25 per cent of the issued share capital on his death in 1957.[144] He remained sceptical of attracting public share capital.

---

[138]   PA 926/1/1/1, Minute Book of the Board of Directors, 7 April 1948.

[139]   PA 926/1/1/1, Minute Book of the Board of Directors, 29 March 1944.

[140]   PA 586/11, General Minute Book, 22 August 1943.

[141]   PA 926/1/1/1, Minute Book of the Board of Directors, 29 March 1944.

[142]   *Machine Tool Review*, Vol. 43, 1955, p. 113.

[143]   See Lloyd-Jones and Lewis, *Alfred Herbert Ltd*, pp. 248–9.

[144]   E. W. Evans, 'Some Problems of Growth in the Machine Tool Industry', pp. 363, 378.

Table 5.11   Alfred Herbert Ltd trading and net profits 1950–65 (£million)

	Trading[a]	Net
1950		0.76
1951		0.93
1952		1.19
1953	3.07	1.35
1954	3.48	1.48
1955	3.98	1.77
1956	4.32	1.80
1957	4.61	1.82
1958	3.33	1.42
1959	2.71	1.34
1960	3.69	1.74
1961	4.18	1.80
1962	4.75	1.99
1963	4.45	1.85
1964	4.77	2.21
1965	5.40	3.11

Source: MTTA, Machine Tool Directory, 1966, p. 146.
Note: a. No information is available on trading profits between 1950 and 1952.

A public company

The financial policy of the company was summed up by Herbert at the 1947 and 1948 AGMs, when he replied to a shareholder concerning a proposal to sub-divide shares into 2s units rather than £1, as a means of attracting increased public subscription. Herbert firmly rejected the proposal, noting in 1947 that this was not consistent with a 'sound' financial policy, which had always been pursued by the directors.[145] In 1948 he condemned the proposal as a recipe for speculation. 'The shares of the company', Herbert insisted, 'should not be looked on as speculative but as investments, and he did not approve of the suggestion'. At the same time, he dispelled any notion of depleting the company's reserve assets and in reply

---

[145] PA 586/11, General Minute Book, 2 April 1947.

to questions in 1948 over the possibility of converting a cash balance of £1.76 million into bonus shares he remained committed to the fact that the reserve was

> one of the pillars of the structure of the company and we should miss it very badly if it was not there. It had temporarily been accumulated because certain investments were sold during the previous year and this resulted in the company realising profits of some £58,000 in last year's accounts. The Directors propose to re-invest some of these funds when they consider that the time is suitable.[146]

Pressed by shareholders in 1949 on the same issue of converting the reserve into bonus shares, Herbert showed an authoritarian style to his governance of the company. He dismissed the shareholders' questions, as he was 'not particularly interested in the possible attitude of the stock exchange in this matter', and insisted that 'the issuing of bonus shares did not have any effect on the amount of money to be distributed, while on the other hand a great deal of trouble might be caused'. Shares were 'a basis for investment and not speculation', and Herbert concluded that 'although his attitude might cause criticism, he was not concerned about criticism, his main interest being to operate the business as efficiently as possible and pay a reasonable dividend.'[147]

In 1951, however, the company did raise additional share capital, as a means of funding expansion. The authorised capital was increased from £1.1 million to £2.1 million by the capitalisation of profits and the issue to shareholders of shares in a ration of one for two. Between 1951 and 1964, the company periodically used this method to raise additional capital. Thus, in 1954 the directors authorised the capitalisation of £4,751,879, from the company's general reserve and distributed bonus shares to existing holders of ordinary shares in a ratio of one to two. The company's authorised capital in 1954 now stood at £6 million, and there were further additions in 1958 and 1964, which raised it to £12 million in 1958, and £18 million in 1964.[148] Director C. W. Clark, who succeeded Herbert as chairman in 1957, summed up the financial policy in 1964:

> It is the profits saved from earlier years which we propose to convert into capital and … such profits have always belonged to the shareholders. These profits have already been used to finance the growth of the Company's business and will therefore be more appropriately designated as capital.[149]

---

[146] PA 586/11, General Minute Book, 12 May 1948.

[147] PA 596, General Minute Book, 26 May 1949.

[148] PA 926/1/1/1, Minute Book of the Board of Directors, 18 October, 6 December 1951; 21 July 1954; 25 April 1958; PA 1558/1/1/1, Minute Book of the Board of Directors of Alfred Herbert Ltd, 1960–80, 6 March 1964.

[149] *Machine Tool Review*, Vol. 52, 1964, p. 47.

The issue of succession

During the 1950s, the company retained its governance rules in terms of financial policy, and pursued a cautious approach to over-expansion. Alfred Herbert, now reaching an advanced age, presided over an ageing managerial board of long-serving directors, and the issue of succession became a major issue by the mid-1950s. Rather than a smooth transition, which had been the hope of Herbert, the board of directors fragmented into a series of cliques. In August 1955, for example, C. W. Clark threatened resignation over the choice of K. W. Norman to replace Joseph Pickin, who had served the company for 60 years, on the board. After a 'lengthy discussion' Clark retracted, but it was a harbinger of a growing power struggle to come. In February 1956, the directors announced the death of A. H. Lloyd, the director of design, after 50 years of service, resulting in Clark again questioning the replacement of directors.[150] Of more serious concern to the deeply retrenched members of the board was the uncertainty over Alfred Herbert's own vision of the succession. In 1957, then aged 90, and in declining health, Herbert appointed his close associate and finance director D. M. Gimson as deputy chair, and Clark and J. C. Blair as joint managing directors, to act in a supporting role. At the same time, and to the consternation of Clark, he extended his prerogative to include the right to appoint and dismiss the deputy chair and managing directors, which gave a sense of insecurity to the recently nominated managing director. Further, the firm had been built upon a family foundation, and although Herbert had no surviving sons he did have two grandsons, who held middle-management positions in the company. In April 1957, Alfred, with 'much pleasure', announced the appointment of his grandsons as deputy directors, with rights to attend the board on invitation by the directors, a matter which raised objections from Clark, who believed that they were not qualified to hold executive positions. What the views of Herbert were on this subject is not known, but after his death on 26 May 1957 the executors of his will authorised the nomination of Gimson as chairman, an acknowledgement that Herbert understood the need for a continuity of management.[151]

The appointment of Gimson was unanimously passed by the board in June 1957, but it did little to reconcile diverse internal interests in the board. Director J. C. Blair commented that 'the eyes of the business world were upon us', and he pleaded for 'a strong and united board', but at the same time directly confronted the authority of the Finance Committee, which he considered had assumed executive powers which should be the prerogative of the board. Supported by J. H. Mahler, a recently appointed director, Blair tabled a resolution to devolve executive policy making from the Finance Committee to the full board, and commented that the devolution of authority was crucial to the 'unity' of the board. On this matter, the future executive roles of Clark and Blair became paramount, with both the

---

[150] PA 926/1/1/1, Minute Book of the Board of Directors, 9 August, 13 September 1955; 9 February 1956.

[151] PA 926/1/1/1, Minute Book of the Board of Directors, 26 April, 5 June 1957.

managing directors insisting that Sir Alfred's instructions to his executors to appoint them in the first place implied that they should have a prominent position in executive decision-making. Accepting this interpretation, Gimson confirmed the appointment of the joint managing directors, and to appease Clark proposed his appointment as deputy chairman, an offer that Clark accepted. This gave Gimson the opportunity to reconsider the 'wide powers' of the Finance Committee, and he widened its constitution to include Clark and Blair. This decision represented a departure from the concentration of executive authority in the hands of a single individual, backed up by a small committee, and although the Committee retained its authority it nevertheless represented a widening of participation at an executive level. Responding to Gimson's suggestion that the Committee should maintain the authority for the purchase of new plant, 'previously authorised by Sir Alfred', Blair insisted that they were a 'Board of engineers' who could provide valuable insight into capital investment policy. This strong stance by Blair led to an alteration in the powers of the Committee ensuring 'that matters of policy should be decided by the Board as a whole'. Effectively, the directors reorganised the board to ensure the permanency of its existing members, and despite the fact that Sir Alfred's will had expressed the wish that his grandsons should be appointed to full directorships this was rejected, the board deferring the decision for future consideration.[152]

The succession of 1957 represented a break with the past, in the sense that the board saw itself as having a more collective function. In this respect, the eulogy given by Gimson at the 1958 AGM was somewhat ironic, when he praised the 'great founder and Chairman', who had presided over every AGM since the establishment of the company, and 'while maintaining the keenest interest in the company's business … appreciated the importance of delegating authority to the fullest extent, and thus ensured that the administration of the business will be continued with the same vigour and efficiency'.[153] The wrangles in the boardroom in 1957 told a different story, of deep frustration with Herbert's governance style, his concentration of decision-making in the Finance Committee and the uncertainty of succession. Nevertheless, a persistence with a personal style of governance continued after Herbert's death, reinforced by the rise of Clark. Gimson's reign lasted only 12 months, and he resigned the chair in 1958 due to ill health, which opened the door for Clark, who became chairman and sole managing director, supported by Blair as deputy chairman.[154] By the late 1950s an elite board had evolved through a combination of merit and reward for long service. In 1957 the accumulated service of the directors totalled 432 years, an average of 39 years for each (Table 5.12).

The board of 1957 was a testimony to the tradition of internal promotion, but during Clark's term of office there was a move towards external recruitment, as the company met the challenge of increased competition from the late 1950s.

---

[152] PA 926/1/1/1, Minute Book of the Board of Directors, 5 June, 2 July 1957.

[153] PA 926/1/1/1, Minute Book of the Board of Directors, 4 March 1958.

[154] PA 926/1/1/1, Minute Book of the Board of Directors, 30 October 1958.

Table 5.12   The Herbert Board of Directors, following the death of Sir Alfred
Herbert in 1957

Director	Responsibility	Years of service
D. M. Gimson	Chairman	54
C. W. Clark	Joint managing director	50
J. C. Blair	Joint managing director	45
W. Core	Sales director	37
O. S. Townsend	Technical director	59
K. W. Norman	Factored division director	22
J. W. Ellson	Chief accountant	38
B. C. Harrison	Design director	33
J. H. Mahler	Combustion engine dept	29
S. A. B. Muirhead	Works director	38
L. J. Hugo	Factored division director	27

Source: *Machine Tool Review*, Vol. 45, 1957, p. 56.

Clark was well aware that the company's managerial capabilities were becoming stretched. Sir Halford Reddish, a director of Portland Cement and Hawker Siddeley, was appointed in a consultative role in 1959, together with E. A. Smith, 43 years of age, and a partner in a leading firm of international management consultants, and a financial director of a public company in civil engineering.[155] A prominent member of the Coventry Chamber of Commerce, V. N. Brailsford joined the board in 1960. Internal promotions, however, were not discarded, and considering the future succession B. C. Harrison was appointed deputy managing director in a supporting role to Clark in 1964. Aware of the need for a smooth succession, Clark was also concerned about the need to inject 'new blood' into top management, and in October 1964 he proposed the appointment of an outsider, Richard Dilworth Young, as deputy chair. Young was a prominent engineer having worked previously for Tube Investments. At the same time, Clark affirmed his intention that Harrison should succeed him as sole managing director, but the appointment of Young led to renewed confusion concerning the succession, which was finally settled in 1966 when Young became chairman with Harrison as managing director.[156]

---

[155] PA 926/1/1/1, Minute Book of the Board of Directors, 28 August 1959; PA 1558/1/1/1, Minute Book of the Board of Directors, 2 December 1960; 24 July 1961; *Machine Tool Review*, Vol. 49 (1961), p. 99.

[156] PA 1558/1/1/1, Minute Book of the Board of Directors, 2 February, 26 October, 11 December 1964; 7 May 1965; 4 March, 8 July 1966; *Machine Tool Review*, Vol. 53, 1965, p. 48.

In the aftermath of Herbert's death, the spirit of co-operation he had constantly evoked evaporated, as the board faced a period of change and uncertainty. The legacy of his long personal control of the company was that it left an ageing executive management to deal with the problems of merger which so influenced the history of the company from the mid-1960s. Young's reign at the company brought major changes, first in 1965 with the acquisition of the machine-tool interests of BSA, and then later in 1967 with its association with Ingersoll, an American producer of numerical controlled production systems. Both these ventures proved failures, and became financial millstones around the company's neck. In particular there was a failure to integrate sales policy and to assimilate staff from the amalgamated firms into the Herbert organisation.[157] All these problems may well have echoed the concerns of Alfred Herbert in the 1920s concerning the problematic nature of the advantages of acquisition. Above all else, as Young observed in 1967, the management lacked the technical capabilities to develop new numerical control machines, and the quantity of managers to create effective administrative structures.[158]

---

[157] See Lloyd-Jones and Lewis, *Alfred Herbert Ltd*, pp. 276–93.
[158] PA 1558/1/1/1, Minute Book of the Board of Directors, 8 December 1967.

Chapter 6
The Relationship between Companies and their Shareholders: Greenwood & Batley and Hadfields

Introduction

The first half of the twentieth century was a period that, according to Chandler, saw a major and crucial divergence between the patterns of share ownership in the UK and the USA. He asserts that this was the point at which the USA made the transition to managerial capitalism whilst the UK remained committed to personal capitalism for several decades longer, with alleged deleterious consequences for its economic progress.[1] A number of chapters in this book discuss Chandler's arguments, with attention paid to the nature of management, and particularly senior management, under personal capitalism. In doing so, we recognise that distinctive business cultures were developed, reflecting the styles of governance groups and the relationships between the members of these groups. The governance of companies reflects the idiosyncratic behaviour of individuals within the organisation. This is not to assume, however, that shareholders did not play a significant and varied role in organisations characterised by personal capitalism. A number of factors are discussed in this chapter that are relevant to the roles played by shareholders in the period 1900–40. One of these was the distribution of share ownership, and the rights and returns offered to investors. This was a period in which the pattern of ownership underwent changes, not all of which are recognised by the conventional model of personal capitalism. The extent to which ownership and control overlapped in UK companies in this period may have been overstated for a number of reasons, which will be discussed later in this chapter.

There were two major Companies Acts during the period 1900 to 1940, in 1907 and 1929, which, although criticised for their failure to improve financial reporting, had some effect on the relationship between shareholders and directors. A number of legal cases also cast light on problems within the governance relationship – notably the 1906 *Newton v Chambers* case, examined in the chapter on corporate governance and elite groups at BSA, and the Royal Mail Steam Packet case of 1931, which reflected the difficulties caused by permissive accounting regulation. The 1920s and 1930s witnessed debates about the desirable role of accounting and auditing in promoting companies' reporting – but it was not until

---

[1]   Chandler, *Scale and Scope*, pp. 288–9.

1947 that legislation, with the cooperation of the accounting professional bodies, was able to settle some of the arguments of the inter-war period.[2] The companies considered in this chapter, Greenwood & Batley Ltd and Hadfields Ltd, contribute to an understanding of the features of shareholding in this period. Both were listed companies, with a large number of shareholders, and the composition of their shareholder groups, their use of financial reporting, and their relationships with investors, all vary in ways that offer insights into the idiosyncrasies of personal capitalism. As discussed previously, Chandler's verdict on British companies has been that they were slow to accept the dispersal of share ownership, and that the persistence of ownership concentration was one of the reasons for the underperformance of British industry in the early twentieth century. It is therefore interesting to look at the evidence available about the shareholder population of listed companies, beginning in the next section with the contemporary discussions of the subject.

Who were the shareholders?

In 1929, *The Economist* published a short article based on its review of large shareholdings in a number of British companies, which is summarised in Table 6.1. The conclusion drawn in the article was that ownership and control had indeed become separated in British companies, with an average holding of £152 of 'all issued ordinary and preference capital … among more than 500,000 individual shareholders'. The mass of shareholders, it claimed, were passive and inarticulate, so that the board of directors had *de facto* if not *de jure* control of the company.[3] Even amongst some of Britain's largest firms – such as Imperial Tobacco, a company formed through a merger of 1901, and Britain's second largest manufacturing firm in 1930 with a market valuation of £130.5 million[4] – large shareholders with holdings of £10,000 or more held only 43 per cent of capital. At the textile firm of Courtaulds, Britain's fourth largest manufacturing concern in 1930, with a market valuation of £51.9 million, share ownership was even more widely dispersed, with just 26.2 per cent of shareholders classified as large owners. The wide dispersion of shareholding, emphasised in Table 6.1 is, of course, a reflection of the limited involvement of institutional investors in British business during this period, which only accelerated with the growth of stock markets from the 1950s.[5] Evidence of a wide dispersion of shareholding, and limited institutional investment, can also be found in the work of Sargant Florence.

---

[2]   See Maltby, 'Was the 1947 Companies Act a Response to a National Crisis?', pp. 31–60.

[3]   *Economist*, 30 March 1929 pp. 691–2.

[4]   See Hannah, *The Rise of the Corporate Economy*, pp. 22, 24, 101–102.

[5]   Wilson, *British Business History*, p. 191; Jeremy, *A Business History of Britain*, pp. 313–14.

Table 6.1   Survey of share ownership distribution in a sample of large- and medium-size companies in Britain

(1) Company	(2) Total shareholders	(3) No. of shareholders each owning £10,000 or more	(4) % of total capital held by shareholders in (3)
Large-size companies:			
Imperial Tobacco	77,200	233	43.0
Courtaulds	28,200	57	26.2
Anglo-Persian	17,100	4	13.1[b]
Brunner Mond[a]	26,200	66	31.4
Vickers	46,400	30	4.8
Dunlop Rubber	51,600	162	20.3
Cunard	14,000	39	30.4
Medium-size Companies:			
General Electric	10,100	11	10.3
Spiller's Milling	8,300	20	21.5
Phoenix Assurance	8,500	18	26.2
Ebbw Vale Steel	7,800	15	29.8
Bass	1,900	21	59.8
Marconi's Wireless	24,600	7	3.8
English Sewing Cotton	9,700	3	2.7
Debenture Corporation	2,000	9	12.2
Cairn Line	2,900	8	20.1
Rover Company	8,300	—	—
Savoy Hotel	2,400	1	1.6

Source: 'Shareholders and Control', *Economist*, 30 March 1929, pp. 691–2.
Notes: a. Subsequently merged in Imperial Chemical Industries; b. Excluding British government's holding.

Writing in 1953,[6] he cited a 1949 survey of shareholdings in large UK companies, providing the distribution of ownership shown in Table 6.2.

---

6   P. Sargant Florence, *The Logic of British and American Industry*.

Table 6.2   Distribution of shareholdings in UK companies, 1949

	% of holdings	% of capital
Individual persons	42.5	36.4
Trustees	4.5	2.4
Banks	3.9	2.9
Insurance companies	10.3	5.6
Investment trusts	8.0	5.3
Other companies	3.7	20.4
Nominees	27.0	26.0

Source: Sargant Florence, *The Logic of British and American Industry*, p. 180.

Sargant Florence's data shows a wide dispersion of shareholding, with 42.5 per cent of shares in UK companies being held by 'individual persons', representing 36.4 per cent of capital. In comparison, financial institutions such as banks, insurance companies and investment trusts accounted for only 22.2 per cent of shares and 13.8 per cent of capital, a symptom of the barriers between industry and city investors in the interwar decades.[7] Although Sargant Florence was obliged to admit that not all investors were individuals, and not all individuals were ineffective, he nevertheless characterised 'the great majority' as 'ignorant, business-shy, or *too* busy – or any two of them, or perhaps all three'.[8] Directors, on this reading, were powerful not because of their concentrated holdings, but because of the absence of intervention by shareholders. As examined in the case study of BSA, the issue of shareholder 'voice' is an important aspect in the study of corporate governance. Certainly, *The Economist* in 1929, and later Sargant Florence in 1953, assumed that the balance of power in corporations rested within the higher echelons of the firm, the individual investor remaining incapable of effecting change, despite a growing dispersal of shareholding in the first half of the twentieth century. For example, Franks, Mayer and Rossi, making a survey of British companies between 1900 and 2000, conclude that 'Ownership of the sample of UK firms incorporated around 1900 was rapidly dispersed with the shareholdings of inside directors more than halving over the 40 years to 1940'.[9] Hannah also concludes that UK shareholding in the late nineteenth and early

---

[7]   Wilson, *British Business History*, pp. 182–8. It is interesting to note that in 1963 'individual persons' accounted for 58.7 per cent of the ownership of UK equities: Jeremy, *A Business History of Britain*, p. 314.

[8]   Sargant Florence, *The Logic of British and American Industry*, p. 180.

[9]   Franks, Mayer and Rossi, 'Ownership: Evolution and Regulation'.

twentieth centuries was more dispersed than that in the USA.[10] He attributes this to a number of significant differences between the UK and US markets. Nominal share values were lower in the UK than in the USA and typical share bargain values were lower: $500 in London compared with $10,000 in New York. This suggests that the UK market was open to a wider range of investors.[11] An important feature, Hannah suggests, was the London Stock Exchange requirement that two-thirds of any new issue should be floated to the public at large. This made it more difficult in the UK than in the USA for vendors, either the owners or promoters of the business, to retain majority control over the company they were launching on the market.[12] Hannah concedes that the USA caught up with the UK by the inter-war years, but suggests that what Berle and Means described in the early 1930s as the divorce of ownership and control in America's largest 200 corporations constituted a 'remarkably fast retreat from personal capitalism' in which the USA caught up with, rather than overtook, the UK.[13]

Dispersed ownership, as Franks et al. point out, is normally associated with 'strong regulation' in the form of protection of investors' rights.[14] Such regulation, including provisions about financial reporting and shareholders' 'anti-director rights', was absent in the UK at the beginning of the twentieth century, and as Franks et al. acknowledge this throws up a paradox for the historian of corporate governance. On the one hand, dispersal is associated with high levels of accountability to ensure investor confidence. On the other hand, how can dispersal be achieved without mechanisms to provide investors with assurance?[15] To explore this paradox the case studies of Greenwood & Batley and Hadfields offer an insight into the behaviour of corporations in relation to the issue of share dispersal and accountability. We begin by reviewing the composition of their shareholder populations, and the characteristics and behaviour of the two companies' shareholders during the period from the early twentieth century to the end of the 1930s, before considering the nature of their relationship with the companies and the structures which underpinned it.

Greenwood & Batley Ltd and Hadfields Ltd: capital structures compared

In 1886, the partnership of Thomas Greenwood and John Batley founded the firm of Greenwood & Batley of Leeds, machine-tool makers and general engineers. Following the death of the co-founder, Thomas Greenwood, in 1873, and the retirement of John Batley, Greenwood's son Arthur took on a major role in

---

[10]   See Hannah, 'The "Divorce" of Ownership', pp. 404–438.

[11]   Ibid., p. 406.

[12]   Ibid., pp. 414–15.

[13]   Ibid., p. 422; Berle and Means, *The Modern Corporation and Private Property*.

[14]   Franks et al., 'Ownership, Evolution and Regulation', p. 1.

[15]   Ibid., p. 54.

the management of the business. In 1888 the concern was converted to a limited company, the original family connections ensured by the appointment of Arthur, a major shareholder, as managing director, together with three co-managing directors: his brother George, his cousin Henry, and John Henry Wurtzburg, a design engineer of long standing. The decision to convert to a public company was to raise additional capital for expansion, and the initial share issue of £300,000 left £35,000, divided into £10 ordinary shares, for factory additions, after the partners received £265,000 for the value of the firm.[16] In 1890, the directors sanctioned an additional issue of part-paid ordinary and preference shares, with further calls in 1893 and 1909, as well as an issue of debentures in 1893. By 1914, the company's issued capital structure consisted of £174,000 of ordinary shares, £100,000 of 7 per cent preference shares and £80,000 in 5 per cent debentures. In 1920, the company increased ordinary share capital to £348,000 by a 1:1 bonus issue, achieved by capitalising reserves, consisting chiefly of £150,000 arising from a fixed asset revaluation. At the same time, in order to widen share participation, the directors authorised the splitting of shares from £10 to £1 nominal value. The 'Notice to the Shareholders' from the directors communicated their intent 'to comply with what appears to be a general desire on the part of shareholders ... of placing your shares on the same basis as those of other industrial undertakings'. Following this new issue, the gearing ratio of Greenwood & Batley was approximately 11 per cent throughout the inter-war period.[17] This lower gearing ratio, which compared to 22 per cent previously, meant that the company was carrying less risk and a lower burden of interest. Consequently, more profit was potentially available to distribute to shareholders as dividend.

Table 6.3 summarises the capital structure of Hadfields Ltd between 1888 and 1937. From its foundation as a public limited company in 1888, down to 1900, the ordinary shares of the company held a nominal value of £10 each, at which date the directors subdivided them and converted them to £1 shares. The company first issued preference shares valued at £78,425 in 1898, and by additional subscriptions the value of these shares was gradually increased to £200,000 in 1901 and £300,000 in 1906. Before the First World War, there was a steady increase in the issue of ordinary shares, followed in 1919/1920 with a major re-capitalisation. This was consistent with the immediate post-war investment boom, associated with stock market speculation and the burdening of companies throughout the depressed economic climate of the inter-war period with overcapitalisation.[18] The next development was the writing-down of share capital in 1935, followed by an exchange of debentures for ordinary shares in 1937. Between 1889 and 1899, and again from 1920 onwards, when the company faced the pressures of the

[16]   R. Floud, 'Greenwood, Arthur', in D. J. Jeremy (ed.), *Dictionary of Business Biography*, Vol. 3 (London, Butterworths, 1985), pp. 642–3.

[17]   West Yorkshire Archive Service (hereafter WYAS), Leeds, GB/NNAF/B6390, Box 63, Annual Reports and Balance Sheets, 1889–1971.

[18]   Hannah, *Rise of the Corporate Economy*, pp. 60–61.

Table 6.3   Changes in the capital structure of Hadfields Ltd, 1888–1937

	Debentures (£)	Ordinary shares of £10 (£)	Ordinary shares of £1 (£)	Preference shares (£)	Comments
1888		33,000			
1889	50,000	90,750			
1891	45,000				
1898				78,425	
1899	Paid off			157,150	
1900				193,250	
1900		Converted to £1 ordinary shares	180,750		Conversion + new issue
1901			200,000	200,000	New issues
1903			250,000		Rights issue
1904			300,000		Rights issue
1906				300,000	
1911			305,135		Rights issue
1912			400,000		New issue
1919			1,600,000		Rights + bonus issues
1920	745,000		1,845,000		Rights issue
1921	1,000,000		1,859,000		
1922	1,039,000		1,860,000		
1935			930,000		Reconstruction
1937	593,000		1,078,000		Exchange debentures/ ordinary

Source: Hadfields Records, Vol. 7, Ordinary, Extraordinary and AGM Minutes, 1889–1919; Vol. 8, Ordinary, Extraordinary and AGM Minutes, 1920–53.

economic downturn, it resorted to debenture finance. Until 1923, the debenture stock placed a heavy financial burden on the company, returning interest of 7.5 per cent in 1923 when they were redeemed and exchanged for 5.5 per cent to save £18,000 annually. As part of the 1935 reconstruction interest was reduced from 5.5 per cent to 4.25 per cent. In 1937, £446,000 debentures were exchanged for ordinary shares. Gearing was thereby much reduced: it had been 29 to 30 per cent throughout the 1920s and 1930s. The reduction of debentures and the writing-down of the ordinary share capital had the effect of reducing the company's capital base to reflect the irretrievable losses it had suffered during the post-war downturn. It marked the beginning of a new era in Hadfields' financing.

Shareholder characteristics

Our understanding of share ownership in the UK in the nineteenth and twentieth centuries is still developing, as indicated earlier in this chapter. A detailed study of the composition of the shareholder populations of Greenwood & Batley and Hadfields is of interest for the light it casts on shareholders' involvement with, and understanding of, their companies' performance. This section of the chapter draws attention to four characteristics of the shareholder groups: the dispersion of shareholdings; the gendered division of share ownership; the location of investors and the retention of shares in a high trust environment; and the importance of directors as large shareholders.

Dispersion of shareholdings

In terms of the composition of shareholding, Greenwood & Batley had 286 ordinary and 216 preference shareholders in 1916, some of whom owned both types of share.[19] By 1933, shareholders totalled 770, (but a breakdown between ordinary and preference shares is not available for this date).[20] Out of the 286 ordinary shareholders in 1916, 68 had 500 or more shares, 45 had 1,000 or more and just 6 shareholders held 5,000 or more. The average ordinary shareholding was £608, suggesting a highly dispersed distribution of equity amongst shareholders. The wide dispersal of holding was also evident for preference shares in 1916. Six large shareholders accounted for 26 per cent of the total number of shares issued, with just 34 out of 216 preference shareholders holding 500 or more shares, 23 holding 1,000 or more and just 3 shareholders holding 5,000 or more. The average preference shareholding was £416.

   In comparison, a survey of the ordinary shareholders' register between 1900 and 1933 indicates that Hadfields had about 7,500 shareholders, about ten times as many as Greenwood & Batley, with an average holding of £250 per shareholder. Similarly to Greenwood & Batley, however, there was a high dispersion of shareholding by size of shareholder. Between 1900 and 1933, 217 large shareholders held 1,700 or more shares. Some 1,800 shareholders held between 101 and 1,699 shares, while

---

   [19]   Information compiled from WYL/298, Greenwood & Batley, List of Shareholders, 25 July 1916.
   [20]   Information compiled from WYL/298, Greenwood & Batley, List of Shareholders, 20 July 1933.

a predominance of small shareholders, totalling 3,400, had between 26 and 100 shares, with a further 2,100 shareholders holding between 1 and 25 shares.[21]

Gendered division of share ownership

A summary of the distribution of shareholders in 1916 at Greenwood & Batley by gender (Table 6.4) shows that women played a significant role; they accounted for 31 per cent of the total number of ordinary shareholders, and 16.3 per cent of ordinary shareholders by value. The average male holding of ordinary shares was £740, compared to £320 for females. Women represented 38 per cent of the total number of preference shareholders, and 18.7 per cent by value, suggesting that they might have been attracted by the more secure return than that offered by the ordinary shares. The average male holding of preference shares was £614 and the average female holding £226. Women also had a significant involvement as shareholders in Hadfields, as outlined in Table 6.5.

Table 6.4   Male and female shareholders in Greenwood & Batley 1916

Share type	No. male shareholders	No. female shareholders	Value male holdings (£)	Value female holdings (£)
Ordinary	197	89	145,721	28,474
Preference	133	83	81,654	18,744

Source: WYAS, GB/NNAF/B6390, Box 63.

Table 6.5   Women ordinary shareholders in Hadfields, 1900–1933

	No of women	Total in sample	Women as % of total
1,700+ shares	29	217	13.4
101–1,699 shares	117	456	25.6
26–100 shares	195	859	22.7
1–25 shares	121	527	23.0

Source: Hadfields Records, Volumes 159–163, Share Registers.

---

[21]   Hadfields Records, Box 9, Abstracts from AGMs and Correspondence, Document dated 5 March 1935.

Location of investors and shareholder trust

The list of ordinary shareholders at Greenwood & Batley in 1916 shows that 74 per cent of them resided in Yorkshire, as did 55 per cent of preference shareholders. Of local Yorkshire investors, there was a predominance of women. Some 91 per cent of females holding ordinary shares were Yorkshire residents, compared to 65 per cent for males, and of preference shareholders located in Yorkshire 66 per cent were male and 34 per cent female. What is of significant importance from the data on location in 1916 is the low level of London investment, with only 10 per cent of ordinary and 13 per cent of preference shareholders having a London address. These patterns of gender and location continued into the inter-war years, as evidenced from an examination of the shareholding schedules for Greenwood & Batley in 1933. In that year, the company had 770 shareholders, of whom 246 or 32 per cent were women, and 524 or 68 per cent male. Of women investors, 39.4 per cent lived in Yorkshire compared with 38.8 per cent of males, while just 12 per cent of all shareholders in 1933 had a London address.

During the period 1900 to 1930 at Hadfields, 44 per cent of all shareholders, 55 per cent of those with 25 shares or fewer, had a Sheffield address, and only 8 per cent were based in London. Hadfields' registers between 1900 and 1933 included eight institutions with a total of 24,093 ordinary shares or 12.9 per cent of the total. Again, institutional investment remained low, and the high number of local shareholders seems to replicate the pattern of investment characterising the Sheffield steel industry in the nineteenth century. As Newton observes, from her study of the origins of public limited companies in Sheffield during the period 1850 to 1885, the shareholders in these concerns were symptomatic of 'a highly localised capital market', representative of a 'high trust' environment which created dedicated investors in personalised 'local networks'.[22] Such local capital networks enabled 'the proliferation of limited liability' while at the same time they enhanced the steel industry's capability to raise external finance.[23]

The local concentration of shareholdings, as discussed later, signifies the parochial nature of British industrial capitalism, with its heavy orientation towards local investment funds and limited flows of capital from metropolitan sources.[24] Indeed, as our case study of Raleigh indicated, local capital networks were the preferred option for public subscription, reducing uncertainty by the reliance of the company on selling shares to business or personal subscribers in the local area.[25] Similarly, Newton, in her study of capital networks in the steel industry in Sheffield from 1850 to 1885, observes that in the public sale of shares company

---

[22] L. Newton, 'Capital Networks in the Sheffield Region, 1850–1885', in J. F. Wilson and A. Popp (eds), *Industrial Clusters and Regional Business Networks in England, 1750–1970* (Aldershot, Ashgate, 2003), p. 153.

[23] Ibid., p. 154.

[24] For a discussion of these issues see Wilson, *British Business History*.

[25] See Lloyd-Jones and Lewis, *Raleigh*, pp. 63–5, 91–2.

promoters preferred 'shareholders who resided in the local area', tapping into 'business or personal networks'.[26] That such a 'high trust' environment continued is evident from the information provided in Table 6.6, which analyses the number of share transactions carried out by largest shareholders at Hadfields between 1912 and 1928, in terms of share allotments, purchases and sales.

Table 6.6   Number of transactions by large Hadfields shareholders (holding 1,700 or more shares) 1912–28

	No. transactions	Comment
1912	91	New issue
1913	25	
1914	54	
1915	25	
1916	72	
1917	34	
1918	37	
1919	516	New issue
1920	292	New issue
1921	158	New issue
1922	139	
1923	149	
1924	103	
1925	62	
1926	32	
1927	59	
1928	139	

Source: Hadfields Records, Vols 159–63, Share Registers,

During this period, there were 217 large shareholders, holding 1,700 shares or more, and the company offered a number of new share issues that would be likely to attract them to take up allotments. The figures suggest that shareholders did not frequently engage in transactions; having acquired a stake in the company, they were not likely to dispose of it very readily. At the local level, the evidence from the Greenwood & Batley share schedules suggests that investors were encouraged or advised to purchase shares by family advice or influence. For example, out of a total of 124 women investors in 1916, 55 per cent had a surname in common with

---

[26]   Newton, 'Capital Networks', p. 153.

one or more other investors, and this was still 50 per cent in 1933. Shareholders remained loyal, with 32 per cent of women and 29.7 per cent of men from the 1916 list retaining their shares in the listings of 1933.

Directors as large shareholders

Despite share dispersion, the managing executive at Greenwood & Batley continued to hold concentrations of shares. For example, in 1916, all six directors of the company held ordinary shares. These represented 19,151, or 11 per cent out of the total number of 174,000 ordinary shares. Five of the six directors also held preference shares, with 13,347, 13.3 per cent, out of 100,000 preference shares concentrated in the hands of the directorship. By 1933, four out of the five directors still held equity in the company. The level of institutional investment in the company remained consistent with our earlier general observations concerning their delayed appearance in British business during the inter-war years. In 1916, four institutions had ordinary shares in Greenwood & Batley, valued at £19,630 or 11.3 per cent of total capitalisation, with just one institutional investor holding preference shares, valued at £7,816 or 7.8 per cent. By 1933, this had risen to 15 institutions holding a mixture of both ordinary and preference shares.

A document drawn up for Hadfields in 1935, before the capital reconstruction of the company, which listed directors' shareholdings, reinforces the point that share ownership was very dispersed. Sir Robert A. Hadfield, the chairman of the board of directors, held 237,540 ordinary shares, some 14 per cent of the total, and only one other director held ordinary shares, totalling just 9,640 or 0.5 per cent of all ordinary shares in 1935. At this point, there were 60 shareholders with 3,000 or more ordinary shares, including Sir Robert's large holding. Between them, they held 570,635 ordinary shares, 31 per cent of the total, 30,000 or 10 per cent of the preference shares, and 24,469 or 2.4 per cent of the debenture stock.[27]

Comparisons of the two companies

From the survey of shareholders in Greenwood & Batley and Hadfields a number of common factors emerge. As suggested in the 1929 *Economist* article, the size of shareholdings was indeed dispersed, with numerous small holdings and relatively few large ones. The geographical pattern of shareholders was very localised, and Londoners were in a minority. This is in line with the conclusion drawn by Davis and Huttenback that Britain 'was not one capital market but two',[28] with investment

---

[27] Hadfields Records, Box 9, Document dated 5 March 1935.

[28] L. Davis and R. A. Huttenback, *Mammon and the Pursuit of Empire: The Political Economy of British Imperialism, 1860–1912* (Cambridge, Cambridge University Press, 1987), pp. 210–11.

in iron, coal and steel by provincials being nearly twice that of Londoners in the early twentieth century.[29] In the case of Sheffield, this replicated the nineteenth-century pattern of local capital investment, with its skewed distribution around the northern industrial districts.[30] Similarly, in centres of British engineering, 'local capital networks were important for supplying capital for formation and further expansion'.[31] The results for Greenwood & Batley and Hadfield suggest a pattern of local support for local companies, with Yorkshire shareholders predominating over Londoners. Women made up a significant proportion of investors. Although we have no details currently for quantities they owned in Hadfield, allowing us to make detailed comparison, they nevertheless had apparently fewer shares than men, and a slight favour for preference over ordinary shares. This meant that they had a more secure prospect of income from their investments but did not have voting power to wield at shareholder meetings. Shareholders were not quick to leave once they had invested – the low volume of transactions in Hadfields and the proportion of shareholders who stayed with Greenwood & Batley suggest that there was an element of 'inertia' or of loyalty in their attitude. A key issue to address is, accordingly, the reasons for the important choices that they made. We begin in the following section by examining share performance in the two companies.

Share performance

Tables 6.7 and 6.8 summarise share price and dividend levels for both Hadfields and Greenwood & Batley during the period 1910 to 1939. In both cases, the records show dramatic fluctuations in share price over the period. As one would expect, high share prices were evident at the end of the First World War, and during the post-war inflationary boom, Hadfields recording a peak price of 162s 6d in 1919, and Greenwood & Batley 320s in 1920.

As in the case studies of Raleigh and BSA in Chapters 2 and 4, the company and its shareholders reaped the benefits of war profits. Thereafter, both Greenwood & Batley and Hadfields registered a sharp decline in share prices, which remained relatively low throughout the 1920s and first half of the 1930s, only moving upwards after 1935 as the momentum of rearmament fuelled a recovery. Hadfields paid no ordinary dividends from 1931 to 1935 inclusive, and furthermore the normal preference dividend of 4.5 per cent was suspended from 1931 to 1934 inclusive. Greenwood & Batley managed only single-figure dividends for most of the inter-war period. Hadfields had to service a high level of long-term debt until it reconstructed its capital in 1935.

---

[29] Ibid., p. 215.

[30] Newton, 'Capital Networks', p. 150.

[31] Lloyd-Jones and Lewis, *Raleigh*, p. 21. See also Lloyd-Jones and Lewis, *Alfred Herbert Ltd*, pp. 29–30.

Table 6.7   Greenwood & Batley ordinary share prices and dividends, 1910–39

	Highest for the year (shillings)	Lowest for the year (shillings)	Dividend (shillings)	Dividend[a] (%)
1910	62/6	62/6	0	0
1911	65/6	60/0	0	0
1912	60/0	43/9	0	0
1913	55/0	55/0	0	0
1914	67/6	55/0	10/0	10
1915	160/0	155/6	25/0	25
1916	200/0	40/0	10/0	10
1917	210/0	175/0	40/0	40
1918	320/0	203/9	35/0	35
1919	265/6	200	30/0	30
1920[b]	32/6	10/0	3/0	15
1921	10/6	8/6	1/0	5
1922	12/6	6/4 $^{1}/_{4}$	1/2	5.8
1923	14/3	10/9	1/0	5
1924	14/0	8/2	1/0	5
1925	12/9	9/4 $^{1}/_{2}$	1/0	5
1926	12/1 $^{1}/_{2}$	10/1 $^{1}/_{2}$	1/0	5
1927	12/6	11/7 $^{1}/_{2}$	1/0	5
1928	13/9	10/7 $^{1}/_{2}$	1/0	5
1929	12/3	10/9	1/0	5
1930	12/0	10/0	1/0	5
1931	11/6	8/1 $^{1}/_{2}$	1/0	5
1932	9/0	6/1 $^{1}/_{2}$	0/6	2.5
1933	15/0	7/0	0/6	2.5
1934	16/3	11/7 $^{1}/_{2}$	0/8.4	3.5
1935	22/3	13/6	0/10.8	4.5
1936	29/7 $^{1}/_{2}$	20/3	0/10.8	4.5
1937	25/0	21/0	1/4.8	4
1938	28/3	19/0	3/0	15
1939	29/1 $^{1}/_{2}$	20/0	3/0	15

Source: Stock Exchanges London and Provincial Ten-year Records of Prices and Dividends 1920, 1928, 1932, 1941.

Notes: a. The dividend figures are for February and August of the relevant year; b. In 1920, shares were split from £10 to £1 nominal value.

Table 6.8   Hadfield Ltd. ordinary share prices and dividends, 1910–39

	Highest for the year (shillings)	Lowest for the year (shillings)	Dividend[a] (%)
1910	69/9	63/0	35
1911	78/0	59/0	35
1912	65/0	56/10 $^1/_2$	35
1913	64/6	57/6	40
1914	65/6	61/0	40
1915	70/0	62/3	45
1916	82/6	67/0	50
1917	110/0	77/6	60
1918	148/9	96/0	60
1919	162/6	37/3	55
1920	45/6	22/6	20
1921	24/6	19/3	10
1922	28/1 $^1/_2$	19/0	10
1923	28/6	19/9	5
1924	21/9	14/9	4
1925	20/0	11/9	2.5
1926	19/3	12/0	3
1927	19/0	13/3	2.5
1928	23/3	16/9	5
1929	18/4 $^1/_2$	8/9	2.5
1930	10/0	5/5 $^1/_4$	2.5
1931	8/9	3/0	0
1932	5/10 $^1/_2$	3/6	0
1933	10/0	3/8 $^1/_2$	0
1934	13/6	8/3	0
1935	19/10 $^1/_2$[b]	8/3	0
1936	37/4 $^1/_2$	18/0	7.5
1937	42/4 $^1/_2$	26/6	17.5
1938	34/0 $^1/_2$	22/6	22.5
1939	31/6	20/0	22.5

Source: Stock Exchanges London and Provincial Ten-year Records of Prices and Dividends 1920, 1928, 1932, 1941.

Notes: a. The dividend figures are March and September of the relevant year, 1910 to 1919, and for April and October from 1920 onwards; b. In 1935, 10s was written off the £1 ordinary shares.

In the context of the uncertain economic environment of the inter-war years, and the two severe downturns in the British economy, the first in the early 1920s, and the second associated with the world economic crisis from 1929 to 1933, the dividends paid to shareholders at both companies do not seem extravagant. Indeed, the evidence suggests that Chandler's assertion that British companies inflated dividend rates in the interests of insider shareholders,[32] a characteristic he identifies with personal capitalism in the British case, is not tenable. The dividend policy of personal capitalist firms in Britain should not necessarily be equated with a propensity to take high ordinary dividends to improve family fortunes or the fortunes of entrenched partnerships of directors, at the expense of the long-run interests of the business. Thus, Dobb, citing evidence from the World Economic Survey on dividends for the UK in the inter-war period, shows that they 'maintained an average figure of more than 6 per cent even in the bad years of 1931–3, as against 10.5 per cent in 1929, and in no year fell much below 6 per cent'.[33] On this basis, the two companies' dividends do not appear unduly generous.

Directors as shareholders

As has been noted earlier, the majority of directors in the companies reviewed here did not have significantly large ordinary shareholdings. During the inter-war period, Sir Robert Hadfield held 14 per cent of Hadfields shares, while another member of the board held just 0.5 per cent of shares. Greenwood & Batley directors had only modest amounts of shares, and collectively they owned just 11 per cent of the ordinary share capital. This makes it unlikely that directors were looking to high dividends as a source of income. In evaluating Chandler's assertion that personal capitalism led to high dividend payments, because of the level of directors' share ownership, it is important to gauge the availability to directors of funds other than dividends.

As Jeremy observes, the issue of executive salaries has become a major issue of corporate governance in the post-privatisation period after 1980, galvanising business, political and public opinion.[34] However, it was not until the Companies Act of 1947 that directors were legally compelled to disclose their salaries in the company financial statements.[35] Jeremy notes that in the inter-war years, in personally managed firms such as Pilkington, Britain's largest glass manufacturer, a 'culture of careful stewardship epitomised the rewards' that long-standing family directors voted to themselves. For example, in 1920, the Pilkington directors

---

[32]   Chandler, *Scale and Scope*, p. 390.

[33]   M. Dobb, *Studies in the Development of Capitalism* (London, Routledge and Kegan Paul, 1978), p. 329.

[34]   Jeremy, *A Business History of Britain*, pp. 315–16.

[35]   See Maltby, 'Was the 1947 Companies Act a Response to a National Crisis?', pp. 31–60.

fixed the annual salary range at £1,700 to £2,500, which was indeed modest in comparison with the large salaries paid to executives at managerially controlled corporations such as ICI and GEC in the 1930s. At the former, the chairman, Sir Harry Gowan, received a salary of £20,000 in 1930, plus a £5,000 expense account, and at the latter the chairman, Lord Hurst, reaped a salary of £100,000 in 1936.[36] The evidence for Greenwood & Batley suggests a 'careful stewardship', the directors voting modest payments during the inter-war years. Directors' salaries stood at £2,500 in 1920 and during the inter-war period rose to £5,000, although these were augmented by bonus payments to the chairman, S. T. Batley, totalling £1,000 in 1918 and 1919, and £500 annually during the 1920s.[37] During the 1920s, the policy of Hadfields relating to salaries was less circumspect, reflecting perhaps the more dominant control of the company's leading personality, Sir Robert A. Hadfield. During the 1920s, the Hadfield directors voted the generous sum of £80,000 annually to Sir Robert, a payment which it was at his discretion to appropriate amongst the 'Chairman, managing directors, directors, managers and other officers and servants'.[38] A payout of £80,000 was the equivalent of a 4 per cent ordinary dividend, but it was concentrated in the hands of a few insiders.

As noted earlier, most directors other than Sir Robert Hadfield did not have large shareholdings. This makes it unlikely that the Hadfields board were looking towards high dividend payouts for income: the £80,000 discretionary fund offered them a source of income that was less dependent on annual profit levels. High dividends were desirable as a means of placating shareholders, but when Sir Robert assured shareholders in 1930 that 'It may console you to remember that if you have received no dividend, we on this side of the table are also shareholders and suffer with you',[39] he was not telling them the whole story. His appeal is rather undermined by the amount voted to him of which the shareholders were unaware. The fact that dividends were public knowledge and directors' salaries were not may have led commentators to over-emphasis the importance of dividends; this is an area where archive research at the level of the individual company may help to modify Chandler's judgement. Thus the final section of this chapter examines the communication with shareholders at the two companies, in the context of the changes in financial reporting during the inter-war period.

Communication with shareholders, and changes in financial reporting

Legal requirements on disclosure were very slow to change during this period from those of the highly permissive nineteenth century. For example, the 1907 Companies Act dealt primarily with the legal recognition of the private company,

---

[36]   Jeremy, *A Business History of Britain*, pp. 507–508.

[37]   Directors' Minute Book, No. 5, Greenwood & Batley, Box 53, ff. 160–69.

[38]   Hadfields Records, Vol. 51, Directors' Private Minute Book, 1904, 1918–47, p. 3.

[39]   *Sheffield Independent*, 18 March 1930.

which defined it as one having fewer than 50 ordinary shareholders, and in which the company did not promote the sale of its shares. The public company, representing any company that was not private, was required to file an audited balance sheet, but not to produce a profit-and-loss account. This had considerable impact on disclosure – particularly the use by companies of secret reserve funds. The low transparency required by company law, in combination with the use of secret reserves, meant that shareholders could not necessarily infer the profit made by a public company. The directors could mask a low profit, in order to pay out a dividend to shareholders, by means of transfers out of the secret into the general reserve fund. A further problem that the 1907 Companies Act did not address was the accounting treatment of groups of companies. Consequently, shareholders in a holding company did not necessarily obtain any information about the composition or performance of the group of subsidiary companies that it controlled.[40]

Of significance to these issues of corporate governance was a major legal case in 1906, *Newton v Chambers*, an event, which as we saw in Chapter 4, had an impact on director–shareholder relations at BSA. The ramifications of the case, however, went well beyond the governance of an individual company. It was recognised as a milestone in financial reporting, and it remained significant in the UK for over 30 years because of its implications for the amount of disclosure that directors needed to offer and that shareholders could reasonably demand.

The outcome of the case at BSA was that the secret reserve remained in place until 1909, and the transparency of financial disclosure remained a contentious issue at the company throughout the inter-war years. Commenting on the importance of the case, Arnold treats it as a contribution to the maintenance of 'existing power imbalances', in the structure of British corporate governance. The use of secret reserves withheld information from investors, creditors and competitors, and the low level of disclosure prevented financial information from being used by trades unions in support of wage bargaining. Companies therefore gauged the degree of disclosure to shareholders in terms of what directors considered to be in the best interests of the company, often deeming it undesirable to make public information that could be of value to competitors or labour organisations.[41] Such an outcome, as Arnold observes, was already evident in 1906, and he cites the warning of Buckley in the *Newton v Chambers case* that 'undue publicity … may often be very injurious to traders, having regard to … complications sometimes arising from the strained relations between capital and labour and the like'.[42] As Arnold concludes, 'The evidence on accounting disclosures, during the first quarter of the twentieth century suggests that the state, during a period of economic and social upheaval, did not believe that it was worth informing the capital markets if it also meant informing the unions'.[43] Summing up the importance of the BSA

---

[40] Maltby, 'Was the 1947 Companies Act a Response to a National Crisis?', p. 35.

[41] Arnold, 'Publishing your Private Affairs to the World', p. 164.

[42] Ibid., citing quotations from Law Report 2 Chancery (1906), pp. 378–9.

[43] Arnold, 'Publishing your Private Affairs to the World, p. 164.

case to the practice of company disclosure, Edwards comments that 'The case, which has since been described as the "charter" for the creators of secret reserves … was partly responsible for secrecy, obscurity, excessive summarisation and distortion becoming common features of financial reporting for the next quarter of a century'.[44]

The permissive nature of financial disclosure raised deep concerns in the public mind, and from the 1920s onwards there was pressure from for companies to tell their shareholders what reserves they had, and for financial reports of groups of companies to disclose the performance of all members of the group. Modernisers promoted the need for full information for the sake of economic efficiency,[45] but evidence given to the 1925 Greene Committee on company law reverted to the arguments of the pre-war period that restricted disclosure was in the interests of the shareholder because it withheld information from competitors. Wilfrid Greene, QC, the chair of the committee, concluded that, 'publicity would very much facilitate the operations of the labour agitator'.[46] The 1929 Companies Act required the publication of profit-and-loss accounts by public companies, but these did not have to be audited, and without a ban on secret reserves they were not informative. In relation to groups, the Act required the holding company to explain how it had accounted for subsidiaries, but not to disclose the profits/losses involved.[47]

Throughout the 1930s, there were expressions of discontent about this situation. It was increasingly difficult for executives to defend a policy of what the financial journalist Samuel called 'obfuscation', following the Royal Mail Steam Packet case of 1931 that highlighted the fraudulent use of secret reserves to hide poor performance. The traditionalist case for letting directors decide what it was safe to disclose was not assisted by advocates such as the chairman of Tube Investments, who told his AGM in 1935 that 'We bring in (to the balance sheet) only just so much as we require to pay the dividends we recommend, and to place to general reserve, or add to the carry forward, so much as we consider will make a pretty balance sheet'.[48] Franks et al. have acknowledged the problem of low levels of disclosure as part of the lack of protection for investors during this period, and they admit this is difficult to reconcile with the pattern of dispersion of shareholding,[49] the latter a central feature of British business generally, and our two case studies in particular. They identify two solutions to the problem. One is the equal treatment of all shareholders, including minorities, during mergers, and

---

[44]   J. R. Edwards, *A History of Financial Accounting* (London, Routledge, 1989), p. 148.

[45]   See Maltby, 'Was the 1947 Companies Act a Response to a National Crisis?', pp. 38–9.

[46]   *The Accountant*, 13 November 1926, p. 681.

[47]   Maltby, 'Was the 1947 Companies Act a Response to a National Crisis?', pp. 38–9.

[48]   *The Accountant*, 14 November 1935, p. 812.

[49]   Franks et al., 'Ownership', p. 30.

the other the geographical proximity of ordinary shareholders. Both, they assert, contributed towards the creation of relationships of trust, and so 'the conditions in which interactions between firms and investors were repeated'.[50] Their findings on proximity are similar to those noted above for Greenwood & Batley and Hadfields. In a sample of companies in 1910 Franks et al. note that 56 per cent of shareholders lived within six miles of the city of incorporation. Preference shareholders tended to live further away than holders of ordinary shares, which may, they suggest 'reflect the higher priority of their claims and the less discretion of management over the size of their dividends'.[51]

The 'informal relations of trust', based on proximity, described by Franks et al.,[52] took a variety of forms. This section of the chapter discusses evidence for each company that shareholders were able to make contacts with directors and needed not to feel overborne by them. Contacts might take the form of questions and statements at annual general meetings, of correspondence or of organised shareholder protests. One such protest was that which resulted in the *Newton v Chambers* case described above. Greenwood & Batley's disappointing performance pre-1914 appears to have triggered shareholder dissatisfaction. A number of shareholders wrote with expressions of this. For example, in 1905, two shareholders wrote asking for details of the directors' remuneration.[53] There were a number of requests for AGMs to be held locally, in Leeds rather than in London, a suggestion that proximity was indeed important for shareholders, in both 1905 and 1913/14.[54] In 1917 A.G. Hopper, a director and the holder of more than 11,000 ordinary and 5,000 preference shares, resigned from the Greenwood & Batley board, apparently over the Board's decision not to proceed with a merger between the company and Nobel's Explosives that had been under discussion since 1916.[55] In July that year, J. Armytage Batley wrote to the Chairman to say that at the next AGM he intended to propose Hopper, W. Nicholson, E. A. Ridsdale and himself as directors. Batley held 50 ordinary and 66 preference shares in his own name, and was also joint holder of 66 preference shares with one other and joint holder of 700 ordinary and 500 preference shares with two others. Neither Nicholson nor Ridsdale held any shares.[56] A Mr F.W. Tennant, a Leeds stockbroker, circulated a number of shareholders in support of their initiative:

> A large body of shareholders with whom I am associated, representing nearly one half of the issued capital and including practically the whole of the Batley, Greenwood and Hopper family interests, have for some time been dissatisfied

[50] Ibid.

[51] Ibid., pp. 30–31.

[52] Ibid., p. 35.

[53] WYL 298, Box 53, Minute Book No. 3, 1905, f. 62.

[54] WYL 298, Box 53 Minute Book No. 3, ff. 81, 290.

[55] WYL 298, Box 53 Minute Book No. 4.

[56] WYL 298, Greenwood & Batley List of Shareholders, 25 July 1916.

with the management of the company, and desire to bring about a complete reorganization to ensure greater economy and efficiency in the interests of the whole body of the shareholders.[57]

The chairman got assurances from directors S. T. Batley (280 ordinary, 600 preference), H. Micklem (3,170 ordinary and 2,990 preference), and T. Greenwood (3,715 ordinary, 775 preference) that they would support him against this initiative. H. Greenwood (8,685 ordinary, 5,627 preference) admitted that he had spoken to the rebels but did not support them. The directors contacted the shareholders refuting the claims in the circular and explaining their total refusal to work with Hopper. They obtained support from the Midland Bank in this. The bank manager's diary records Greenwood & Batley's expression of thanks for its assistance.[58] There was no further mention of this, which suggests that the next AGM repelled the takeover.[59]

This is an interesting episode for a number of reasons. It emphasises the importance of family connections in investment. The three families named in Tennant's circular each had a block of shares: Batleys owned a total of 10,900 ordinary shares and 6,800 preference shares; Greenwoods owned 12,410 ordinary shares and 6,616 preference shares; Hopper held 13,305 ordinary shares and 6,440 preference shares; in addition, a Miss Hopper-Greenwood held 1,560 ordinary shares and 1,890 preference shares. But the families were split – the Batley and Greenwood board members did not share the views of Tennant's 'large body'. This dispute is a reminder that families did not necessarily agree, and also that a large block of family shares might be outvoted: 'practically the whole of the Batley, Greenwood and Hopper families' (leaving out the directors) held only 13 per cent of Greenwood & Batley's shares. Family ownership did not necessarily mean family control. Minority shareholders were not necessarily confronted by a united family block, even when families were closely implicated in ownership.

The Hadfields AGMs suggest a cordial relationship between directors and shareholders. They were invariably held in Sheffield and for most of the period at the Royal Victoria Hotel or The Station Hotel, and were thus accessible for shareholders from out of town. They were well attended according to the record kept in the Hadfields minute book – as many as 262 shareholders in 1921, and generally more than a hundred. Shareholders did make some attempt to engage in a debate about financial performance, but only in the early years of the company. In 1905, a Mr Foster called for a bonus issue to be made out of the special reserve, to improve the return. In reply, Robert Hadfield told him that this 'was a very delicate question' although 'the matter did have their attention'.[60] He made the same

[57]   WYL 298, Box 53 Minute Book No. 4.

[58]   HSBC 347/8, f. 187, Murray Diary, February 1911–January 1916, entry for 17 July 1917.

[59]   WYL 298, Box 53 Minute Book No 4.

[60]   *Sheffield Independent*, 15 March 1905.

response to a similar proposal the following year – but it was not until 1911 that the company made another share issue. There is no evidence of searching questions or of discussion of financial issues at the Hadfields AGMs of the period; the directors' commentary was intended to forestall rather than invite further discussion. Hadfields suffered from poor results for much of the inter-war period, with the market value of ordinary shares lower than their nominal value between 1929 and 1935, when they were written down by 50 per cent in value. Despite this dismal performance, there is no evidence that relationships between the shareholders and the directors were damaged; the detailed accounts of the company's AGMs in the Sheffield press give no indication of protests or hostile questions.[61]

A discussion at a Hadfields directors meeting in 1911 suggests the directors' expectation of their ability to maintain a good relationship. The directors were discussing the pricing of a new share issue, and the desirability or otherwise of adding a £1 premium to the £1 nominal value of shares. The Company Secretary's notes of the meeting summarised the conclusion:

> AJ: If issue at a big premium, shareholders expect big dividend.
> HB: Suggest Chairman delicately tell shareholders at Annual General Meeting.
> WHD: If Sir Robert says shares are worth price – shares will go up immediately.[62]

The directors plainly expected that shareholders were prepared to trust them.

Conclusion

The relationship between shareholders and directors is a crucial component of personal capitalism. Many commentators, from the 1920s onwards, have depicted shareholders as passive and compliant, at the mercy of close-knit boards of family members. Certainly there is evidence in the companies reviewed above that shareholdings were dispersed and that shareholders tended to retain their shares for long periods. But shareholders were also capable of complaining vehemently if they were dissatisfied with directors' performance. The *Newton v Chambers* case of 1906 also showed that small shareholders could make a significant protest if they considered that directors were infringing their rights. And the attempt by Greenwood & Batley shareholders to reconstruct the board is also a reminder that tensions could arise within groups of directors and shareholders notionally linked by family loyalties. Hannah comments of the early twentieth century that 'what happened between owners and managers was … a slow and equivocal separation agreement'. Part of that evolution, he comments, was of 'routines of trust, reciprocity and quality certification which sometimes succeed and sometimes

---

[61]   Maltby, 'Hadfields Ltd.: Its Annual General Meetings', pp. 415–39.
[62]   Hadfield Records, Hadfields 113, Meeting, 20 November 1911.

fail'.[63] The features of share ownership in the period left directors in a strong position, but not an impregnable one. Variation between companies, rather than conformity to a single pattern, was the prevailing theme.

---

[63]   Hannah, 'The "Divorce" of Ownership', p. 426.

Bibliography

Primary sources

Business records

Birmingham Small Arms Ltd (BSA)

Birmingham Archive:
MS/137/A/91/114, Minute Books of BSA Directors No.5, 1917–20.
MS/321/A/1, BSA Directors Reports, Speeches of Chairman, 1914–19.
Coventry Archive:
PA 594/1/1/2/2–4, BSA Meeting File, Ordinary and AGM, 1918–21.
PA594/1/1/2/6–18, BSA, Notes and Transcripts of AGMs, 1922–35.
PA 594/1/1/3/3, BSA Board Minutes, 29 February 1924, Memorandum on BSA
    Tools and Burton, Griffiths Ltd.
PA 594/1/1/3/58, BSA Board Minutes, 30 November 1928, Report by F. W. Turrell,
    Managing Director BSA Tools on Organisation of Sales.
PA594/2/1/1/2, Directors Declaration of Interest under Companies Act, 1929.
PA 594/2/1/2/10, Part 1, Correspondence File of Sir Alexander Roger.
PA594/2/1/2/23, Correspondence File of A. H. J. Pollen.
PA594/2/1/59, Correspondence File, E. M. Griffiths, including Correspondence of
    T. S. Walker, 1921–32.
PA 594/4/4/1/6, Part 1, File and Agreements between ADC, Daimler and AEC.
PA594/9/1/3/2, Correspondence on Proposed Restructuring, 26 July 1932.
PA 926/12/1/1, Burton, Griffiths and Co., General Minute Book.
Hong Kong and Shanghai Banking Corporation (HSBC) Archives, London:
30/100, Diary of H. A. Astbury.
358/13, Coventry Reference Book, 1923–37, 7 March 1931.
Solihull Library:
BSA 19, The Birmingham Small Arms & Metal Company Limited, Shareholders'
    Minute Book covering the period 1897–1952.
Modern Record Centre (MRC), University of Warwick:
MSS 19A/1/1/1/13, BSA Board Meeting, 19 March 1920.
MSS 19A/1/2/16–17, Reports.
MSS 19A/1/2/42, letter from Percy Martin to BSA, January 1920.
MSS 19A/1/2/56, Report to Sir Alexander Roger, by D. H. Allan, 3 February
    1933.
MSS 19C/11 BSA Directors Minutes, Board Meetings, 1920.
MSS 19C/31/1, Notices of EGM, 1906.

Greenwood & Batley Ltd
West Yorkshire Archive Service, Leeds:
GB/NNAF/B6390, Box 63, Annual Reports and Balance Sheets, 1889–1971.
WYL/298, Box 53, Directors' Minute Book, No. 5, Greenwood & Batley.
WYL/298, Box 53, Minute Book No. 3, Greenwood & Batley.
WYL/298, Box 53, Minute Book No. 4, Greenwood & Batley.
WYL/298, Greenwood & Batley, List of Shareholders.
Hong Kong and Shanghai Banking Corporation (HSBC) Archive, London:
347/8, Murray Diary, 1916–17.

Hadfields Ltd
Sheffield Archive: There are no piece numbers for individual boxes, which contain
    a vast amount of business records of various types. The records are indicative
    of the content of the boxes.
Box 6, Circulars and Memorandums to Shareholders, on Capital Reconstruction
    Scheme, 1935.
Box 9, Abstracts from AGMs, and Correspondence.
Box 45, Draft Report on Bean Cars Ltd by Sir Harold Peat, 1928.
Box 46, Bundle of Documents on National Motor Co. Merger.
Box 47, Report on Investigation into the Bean Car Organisation by Camm,
    Metcalf, 1927.
Box 53, Extract from Autobiography of W. F. Kett, written in the 1950s.
Box 55, Correspondence and Memorandums.
Box 58, AGM, 3 April 1922, and Correspondence and Memorandums.
Box 64, Correspondence and Memorandums concerning C. Sinclair, 1923–24;
    Report by P. Brown and A. H. B. Clerke, 18 August 1920.
Box 66, Correspondence and Memorandums, 1928.
Box 70, Report by J. B. Thomas on Bean Cars, 12 November 1928.
Box 101, Correspondence with Urwick, Orr and Partners (management
    consultants), 1944–45.
Box 103, Correspondence between R. A. Hadfield and J. Mallaband, 1888.
Box 113, Meeting, 20 November 1911.
Box 116, AGM, March 1928.
Box 122, Extract of Minutes of Directors' Meeting, 6 December 1929, and
    Correspondence files with William Deacons Bank, 1926–28.
Box 124, Hadfield AGM, 1917–38.
Box 130, Minutes of Local Directors, 1929–44.
Box 132, Urwick, Orr and Partners Report, March 1945.
Box 135, Wallace Clark (management consultant) Correspondence and Reports,
    1936.
Box 135, Reports on Wages and Costing Systems', Jeffrey's Reports, 1924 and
    1925.
Volume 7, Ordinary, Extraordinary and AGM Minutes 1889–1919.
Volume 8, Ordinary, Extraordinary and AGM Minutes 1920–53.

Volume 51, Directors' Private Minute Book, 1904, 1918–47.

Volume 93, Hadfields Steel Foundry Co. Ltd, Board Minutes No. 2, 1904–36.

Volume 94, Hadfields Steel Foundry Co. Ltd, Board Minutes, 1888–1904.

Volumes 159–63, Hadfields Ltd, Share Registers.

Sheffield Central Library (Local History):

338.4SQ, Hadfields Ltd, Report of AGM, 28 March 1919.

623.4 SSTQ, *The Hadfield System as Applied to War Material* (n.d., most probably 1911).

Alfred Herbert Ltd

Private records:

Machine Tool Trade Association.

Coventry Archives:

PA 586/11 General Minute Book, 1887–1951.

PA 926/1/1/1, Alfred Herbert Ltd, Minute Book of the Board of Directors, 1944–60.

PA 926/1/4/1–3, Minute Books of the Departmental Board of Directors, 1911–41.

PA 926/1/5/16/15, Alfred Herbert to Wilshere & Sons, 27 February 1903.

PA 926/1/5/17/7, Alfred Herbert to Wilshere & Sons, 24 December 1903.

PA 926/1/5/33–42, Alfred Herbert Ltd, Financial Accounts.

PA 1270/1/1–3, Memorandums and Articles of Association of Alfred Herbert Ltd, 1894–1954.

PA 1270/3/1/1, J. Pickin to C. W. Clark, 23 September 1925; C. W. Clark to J. Pickin, 6 October 1925.

PA 1270/4/1, Oscar Harmer for the Alfred Herbert Testimonial, 22 July 1917.

PA 1270/7/1, Speeches of C. W. Clark.

PA 1270/9/1, Alfred Herbert News.

PA 1270/9/11, Shots at the Truth by Sir Alfred Herbert, 'Experience', reprinted from the *Machine Tool Review*, January–February 1940.

PA 1558/1/1/1, Minute Book of the Board of Directors of Alfred Herbert Ltd, 1960–80.

Raleigh Ltd

Nottinghamshire Archives, Raleigh Records:

DDRN 1/1/1–6, Raleigh Cycle Co. Ltd, Directors and General Meetings, Minutes 1891–1908.

DDRN 1/2/1–6, Raleigh Cycle Co. Ltd, Board and General Meetings, Minutes with Fortnightly Reports, 1915–44.

DDRN 1/3/1, Minute Book of the Raleigh Cycle Holding Co. Ltd from 1934.

DDRN 1/13/1, Promotional Material sent to LDV Agents, October 1932.

DDRN 1/19, Promotional Material sent to Agents, 1935.

DDRN 1/23/1, Sturmey-Archer Gears, Minutes.

DDRN 1/39/6, Report of Directors, 1904.

DDRN 1/40/6, Auditors Reports and Balance Sheets, 1916.

DDRN 2/7/1 Forms of Notes and Cuttings, and circulars to Shareholders, 1896–1908.

DDRN 3/1/1–3, Company Ledgers.

DDRN 3/1/2/2, Raleigh Cycle Agreement for Sale or Purchase of Business upon Reconstruction, 4 March 1896.

DDRN 3/11/11, Auditors Reports and Accounts, 1929.

DDRN 4/1010/1/8, The Book of the Raleigh (the company's sales catalogue) for 1904 Season.

DDRN 5/1/6, Press Cuttings 1931–34.

DDRN 7/2/7, History of the Raleigh Cycle Co. Ltd, n.d.

DDRN 7/2/12, Sir Harold Bowden, Manuscripts of the History of the Raleigh Company, n.d., unpublished.

DDRN 7/2/27, Raleigh Company Executives, 1887–1962.

DDRN 10/3/1/3/1, Agreement between Old Raleigh Co. Incorporated 1891 and the New Company Incorporated 1896, Supplement, 29 April 1896.

DDRN 10/3/4/6/1, Memorandum and Articles of Association of the Raleigh Cycle Co., Incorporated 15 February 1899.

DDRN 10/3/4/13–15, Agreements between Frank Bowden and the Raleigh Cycle Co., 1908.

DDRN 10/3/8, Allotment Book Register of Members and Annual Share Ledger of the Raleigh Cycle Co Ltd.

DDRN 10/3/9/3, Prospectus of the Raleigh Cycle Co. Ltd, 1891.

Newspapers and trade journals

Bicycling News
Guardian
The American Machinist
Motor Cycle and Cycle Trader
Motor Export Trader
Nottingham Daily Express
Machine Tool Review (published by Alfred Herbert Ltd.), located in Coventry Central Library
Sheffield Independent
Sunday Express
The Times

Financial, accounting and legal journals

The Accountant
The Economist
Financial News
Law Reports 2 Chancery, 1906, pp. 378–87
The Financial Times

The Financial World
The Statist
Stock Exchange Official Intelligence Book, 1907
Stock Exchange Year Book, 1945
Stock Exchanges London and Provincial, Ten Year
Record of Prices and Dividends, 1920, 1928, 1932, 1941

Secondary sources

Aldcroft, D. H., 'The Performance of the British Machine-Tool Industry in the Inter-war Years', *Business History Review*, Vol. 40, No. 3 (1966), pp. 281–96.

Alford, B. W. E., 'Lost Opportunities: British Businessmen during the First World War', in N. McKendrick and R. B. Outhwaite (eds), *Business Life and Public Policy. Essays in Honour of D .C. Coleman* (Cambridge, Cambridge University Press, 1986), pp. 205–227.

Alvesson, M., *Cultural Perspectives on Organisations* (Cambridge, Cambridge University Press, 1993).

Arnold, A. J., '"Publishing your Private Affairs to the World": Corporate Financial Disclosures in the UK 1900–24', *Accounting, Business and Financial History*, Vol. 7, No. 2 (1997), pp. 143–73.

——, 'Innovation, Deskilling and Profitability in the British Machine Tool Industry, 1887–1927', *Journal of Industrial History*, Vol. 1, No. 2 (1999), pp. 5–73.

—— and D. R. Matthews, 'Corporate Financial Disclosures in the UK, 1920–1950: The Effects of Legislative Change and Managerial Disclosure', *Accounting and Business Research*, Vol. 32 (2002), pp. 3–16.

Back, W., 'The Natural History of the Industrial Organiser', *The Accountant*, 21 June 1924, pp. 1,020–22.

Beeley, S., *A History of Bicycles: From Hobby Horse to Mountain Bike* (London, Studio Editions, 1992).

Bendix, R., *Work and Authority in Industry* (New York, Wiley, 1956).

Berle, A. A. and G. C. Means, *The Modern Corporation and Private Property* (New York, Macmillan, 1932).

Bowden, G. H., *The Story of the Raleigh Cycle* (London, W. H. Allen, 1975).

Bowden, H., 'The Four "Ms" of Industry: Men, Management, Machines and Money', Address to Birmingham Rotary Club reported in *Birmingham Gazette*, 16 October 1934, pp. 21–4.

Bowden, S. and D. Higgins, 'British Industry in the Inter-War Years', in R. Floud and P. Johnson (eds), *The Cambridge Economic History of Modern Britain*, Vol. II, *Economic Maturity, 1860–1939* (Cambridge, Cambridge University Press, 2004), pp. 374–402.

Boyce, G. and S. Ville, *The Development of Modern Business* (Basingstoke, Palgrave, 2002).

Breeley, H. W. and G. W. Troup, 'The Machine Tool Industry', in D. Burn, (ed.), *The Structure of British Industry: A Symposium*, Vol. 1 (Cambridge, Cambridge University Press, 1958), pp. 360–85.

Camfferman, K. and S. A. Zeff, 'The Apotheosis of Holding Company Accounting: Unilever's Financial Reporting Innovations from the 1920s to the 1940s', *Accounting, Business and Financial History*, Vol. 13, No. 2 (2003), pp. 171–206.

Cannons, M. J., 'Eadie, Albert', in D. J. Jeremy (ed.), *Dictionary of Business Biography* (London, Butterworths, 1985), pp. 222–4.

Casson, M., 'Entrepreneurship and Business Culture', in J. Brown and M. B. Rose (eds), *Entrepreneurship, Networks and Modern Business* (Manchester, Manchester University Press, 1995), pp. 30–54.

——, 'An Economic Approach to Regional Business Networks', in J. F. Wilson and A. Popp (eds), *Industrial Clusters and Regional Business Networks in England, 1750–1970* (Ashgate, Aldershot, 2003), pp. 19–43.

Chandler, A. D., Jnr., *The Visible Hand: The Managerial Revolution in American Business* (Cambridge, MA, Harvard University Press, 1977).

——, *Scale and Scope: The Dynamics of Industrial Capitalism* (Cambridge, MA, Harvard University Press, 1990).

Channon, D.F., *The Strategy and Structure of British Enterprise* (London, Macmillan, 1973).

Cheffins, B. R., 'History and the Global Corporate Governance Revolution: The British Perspective', *Business History*, Vol. 43, No. 4 (2001), pp. 87–118.

——, *Corporate Ownership and Control, British Business Transformed* (Oxford, Oxford University Press, 2009).

Church, R., 'Family Firms and Managerial Capitalism: The Case of the International Motor Industry', in R. P. T. Davenport-Hines (ed.) *Business in the Age of Depression and War* (London, Frank Cass, 1990), pp. 311–26.

——, 'The Limitations of the Personal Capitalism Paradigm', *Business History Review*, Vol. 64, No. 4 (1990), pp. 703–710.

——, 'The Family Firm in Industrial Capitalism: International Perspectives on Hypothesis and History', *Business History*, Vol. 35, No. 4 (1993), pp. 17–43.

——, 'Demonstrating Nuffield: The Evolution of Managerial Culture in the British Motor Car Industry', *Economic History Review*, Vol. 49, No. 3 (1996), pp. 561–83.

Coleman, D. C., 'Gentlemen and Players', *Economic History Review*, Vol. 26, No. 1 (1973), pp. 92–116.

——, *Courtaulds: An Economic and Social History*, Volume II (Oxford, Oxford University Press, 1980).

Collins, M., *Banks and Industrial Finance in Britain, 1800–1939* (Basingstoke, Macmillan, 1991).

—— and M. Baker, *Commercial Banks and Industrial Finance in England and Wales, 1860–1913* (Oxford, Oxford University Press, 2004).

Cottrell, P. L., *Industrial Finance 1830–1914: The Finance and Organisation of British Manufacturing Industry* (London, Methuen, 1980).

Davenport-Hines, R. P. T., *Dudley Docker: The Life and Times of a Trade Warrior* (Cambridge, Cambridge University Press, 1984).

——, 'Pollen, Arthur Joseph Hungerford', in D. J. Jeremy (ed.), *Dictionary of Business Biography* (London, Butterworths, 1985), pp. 753–7.

——, 'Roger, Sir Alexander Forbes Proctor', in D. J. Jeremy (ed.), *Dictionary of Business Biography* (London, Butterworths, 1985), pp. 967–9.

——, 'Rogers, Sir Hallewell', in D. J. Jeremy (ed.), *Dictionary of Business Biography* (London, Butterworths, 1985), pp. 923–7.

—— (ed.), *Business in the Age of Depression and War* (London, Frank Cass, 1990).

Davies, J. M., 'A Twentieth Century Paternalist: Alfred Herbert and the Skilled Coventry Workmen', in B. Lancaster and T. Mason (eds), *Life and Labour in a Twentieth Century City: The Experience of Coventry* (Coventry, Cryfield Press, n.d.).

——, 'Social Relations in an Engineering Factory: Alfred Herbert Ltd, 1887–1922', MA thesis, University of Warwick (1983).

Davis, L. and R. A. Huttenback, *Mammon and the Pursuit of Empire: The Political Economy of British Imperialism, 1860–1912* (Cambridge, Cambridge University Press, 1987).

Demaus, A. B. and J. C. Tarring, *The Humber Story, 1868–1932* (Stroud, Alan Sutton, 1989).

Dicksee, L. R., *Published Balance Sheets and Window Dressing* (London, Gee & Co., 1927). Reprinted in L. R. Dicksee, *Business Methods and the War: The Fundamentals of Manufacturing Costs; Published Balance Sheets and Window Dressing* (New York, Arno Press, 1980).

Dobb, M., *Studies in the Development of Capitalism* (London, Routledge and Kegan Paul, 1978).

Dosi, G., R. R. Nelson and S. G. Winter, 'Introduction: The Nature and Dynamics of Organizational Capabilities', in G. Dosi, R. R. Nelson and S. G. Winter (eds), *The Nature and Dynamics of Organizational Capabilities* (Oxford, Oxford University Press, 2000), pp. 1–24.

Edwards, J. R., 'The Accounting Profession and Disclosure in Published Reports, 1925–1932', *Accounting and Business Research*, Vol. 6 (1976), pp. 289–303.

——, *A History of Financial Accounting* (London, Routledge, 1989).

Evans, E. W., 'Some Problems in the Growth of the Machine Tool Industry', *Yorkshire Bulletin of Economic and Social Research*, Volume 18 (1966), pp. 45–63.

Fitzgerald, R., 'The Competitive and Institutional Advantage of Holding Companies: British Business in the Inter-war Years', *Journal of Industrial History*, Vol. 3, No. 2 (2000), pp. 1–30.

Floud, R., *The British Machine Tool Industry, 1850–1914* (Cambridge, Cambridge University Press, 1976).

——, 'Greenwood, Arthur', in D. J. Jeremy (ed.), *Dictionary of Business Biography* (London, Butterworths, 1985), pp. 642–3.

Foreman-Peck, J., 'Exit, Voice and Loyalty as Responses to Decline: The Rover Company in the Inter-War Years', *Business History*, Vol. 23, No. 2 (1981), pp. 191–210.

Franks, J., C. Mayer, and S. Rossi, 'Ownership: Evolution and Regulation' (25 March 2005). ECGI – Finance Working Paper No. 09/2003; EFA 2004 Maastricht Meetings Paper No. 3205; AFA 2003 Washington, DC Meetings.

Fridenson, P., 'Business Failure and the Agenda of Business History', *Enterprise and Society*, Vol. 15, No. 4 (2004), pp. 562–82.

Frost, G. H., *Munitions of War. A Record of the BSA and Daimler Co. during the First World War* (Birmingham and Coventry, BSA and Daimler, n.d.).

Griffiths, J., 'Give My Regards to "Uncle Billy": The Rites and Rituals of Company Life at Lever Brothers, c. 1900–1990', *Business History*, Vol. 37, No. 4 (1995), pp. 25–45.

Hannah, L., *The Rise of the Corporate Economy* (London, Methuen, 1983).

——, 'Scale and Scope: Towards a European Visible Hand', *Business History*, Vol. 32 (1991), pp. 297–310.

——, 'Pioneering Modern Corporate Governance: A View from London in 1900', *Enterprise & Society*, Vol. 8, No. 3 (2007), pp. 642–86.

——, 'The "Divorce" of Ownership from Control from 1900 Onwards: Re-calibrating Imagined Global Trends', *Business History*, Vol. 49, No. 4 (2007), pp. 404–438.

Harrison, A. E., 'Growth, Entrepreneurship and Capital Formation in the United Kingdom's Cycle and Related Industries, 1870–1914', University of York, unpublished PhD thesis (1977).

——, 'Joint Stock Company Floatation in the Cycle, Motor Vehicle and Related Industries 1882–1914', *Business History*, Vol. 23, No. 2 (1981), pp. 165–90.

——, 'The Origins and Growth of the UK Cycle Industry', *Journal of Transport History*, Vol. 6, No. 1 (1985), pp. 41–70.

Hermsen, M. L., P. J. Niehoff and M. R. Uhrynuk, 'An Extraordinary Expansion', *Accountancy*, Vol. 130, Issue 1,310 (October 2002), pp. 110–12.

Hirschman, A. O., *Exit, Voice and Loyalty. Responses to Decline in Firms, Organisations and States* (Cambridge, MA, Harvard University Press, 1970).

Hodge, Margaret, 'Fit for Purpose', *Accountancy*, Vol. 139, Issue 1,365 (May 2007), p. 105.

Hodgson, G. M., *Economics and Evolution: Bringing Life Back to Economics* (Cambridge, Cambridge University Press, 1993).

——, 'On the Evolution of Thorstein Veblen's Evolutionary Economics', *Cambridge Journal of Economics*, Vol. 22 (1999), pp. 463–77.

Hofstede, G., *Cultures and Organisations. Intercultural Cooperation: Software of the Mind* (London, McGraw-Hill, 1994).

Jeremy, D. J. (ed.), *Dictionary of Business Biography* (London, Butterworths, 1985).

——, *A Business History of Britain 1900–1990s* (Oxford, Oxford University Press, 1997).

Johnman, L., 'The Largest Manufacturing Firms of 1935', in R. P. T. Davenport-Hines (ed.) *Business in the Age of Depression and War* (London, Frank Cass, 1990), pp. 20–39.

Kay, J., *The Business of Economics* (Oxford, Oxford University Press, 1996).

Keasey, K., H. Short and M. Wright, 'The Development of Corporate Governance Codes', in K. Keasey, S. Thompson and M. Wright (eds.), *Corporate Governance* (Oxford, Oxford University Press, 1997), pp. 21–44.

——, S. Thompson and M. Wright (eds), *Corporate Governance* (Oxford, Oxford University Press, 1997).

——, S. Thompson and M. Wright, 'Introduction', in K. Keasey, S. Thompson and M. Wright (eds.), *Corporate Governance* (Oxford, Oxford University Press, 1997), pp. 1–19.

Kininmonth, K. W., 'The Growth, Development and Management of J. & P. Coats Ltd, c.1890–1960: An Analysis of Strategy and Structure', *Business History*, Vol. 48, No. 4 (2006), pp. 551–79.

Kitchen, J. and R. H. Parker, *Accounting Thought and Education: Six English Pioneers* (London, Institute of Chartered Accountants in England and Wales, 1977).

Konstant, P. C., 'Exit, Voice, Loyalty in the Course of Corporate Governance and Counsel's Changing Role', *Journal of Socio-Economics*, Vol. 28 (1999), pp. 203–246.

Langlois, R., 'Personal Capitalism and Charismatic Authority: The Organisational Economics of a Weberian Concept', *Industrial and Corporate Change*, Vol. 7, No. 1 (1997), pp. 195–213.

—— and P. L. Robertson, *Firms, Markets and Economic Change: A Dynamic Theory of Business Institutions* (London, Routledge, 1995).

Lipartito, K., 'Culture and the Practice of Business History', *Business and Economic History*, Vol. 32, No. 2 (1995), pp. 1–44.

Lloyd-Jones, R. and M. J. Lewis, 'British Industrial Capitalism During the Second Industrial Revolution: A Schumpeterian Approach', *Journal of Industrial History*, Vol. 1, No. 1 (1998), pp. 73–110.

—— and M. J. Lewis, *Raleigh and the British Bicycle Industry: An Economic and Business History, 1870–1960* (Aldershot, Ashgate, 2000).

—— and M. J. Lewis, 'Business Networks, Social Habits and the Evolution of a Regional Industrial Cluster: Coventry, 1880s–1930s', in J. F. Wilson and A. Popp (eds), *Industrial Clusters and Regional Business Networks in England, 1750–1970* (Ashgate, Aldershot, 2003), pp. 229–50.

—— and M. J. Lewis, *Alfred Herbert Ltd and the British Machine Tool Industry* (Aldershot, Ashgate, 2006).

—— and M. J. Lewis, '"A New Paradigm of British Business History": A Critique of Toms and Wilson', *Business History*, Vol. 49, No. 1 (2007), pp. 98–105.

——, M. J. Lewis, J. Maltby and M. Matthews, 'Control, Conflict and Concession: Corporate Governance at Birmingham Small Arms, 1906–1933', *Accounting Historians Journal*, Vol. 32, No. 1 (2005), pp. 149–84.

——, M. J. Lewis, J. Maltby and M. Matthews, 'Corporate Governance in a Major British Holding Company: BSA in the Interwar Years', *Accounting, Business and Financial History*, Vol. 16, No. 1 (2006), pp. 69–97.

McIvor, A. J., 'Employers Organisations and Strike Breaking in Britain, 1880–1914', *International Review of Social History*, Vol. 29 (1984), pp. 20–45.

MacNeil, I. and Xiao Lu, 'Comply or Explain: market Discipline and Non-Compliance with the Combined Code' (2005), http://papers.ssrn.com/sol3/Delivery.cfm/SSRN_ID726664_code282794.pdf?abstractid=726664&mirid=1 (accessed 10 November 2008).

Maltby, J., '"A sort of Guide, Philosepher and Friend": The Rise of the Professional Auditor in Britain', *Accounting, Business & Financial History*, Vol. 9, No. 1 (1999), pp. 29–50.

——, 'Was the 1947 Companies Act a Response to a National Crisis?', *Accounting History*, Vol. 5, No. 2 (2000), pp. 31–60.

——, 'Hadfields Ltd: Its Annual General Meetings, 1900–1939 and their Relevance to Corporate Social Reporting', *British Accounting Review*, Vol. 36, No. 4 (2004), pp. 415–39.

Marrison, A., *British Business and Protection, 1903–1932* (Oxford, Oxford University Press, 1996).

Matthews, M., T. Boyns, T. Edwards and J. Richard, 'Chandlerian Image or Mirror Image? Managerial and Accounting Control in the Chemical Industry: The Case of Albright & Wilson, c. 1892 to c. 1923', *Business History*, Vol. 45, No. 4 (2003), pp. 24–52.

Middlemas, K., *Politics in Industrial Society: The Experience of the British System since 1911* (London, Andre Deutsch, 1979).

Millward, A., 'The Cycle Industry in Birmingham, c1890–1920', in B. Tilson (ed.), *Made in Birmingham 1859–1985* (Studley, Warwick and Brewin, 1989).

Nelson, R. R., *The Sources of Economic Growth* (Cambridge, MA, Harvard University Press, 2000).

Newton, L., 'Capital Networks in the Sheffield Region, 1850–1885', in J. F. Wilson and A. Popp (eds), *Industrial Clusters and Regional Business Networks in England, 1750–1970* (Ashgate, Aldershot, 2003), pp. 130–54.

O'Sullivan, M., *Contests for Corporate Control: Corporate Governance and Economic Performance in the USA and Germany* (Oxford, Oxford University Press, 2001).

Quail, J., 'The Proprietorial Theory of the Firm and its Consequences', *Journal of Industrial History*, Vol. 3, No. 1 (2000), pp. 1–22.

Reader, W. J., '*Imperial Chemical Industries: A History*, Vol. II (Oxford, Oxford University Press, 1975).

Rose, M. B., 'Beyond Buddenbrooks: The Family Firm and the Management of Succession in Nineteenth Century Britain' (Lancaster University Management School, Discussion paper EC4/91, 1991), pp. 2–16.

Samuel, H. B., *Shareholders' Money, An Analysis of Certain Defects in Company Legislation with Proposals for their Reform* (London, Pitman & Sons, 1953).

Sargant Florence, P., *The Logic of British and American Industry: A Realistic Analysis of Economic Structure and Government* (London, Routledge and Kegan Paul, 1953).

Schein, E. H., *Organisational Culture and Leadership: A Dynamic View* (San Francisco, McGraw Hill, 1985).

Schmitz, C., *The Growth of Big Business in the United States and Western Europe, 1850–1939* (London, Macmillan, 1993).

Shaw, C., 'The Largest Manufacturing Firms of 1907', in R. P. T. Davenport-Hines (ed.), *Business in the Age of Depression and War* (London, Frank Cass, 1990), pp. 1–19.

Sheikh, S. and S. K. Chatterjee, 'Perspectives on Corporate Governance', in S. Sheikh and W. Rees (eds), *Corporate Governance and Corporate Control* (London, Cavendish, 1995), pp. 1–20.

Singleton, J., 'The Tank Producers: British Mechanical Engineering in the Great War', *Journal of Industrial History*, Vol. 1, No. 1 (1998), pp. 86–106.

Spicer, E. E. and E. C. Pegler, *Practical Auditing* (London, H. Foulks Lynch & Co., 1914).

St Nixon, J., *Daimler 1896–1946* (London: G. T. Foulis and Co., n.d.).

Strachan, H., *The First World War*, Vol. 1, *To Arms* (Oxford, Oxford University Press, 2001).

Supple, B., 'Scale and Scope: Alfred Chandler and the Dynamics of Industrial Capitalism', *Economic History Review*, Vol. 44, No. 3 (1990), pp. 500–514.

Teece, D., 'Economies of Scope and the Scope of the Enterprise', *Journal of Economic Behaviour and Organisation*, Vol. 1, No. 3 (1980), pp. 223–47.

Thackery, B., *The AEC Story: Part One* (Glossop, Venture Publications, 2001).

Thoms, D. and T. Donnelly, *The Motor Car Industry in Coventry since the 1890s* (London, Croom Helm, 1985).

Tricker, R. I. *Corporate Governance* (Aldershot, Gower, 1984).

The Turner Review: A Regulatory Response to the Global Banking Crisis March 2009 www.fsa.gov.uk/pubs/other/turner_review.pdf (accessed on 2 April 2009).

Tweedale, G., *Giants of Sheffield Steel: The Men who made Sheffield the Steel Capital of the World* (Sheffield, Sheffield City Libraries, 1986).

——, 'Business and Investment Strategies in the Inter-War British Steel Industry: A Case Study of Hadfields Ltd and Bean Cars', *Business History*, Vol. 29 (1987), pp. 47–72.

——, *Sheffield Steel and America: A Century of Commercial and Technological Interdependence, 1830–1939* (Cambridge, Cambridge University Press, 1987).

——, *Steel City: Entrepreneurship, Strategy and Technology in Sheffield 1743–1993* (Oxford, Clarendon, 1995).

Wilson, J. F., *British Business History, 1720–1994* (Manchester, Manchester University Press, 1995).

—— and A. Popp (eds), *Industrial Clusters and Regional Business Networks in England, 1750–1970* (Ashgate, Aldershot, 2003).

—— and A. W. J. Thompson, *The Making of Modern Management in Historical Perspective* (Oxford, Oxford University Press, 2006).

Index

Modern Economic and Social History Series

General Editor
Derek H. Aldcroft, University Fellow, Department of Economic and Social
History,
University of Leicester, UK

Derek H. Aldcroft
Studies in the Interwar European Economy
1 85928 360 8 (1997)

Michael J. Oliver
Whatever Happened to Monetarism?
Economic Policy Making and Social Learning in the United Kingdom Since 1979
1 85928 433 7 (1997)

R. Guerriero Wilson
Disillusionment or New Opportunities?
The Changing Nature of Work in Offices, Glasgow 1880–1914
1 84014 276 6 (1998)

Roger Lloyd-Jones and M.J. Lewis with the assistance of M. Eason
Raleigh and the British Bicycle Industry
An Economic and Business History, 1870–1960
1 85928 457 4 (2000)

Barry Stapleton and James H. Thomas
Gales
A Study in Brewing, Business and Family History
0 7546 0146 3 (2000)

Derek H. Aldcroft and Michael J. Oliver
Trade Unions and the Economy
1870–2000
1 85928 370 5 (2000)

Ted Wilson
Battles for the Standard
Bimetallism and the Spread of the Gold Standard in the Nineteenth Century
1 85928 436 1 (2000)

Patrick Duffy
The Skilled Compositor, 1850–1914
An Aristocrat Among Working Men
0 7546 0255 9 (2000)

Robert Conlon and John Perkins
Wheels and Deals
The Automotive Industry in Twentieth-Century Australia
0 7546 0405 5 (2001)

Geoffrey Channon
Railways in Britain and the United States, 1830–1940
Studies in Economic and Business History
1 84014 253 7 (2001)

Sam Mustafa
Merchants and Migrations
Germans and Americans in Connection, 1776–1835
0 7546 0590 6 (2001)

Bernard Cronin
Technology, Industrial Conflict and the Development of Technical Education in
19th-Century England
0 7546 0313 X (2001)

Andrew Popp
Business Structure, Business Culture and the Industrial District
The Potteries, c. 1850–1914
0 7546 0176 5 (2001)

Scott Kelly
The Myth of Mr Butskell
The Politics of British Economic Policy, 1950–55
0 7546 0604 X (2002)

Michael Ferguson
The Rise of Management Consulting in Britain
0 7546 0561 2 (2002)

Alan Fowler
Lancashire Cotton Operatives and Work, 1900–1950
A Social History of Lancashire Cotton Operatives in the Twentieth Century
0 7546 0116 1 (2003)

John F. Wilson and Andrew Popp (eds)
Industrial Clusters and Regional Business Networks in England, 1750–1970
0 7546 0761 5 (2003)

John Hassan
The Seaside, Health and the Environment in England and Wales since 1800
1 84014 265 0 (2003)
Marshall J. Bastable

Arms and the State
Sir William Armstrong and the Remaking of British Naval Power, 1854–1914
0 7546 3404 3 (2004)

Robin Pearson
Insuring the Industrial Revolution
Fire Insurance in Great Britain, 1700–1850
0 7546 3363 2 (2004)

Andrew Dawson
Lives of the Philadelphia Engineers
Capital, Class and Revolution, 1830–1890
0 7546 3396 9 (2004)

Lawrence Black and Hugh Pemberton (eds)
An Affluent Society?
Britain's Post-War 'Golden Age' Revisited
0 7546 3528 7 (2004)

Joseph Harrison and David Corkill
Spain
A Modern European Economy
0 7546 0145 5 (2004)

Ross E. Catterall and Derek H. Aldcroft (eds)
Exchange Rates and Economic Policy in the 20th Century
1 84014 264 2 (2004)

Armin Grünbacher
Reconstruction and Cold War in Germany
The Kreditanstalt für Wiederaufbau (1948–1961)
0 7546 3806 5 (2004)

Till Geiger
Britain and the Economic Problem of the Cold War
The Political Economy and the Economic Impact
of the British Defence Effort, 1945–1955
0 7546 0287 7 (2004)

Anne Clendinning
Demons of Domesticity
Women and the English Gas Industry, 1889–1939
0 7546 0692 9 (2004)

Timothy Cuff
The Hidden Cost of Economic Development
The Biological Standard of Living in Antebellum Pennsylvania
0 7546 4119 8 (2005)

Julian Greaves
Industrial Reorganization and Government Policy in Interwar Britain
0 7546 0355 5 (2005)

Derek H. Aldcroft
Europe's Third World
The European Periphery in the Interwar Years
0 7546 0599 X (2006)

James P. Huzel
The Popularization of Malthus in Early Nineteenth-Century England
Martineau, Cobbett and the Pauper Press
0 7546 5427 3 (2006)

Richard Perren
Taste, Trade and Technology
The Development of the International Meat Industry since 1840
978 0 7546 3648 9 (2006)

Roger Lloyd-Jones and M.J. Lewis
Alfred Herbert Ltd and the British Machine Tool Industry, 1887–1983
978 0 7546 0523 2 (2006)

Anthony Howe and Simon Morgan (eds)
Rethinking Nineteenth-Century Liberalism
Richard Cobden Bicentenary Essays
978 0 7546 5572 5 (2006)

Espen Moe
Governance, Growth and Global Leadership
The Role of the State in Technological Progress, 1750–2000
978 0 7546 5743 9 (2007)

Peter Scott
Triumph of the South
A Regional Economic History of Early Twentieth Century Britain
978 1 84014 613 4 (2007)

David Turnock
Aspects of Independent Romania's Economic History with Particular Reference
to Transition for EU Accession
978 0 7546 5892 4 (2007)
David Oldroyd
Estates, Enterprise and Investment at the Dawn of the Industrial Revolution
Estate Management and Accounting in the North-East of England, c.1700–1780
978 0 7546 3455 3 (2007)

Ralf Roth and Günter Dinhobl (eds)
Across the Borders
Financing the World's Railways in the Nineteenth and Twentieth Centuries
978 0 7546 6029 3 (2008)

Vincent Barnett and Joachim Zweynert (eds)
Economics in Russia
Studies in Intellectual History
978 0 7546 6149 8 (2008)

Raymond E. Dumett (ed.)
Mining Tycoons in the Age of Empire, 1870–1945
Entrepreneurship, High Finance, Politics and Territorial Expansion
978 0 7546 6303 4 (2009)